John Berryman and the Thirties

John Berryman and the Thirties

A Memoir

E. M. Halliday

Afterword by Paul Mariani

The University of Massachusetts Press
Amherst, 1987

Copyright © 1987 by
The University of Massachusetts Press
All rights reserved
Printed in the United States of America
LC 87–10910
ISBN 0–87023–584–2 cloth; 585–0 paper
Set in Linotron Galliard
Printed by Cushing-Malloy and
bound by John Dekker & Sons

Library of Congress Cataloging-in-Publication Data
Halliday, E. M. (Ernest Milton), 1913–
    John Berryman and the thirties.

    1. Berryman, John, 1914–1972—Friends and
associates. 2. Poets, American—20th century—
Biography. 3. Halliday, E. M. (Ernest Milton),
1913–   . I. Title.
PS3503.E744Z594 1987   811'.54 [B]   87–10910
ISBN 0–87023–584–2 (alk. paper)
ISBN 0–87023–585–0 (pbk. : alk. paper)

British Library Cataloguing in Publication Data are available

In affectionate memory of

Winann Vaughan Andrade
John Berryman
Bhain Campbell
Lois Halliday Clapp
Sally Pierce Dow
Jim Green
Beverley Cline Halliday
Paul Probert
Hedda Rowinski Rosten
Rosalie Stech Sullivan
Mark Van Doren
Jeanne Curtis Webber

By brooks too broad for leaping
The lightfoot boys are laid;
The rose-lipt girls are sleeping
In fields where roses fade.
                —A. E. Housman

Contents

Acknowledgments

Since this memoir would have been impossible without John Berryman's letters to me, I first of all want to thank Kate Donahue Berryman for permission to publish excerpts from them, as well as permission to use previously unpublished poems that John sent me. More thanks go to her for kind hospitality at her pleasant home in Minneapolis. Florence Johnston Miller also extended a helping hand by permitting me to quote from Bhain Campbell's poems and letters.

For assistance in finding letters, appropriate pictures, and other pertinent documents, I am grateful to Alan Lathrop, curator of the Manuscripts Division, University of Minnesota Libraries, and to his able assistant Vivian Newbold; to Paul Palmer, curator of the Columbiana Library, Columbia University; Andrea Beauchamp, Hopwood Program Coordinator, University of Michigan; librarians of the New York Public Library; Jane Atherton Roman; Norman Rosten; Eileen Simpson; Barbara Thomas. Except where otherwise credited, illustrations are from the author's collection.

Many friends and acquaintances who knew John Berryman or Bhain Campbell or both, spent time reminiscing with me about events recounted in this narrative; I particularly want to thank Elsie Pierce Begle; Mannie Bilsky; Bart Breed; NC Breese; John Malcolm Brinnin; Dorothy Rockwell Clark; Beryl Eeman; Frank Fletcher; Harry Garvin; Robert Giroux; Dorothy Halliday Hefferline; Mary Jane Christenson Heming; Ellen Mayo Hill; Garnette Snedeker Kroeger; Arthur Miller; Florence Johnston Miller; Miriam Ostroff; Harriet Renaud; Warner G. Rice; Jane Atherton Roman; Norman Rosten; Elspeth Davies Rostow; Eileen Simpson; Annette Johnston Slocombe; and Dorothy Van Doren. Incidentally, the scant references in this book to Robert Jefferson Berryman reflect only the fact that, because he was five years junior to his brother John, I hardly knew him.

Marc Bailin, Christopher Benfey, Robert Giroux, Richard Kelly, Paul Mariani, Charles L. Mee, Jr., Virginia Peckham, Henri Peyre, Norman

Rosten, Charles Thornbury, and M. S. Wyeth, Jr., have individually discussed aspects of the book with me and made helpful suggestions.

At the University of Massachusetts Press, Bruce Wilcox, Pam Wilkinson, and Catlin Murphy have all been extremely efficient and good natured.

The book's epigraph is from *A Shropshire Lad* in *The Collected Poems of A. E. Housman*, Copyright © 1965 by Holt, Rinehart and Winston, Inc., and is reprinted by permission of Henry Holt and Company, Inc. The epigraphs for chapters 1, 3, 4, 5, and 7 are excerpts from *Love & Fame* by John Berryman, Copyright © 1970 by John Berryman, reprinted by permission of Farrar, Straus & Giroux, Inc., and Kate Berryman. The epigraph for chapter 2 is an excerpt from *The Dream Songs* by John Berryman, Copyright © 1965, 1966, 1967, 1968, 1969 by John Berryman, reprinted by permission of Farrar, Straus & Giroux, Inc., and Kate Berryman.

Preface

Joel Conarroe, in his excellent study of John Berryman's poetry,* remarks: "The details of artists' lives have a strong attraction for us; this is especially true of a writer as brilliant, as troubled, and as flamboyant as Berryman." He goes on to show that in Berryman's best work, the famous Dream Songs that won him the Pulitzer Prize, the very warp and woof of the poet's life became the essential stuff of the poetry: "He was a spiritual historian, and his great poem, like Whitman's, was mainly the outcroppings of his own emotional and personal nature. . . . " We thus can know a great deal about the poet's life and character through the tribulations, anxieties, pleasures, hopes, and regrets of Henry, the protagonist of the Dream Songs and Berryman's alter ego.

In Berryman's earlier work, however, such a correlation is seldom to be found: as Conarroe demonstrates, before 1948 most of John's poetry is "humorless, abstract, often bloodless," because he did not allow his intensely emotional, tempestuous nature to express itself in his poems. For him, therefore, more than for poets whose writing does not exhibit so drastic a change of mode in mid-career, a biographical account of his youth may be especially significant. I had the luck to know John intimately during the decade (1933–43) preceding that of his marriage to Eileen Simpson, who has well recounted the events of his life from 1943 to 1953. It was also my good fortune to have as a close friend and to introduce to John the young poet Bhain Campbell, who perhaps more than any other individual during that earlier period impressed himself on John's poetic consciousness, despite his untimely death in 1940.

It might be said, I think, that the story of the relationship among us three, with its interwoven threads drawn from the lives of others in our youthful crew of half a century ago, tapestries the early days of Henry, the ambiguous hero of the Dream Songs.

John Berryman: An Introduction to the Poetry (New York: Columbia University Press, 1977).

John Berryman and the Thirties

ONE
Morningside Heights,
1933–34

She set up a dazing clamour across this blood
in one of Brooks Hall's little visiting rooms.
In blunt view of whoever might pass by
we fondled each other's wonders.
                —"Cadenza on Garnette"

I first met John Berryman on a sunny day in February 1933. It was the start of the second semester of our freshman year at Columbia College, and it was somewhat prophetic that our first encounter had to do with a girl whom both of us were after. Her name was Flora, and she was endowed with blonde ringlets and skin like vanilla ice cream. I met her when, rather desperate for female company, I had gone to a tea dance in one of the Columbia dormitories even though I had never learned to dance. I stood in the stag line in a state of great longing but little nerve for about an hour, and then Flora literally bumped into me—on the way to the powder room, she explained apologetically. Would I like to dance? I told her I didn't know how, which struck her as a great piece of wit; but when I said no, I really did *not* know how to dance, she said, "Well, come 'round and see me at Brooks Hall, and we'll *do* somethin' about that!"

I went over to the dormitory at Barnard College, across Broadway from Columbia, the very next day, and asked if I could see Flora. While I was waiting in the foyer, I became aware of a slim, good-looking guy with a sophisticated air who was pacing up and down and regarding me with some interest. Flora suddenly appeared, like a vision out of a Civil War romance, and we both headed for her. "Oh my goodness," she said, "I do believe I have two visitors at the same time!"

John, who actually had a date with Flora as opposed to my having

E. M. ("Milt") Halliday, 1933. "Had I
gone out for football? I ought to, he
said; I was big enough."

just chanced it, was very debonair about the whole thing, rejecting my
offer to go on my way, and after a half-hour stroll with Flora between us,
he went with me to a drugstore on Broadway for a cup of coffee and
further conversation. In short order he learned that I had graduated from
Andover the previous year. This was not a fact of which I was unduly
proud, although I did realize that in the entire Columbia freshman class
I was one of two from that famous prep school. (At least half of my class
at Andover went off to Yale like lemmings, just as most Exeter graduates
in that era swarmed to Harvard.) John, who had come from South Kent,
a small school in Connecticut, was obviously impressed to have met "an
Andover man," and from that moment on treated me like a good friend.
Had I gone out for football? I ought to, he said; I was big enough. He
didn't have the weight for that, but was out for track, having had some
experience at South Kent. Did I live on campus? Oh, with my parents in
Brooklyn Heights. Same with him, only his mother's apartment was in
Manhattan, on the Upper East Side; I must come over soon. Did I have
my second-semester schedule made out yet? Maybe we'd be in the same
section of C.C. (Contemporary Civilization, Columbia's celebrated and
required course for freshmen, which met five times a week). German! He
didn't speak a word of German, but had taken a lot of French, and was
taking more at Columbia. What other Barnard girls did I know besides
Flora? She was a honey, he said, but there were dozens of other honeys.
Did I have a girl friend in Brooklyn?

This was a touchy subject with me, and I suspect I tried to put on an air of cosmopolitan nonchalance. In fact, however, as I confessed to John in the ensuing weeks of our growing friendship, my experience with females had so far been painfully scant. Andover had been nearly as monosexual as a monastery; and before that, at Pleasantville High in Westchester County, I had been steered away from rubbing elbows (or anything else) with girls by a lugubrious set of circumstances which I will not go into here except to say that, quite against my true desires, I went all through high school without ever dating a girl or going to a dance.

While I was away at Andover, my mother had persuaded my father that with the children gone, his long commute from Westchester to his job with the Congregational Board of Home Missions in New York was unnecessary: she wanted to move back to the city, where such amenities as museums and libraries and Macy's were more accessible. They compromised on an apartment in Brooklyn Heights that had a fine view of the harbor from the roof, so that Dad could go up there on summer evenings and smoke his pipe and look at the Statue of Liberty and think long thoughts.

My father's financial condition, however, had not improved with the move, and now, with the Depression really digging in, I was told that the University of Michigan—where I already had been admitted—was out of the question unless I could earn enough during the summer to pay for my tuition. I spent two or three weeks looking for work and met nothing but disdainful rejection: I was competing with men who had wives and children and were getting desperate. My father, who among other efforts to increase the family income taught public speaking in an evening course at Columbia, said that he might be able to swing tuition there if I'd be content to live at home and go to college on the subway. I was sure that it was too late and Columbia would turn me down, but the registrar quickly scanned my Andover credentials and said they'd be glad to put me in their class of 1936.

The Columbia campus in the fall of 1932 was vibrating with political harmonics on top of the usual thrumming over the freshman-sophomore tug-of-war, fraternity rushing, varsity football, and what the Barnard girls were up to. Fervent advocates of Franklin D. Roosevelt handed out leaflets explaining why only he and the Democratic party could pull the country

Dr. Ernest M. Halliday, flanked by his daughters, Dorothy (left) and Lois, 1933. The Hallidays lived in "an apartment in Brooklyn Heights that had a fine view of the harbor from the roof."

out of the Depression, while uneasy young Republicans urged hanging on with Hoover. The radio in the lounge of Hartley Hall was heard assuring everyone, in the voice of Hoover himself, that grass would grow in the streets if the Democrats won; soon after, the suave sonority of FDR intoned that as a president, Hoover was a good engineer: "He has ditched, dammed, and drained the country." A political force of which I had previously been almost unaware made waves in October, when a Columbia straw vote showed Norman Thomas leading heavily over Hoover and Roosevelt, in that order. My mother remarked that this didn't surprise her—"College students nowadays are nearly all socialists, I guess." But this was amply contradicted a week or so later when the results of the college straw vote across the country came in: Hoover had won easily, with FDR a poor second and Norman Thomas practically invisible. I began to realize that the student body at Columbia was not exactly run-of-the-mill, and even the dignified president, Nicholas Murray Butler, alarmed my teetotaling father by predicting publicly that prohibition was doomed.

But despite the stir of the national election and Roosevelt's sweep in

John Berryman, 1934. "John, with his lean build but broad shoulders, his sharply cut jaw, and his quizzical hazel eyes flickering behind his metal-framed glasses, radiated charisma."

November, and even though it was gratifying to belong to the category "college man," I felt quite out of things during my first semester at Columbia. Departing for Brooklyn every afternoon after my last class, I had the bleak feeling that I was going back to the boondocks just when events of interest were beginning to happen on Morningside Heights. Above all, the transformation of my life with respect to girls, which I had confidently expected college to bring almost automatically, was not taking place.

This autumn of discontent was threatening to turn into a long winter when I met John Berryman. I was very glad to find that he apparently took our close friendship for granted from the start, for he struck me as more knowledgeable about girls than anyone I'd ever met. We were both soon convinced that together we would surmount with éclat any obstacle that Columbia or life might present. John, with his lean build but broad shoulders, his sharply cut jaw, and his quizzical hazel eyes flickering behind his metal-framed glasses, radiated charisma. I did not know the word at the time, but I strongly felt the phenomenon. A year or so later, when I read *Tender is the Night*, I decided that John had an extraordinary amount of the attribute by which Fitzgerald characterized Dick Diver: poise.

A partial view of the Columbia campus in the thirties. "Our class schedules inevitably differed, but John and I met every day...." This spot, just outside our main classroom building, was a nice place to meet; you could watch a tennis match while waiting. Columbiana Library

Our class schedules inevitably differed, but John and I met every day for Cokes or coffee, and usually arranged some joint enterprise for the afternoon or evening. He even made the trip to Brooklyn Heights to meet my family—he and my sister Lois took to each other immediately—and I went often to his home on East 84th Street. It was there that I had my first taste ever of an alcoholic beverage—beer from a consignment that John's mother said had been recommended by "my bootlegger" as better than average. I had imagined that beer would be something like sarsaparilla, and was jarred by its bitter, yeasty effrontery. This was nothing compared to my first martini, which John concocted one afternoon when he and I found his parents' apartment unoccupied, with a note from his mother about an unexpected dinner invitation and something or other for his supper in the icebox. I really did not like the bite of the gin and vermouth, but by the time I got down to the olive I was feeling so elevated, and the conversation had turned so brilliant, that I was ready for a refill. John decided, however, that so much gin missing from the bottle might be noticed, and we went off in a pleasant haze to see *42nd Street* for the second time, totally forgetting supper.

Mr. Berryman, whom John called Uncle Jack, struck me as a white-haired nice old guy who was baffled by many of the interests and activities of his stepson. He was either retired or unemployed, I believe; at any rate he was often around the apartment when John's mother was off at her job, which seemed to have something to do with interior decorating or advertising. Mr. Berryman would turn the pages of the *Wall Street Journal* and half-listen with bemused tolerance to our discussions of *Oedipus Rex*, Ruby Keeler, or *The Counterfeiters*, which I had been reading in English and John, one-upping me handily, in French. (He was also writing poetry in French in those days, claiming that it was an easier language in which to find rhymes without stretching the sense.) Uncle Jack did try valiantly to play the role of stepfather, instructing us in what he considered to be useful lore of various kinds. One Saturday morning, for example, when John's mother was away on a trip, he showed us the proper way to make scrambled eggs (very slowly); and one night he announced that I ought to see a speakeasy "before there aren't any more of them." This turned out to be less exciting than I had hoped, since the place he took us to, once he had negotiated with the doorman, had all the appearances of an ordinary restaurant except that there was a small bar. Nobody, to my disappointment, was drunk or disorderly.

Mrs. Berryman, John's mother, embodied everything suggested by the word "sophisticated," and I sometimes thought of her when I heard Duke Ellington's "Sophisticated Lady"—a new song, then—on the radio. She was naturally a good-looking woman, I think, but in any event she was always skillfully made up, and she wore what impressed me as elegant if slightly bizarre costumes. She spoke in a bright, cheerful way, perking the conversation with quips and with allusions to what the *New Yorker* called "goings on about town"; indeed, it was through her that I first became acquainted with that magazine. The ambiance of her living room was quite different from that of my parents' home in Brooklyn Heights, where a warm but altogether soberer mood prevailed. Now and then she would casually recount, scotch highball in hand, a joke that would have been considered decidedly off-color in my family; I recall one, for instance, about a drunk who comes home very late singing the Cole Porter song, "It's delightful, it's delicious, it's delovely," and in answer to his wife's inquiry as to where he's been says, "Oh, I just got delaid." Occasionally I was invited to stay for dinner, and there again I found things almost exotic, judged by what I was familiar with. The steak, much thicker than in Brooklyn, came from the broiler charred nearly black but amazingly rare inside; the salad had raw mushrooms and watercress; there was cheese and fruit for dessert instead of homemade lemon gelatine with whipped cream (my mother never fooled around with Jello).

I early became aware that John's mother was almost obsessively devoted to his welfare and success. Although, as I also learned early, her income was not adequate to her style of living, she saw to it that John was well dressed and well laundered. His wardrobe was not much more extensive than mine, but the quality was distinctly better. It was John who engendered in me a lifelong disdain for padding in the shoulders of suits and jackets; he also tried—unsuccessfully—to persuade me that a well-chosen necktie was an essential article of clothing. I had been obliged to wear a tie at Andover, and ever after avoided it whenever I could; nor would I, to John's annoyance, concede that the gold collar clip he usually wore in those days was anything but a nuisance. I disliked what I called personal hardware, and he used to laugh at me because when my father gave me a wristwatch for my birthday, I took to carrying it in my jacket pocket, fishing it out by the leather strap when I wanted to know what time it was.

Both John and I and most of our friends, with the exception of Tom McGovern, a budding politician who had been chosen vice president of our class, took less interest in the Contemporary Civilization course than in literature, films, and girls, yet it was certainly a lively bill of fare. On the principle that important matters that are interwoven in real life ought not to be too artificially separated for study purposes, it was an intricate amalgamation of political science, economics, sociology, and history. Our instructors tried to tie current events in with the past, and this became more and more evident as the New Deal picked up momentum. With a squad of Columbia professors, headed by Raymond Moley and Rexford

Tugwell, active in Roosevelt's "Brain Trust," the Contemporary Civilization course seemed to have a pipeline to Washington. Hardly a week went by without the distribution of loose-leaf addenda to our texts so that we could keep up with the NRA, the AAA, the WPA. This seemed quite appropriate to us, for we had by now comfortably accepted the notion that Columbia was academically well out in front of the rest of the country, with Harvard, Yale, Princeton, et cetera, panting along behind.

It's true that I had a few doubts about this when it came to German. John had urged me to switch to his French course, but I was reluctant to forgo the rewards of the benign sadism I had undergone in beginning German at Andover, for I had placed at the sophomore level at Columbia after just that one year of study. My instructor, however, soon had me longing for the satirical wit of my old Andover teacher. A slender, ramrod-straight young man whose name I happily have forgotten, with ice-pick eyes and shiny, slicked-down hair parted in the exact middle, he addressed us in staccato German and correct but heavily accented English, his upper lip permanently curled in a sneer. Contemptuous critiques of our mistakes in his native tongue often escalated into sarcastic assessments of the soft and unmanly character of American youth: stepping smartly around the front of the classroom with (so help me) periodic clicking of his heels, he would imply that any young Nazi would make us look like cream puffs. Since there were several members of the class, including me, who in all probability could have tossed him out of the window single-handed, this tended to annoy us and did not promote our desire to become fluent in German. I particularly remember his behavior in March 1933, when the electoral triumph of the Nazis in the Reichstag had him levitating with happiness. He haughtily informed us that in June he was going back to serve *das Vaterland*, which made all of us feel a lot better.

The course I most enjoyed in my freshman year was English, even though the instructor was a very difficult man to get an A from. He was young, with close-cropped hair and a rather melancholy air, yet class discussions were stimulating, for he spoke with quiet eloquence and steadily stressed the view that literature could be meaningful only as it referred to the rest of life. Handing in an essay that I was sure would have earned me a top grade at Andover, I was disturbed to get it back with a couple of succinct comments on its structure and cogency, followed by "You can do better than this. B − ." It was years later before I realized that it had been my good fortune to be exposed to one of the best critical minds of the time, for the instructor's name was Lionel Trilling.

AS JOHN BECAME aware that my intense interest in girls was matched only by my lack of experience with them, he drew up a program for my rehabilitation. "Halliday," he said, "you've got to learn to dance. Right away." He reminded me that there was a dance every Friday afternoon at John Jay Hall, the largest of the dormitories, and that a date was unnecessary: "Christ, Milt, whole platoons of women come over from Barnard for every dance, and you can cut-in on any girl any time. Get your sister to teach you a basic step. We've got no time to lose, my boy."

Lois, after two exuberant years at the University of Michigan, had been obliged by the Depression to stay home, and was now enrolled as a day student at Hunter College in Manhattan. After a chat with John on the phone, she announced that she'd be "thrilled" to be my dance instructor, and we began forthwith. She picked out four or five phonograph records from her collection, pushed the furniture aside in the family living room, and took off her shoes—because, she explained, at 5′10″ she surely was taller than most of the girls I'd be dancing with. (This thoughtful provision was rescinded after I had stepped on her stockinged toes a few times.) A simple box step was the foundation of my terpsichorean education; Lois insisted that I forget about waltzes, tangoes, and so forth until much later. "The most important thing," she emphasized, "is to lead the girl very definitely, and never miss a beat. No, Milt, really *grab* me."

The lessons went so well that after about a week Lois said it was time to go public. She had saved a few dollars from baby-sitting receipts, and we were going out to dinner at a place in Greenwich Village where they had a nice dance floor and a swell band—and no cover, no minimum. "It will be great, Milt; no one will guess that we're brother and sister." I told her I couldn't afford it on my allowance of $2.50 a week, but she said the whole thing would be her Easter present to me. So one March evening we took the subway to Sheridan Square and sauntered into the Greenwich Village Inn—that is, if it's possible to saunter tensely: I was quite nervous about my debut. Among other things, it was the first time I had ever checked my coat anywhere.

But it all worked out as Lois had foretold. I don't remember what we ate, but the dance music was smooth and easy, and I box-stepped around the floor with what she assured me was great aplomb, missing no beats. Nobody stared at us, although the handsome drummer kept raising a leering eyebrow at Lois as we went by, which pleased her enormously. We seemed to dance especially well to a number called "Street of Dreams," so at Lois's request the band repeated it twice before we left the place. I still have an old 78-r.p.m. recording of that song, and play it fondly from time to time.

John was delighted when I informed him I was ready to take on the Barnard girls at the weekly tea dance. He advised me on what to wear, urged me to take a shower before leaving for Columbia on Friday morning, and suggested that for once I allow plenty of time so I wouldn't have to run: "I don't want you presenting a wilted appearance, you know." I found the prospect of dancing with girls who were not my sister exciting but a bit daunting, and I went with John to the East Lounge of John Jay with less confidence than I had hoped for. There was a small but very live student band for the dance, and there was what I thought a most stirring collection of pretty girls. The stag line was correspondingly long, of course, and I noted the amazing frequency with which some of the girls changed partners with no break in the music. "Now, watch how it's done," John said. "See, you just tap the guy lightly on the shoulder and say, 'May I cut?' And then he disappears and you just step right in there. There's nothing to it." "But what if he says 'No' when I say 'May I cut'?" "He won't," John said. "It just isn't done. That's what these dances are all about, getting to know girls. Now, see that tall blonde? I know her, and she's a swell dancer. I'm going to cut in; then after about two minutes, you cut me. Here goes."

Sure enough, John was presently whirling around with the blonde, maneuvering her in my direction and looking at me over her shoulder with an encouraging grin. I stepped out, tapped his shoulder, and a minute later was showing the blonde everything I knew about the fox trot, which didn't take long. To my great pleasure, she followed me easily and seemed to enjoy it. Hallelujah! I even managed to talk to her without losing track of the rhythm, and we had just exchanged names and minimal vital information when I felt a tap on my shoulder and had to relinquish her to somebody else. But my adrenalin and, doubtless, other hormonal secretions were really flowing now, and not quite believing my own audacity, I danced with one good-looking girl after another, transported by the sway of the music, the feel of warm female bodies close to mine—each so surprisingly different from the one before—and a sense of taking part in a kind of tribal ritual that might lead us all to sacred blessedness. The only thing bothering me was that a couple of times the girl I had in my arms moved in with such nether intimacy that I quickly got an erection. Spotting John at the side of the room a few minutes later, I consulted him about this: should I kind of pull away, or what? "Hell no," said John. "Hold it right in there. If *she* pulls away, that's her tough luck and she's probably a prude anyway. If she *doesn't* pull away, my boy, be damned sure to get her name and phone number. Now follow me: that brunette with the big breasts was just giving me her name when I got cut. Cut me in about three minutes." He headed for the brunette, who at that moment was executing a nifty two-step just in front of a carved oaken panel above the big lounge fireplace whose gilded letters read (and still do):

HOLD FAST TO THE
SPIRIT OF YOUTH
LET YEARS TO COME
DO WHAT THEY MAY

WITH MY NEW savoir-faire and a few names and phone numbers in my new address book, I soon screwed up my courage and actually asked a girl out on a date. Since John not only said he didn't mind, but positively exhorted me to pursue Flora, I cultivated her acquaintance for a week or so, sitting beside her in one of the alcoves on the first floor of Brooks Hall where a degree of privacy was possible if one remembered that somebody (even, possibly, the housemother) might walk past at any moment; I was elated when she cheerfully accepted my invitation to dinner. This meant the long subway ride to Brooklyn Heights, since I was far short of the means to take her to a restaurant; my mother, of course, had supported the invitation. I knew that the dinner, however unpretentious, would be bounteous.

The whole family, as a matter of fact, put themselves out to be hospitable to Flora: what took me by great surprise was the behavior of my father. Since he had always assumed a rather severe and critical posture toward the boy friends that Lois and Dorothy brought to the house, I expected him to show the same disposition toward my date. Instead, she no sooner crossed our threshold than Dad became a courtly and polished bon vivant, helping Flora out of her coat, ushering her to the best chair in the living room with a bow, sending me to the kitchen to fetch her a glass of cider, and making solicitous inquiries about her home town, her family, her reasons for coming to Barnard. At the dinner table he carved the roast beef with a flourish, all the while tossing off urbane remarks and witticisms that almost made me wonder if he might have honored the event with a surreptitious snort of brandy, and favored Flora with some of his best jokes—clean, of course—delivered with unusual verve. I felt outmaneuvered, and was pleased to have the apple pie and coffee finally cleared away and to get Flora into her coat for an ascent to the roof to see the harbor and the Manhattan skyline. (It truly was a fine view, "worth the trip," as the *New Yorker* used to say in advising readers to visit the Bossert Hotel Roofgarden, just a block away.) On our apartment-house roof, the March wind was whipping keenly, and Flora kept burbling about how "sweet" my father was; nevertheless she not only kissed me but stuck her tongue in my mouth, which seemed to make up for everything. The family, next day, offered kudos for my choice of Flora, though Lois suggested that her hair was bleached, and Mother muttered something about, "Your *father* certainly liked her—why, I don't know *when* I've seen him act like that!" As for John, he reacted to my account of the evening with the prediction that Flora's maidenhood was imminently doomed.

READING SHAKESPEARE AND Shaw and O'Neill and discussing them with John had nudged me into an epiphany: I was living in one of the great theatrical centers of the world. Except for high-school productions and a performance of *The Merchant of Venice*, to which Father took the whole family because he had once directed the play at the University of Illinois and knew most of it by heart, my exposure to the stage had been nil. I began to take an interest in Broadway, but assumed that the cost of tickets was beyond me, and settled for reading reviews in the *New York*

Times and the *New Yorker*. Around Christmas of 1932, my sister Dorothy, who sang in a choral group in Brooklyn Heights, took up with a handsome baritone who was in the chorus of a new musical at the Alvin Theatre and was also understudy to one of the stars, Reinald Werrenrath ("the most misspelled baritone in American musical history," Robert Benchley wrote). The show was *Music in the Air*, with a marvelous score by Jerome Kern including the entrancing "The Song is You," and Dorothy's connection soon generated a few free tickets (I think she saw the show five times). I was captivated by *Music in the Air*, and despite a somewhat absent-minded plot that required a troupe of attractive people to wander about the stage in dirndls and leather shorts, bursting into song on slender provocation, I have always wished the show might be revived. I had not known what a spell a live professional performance could weave, and I was excited to note in the theater lobby that second-balcony seats could be had for fifty-five cents, including tax.

I communicated this economics bulletin to John, and we decided that even on our sparse income we could now and then see a play. Yet freshman year went by without our ever managing to do that together. One thing that interfered was my brief but expensive infatuation with a spectacularly pretty seventeen-year-old named (I think) Sandra, whom John and I met at one of the big dances at Columbia. Stage-struck as I was by *Music in the Air*, I was enthralled to hear that she was currently rehearsing as a chorus girl in *Earl Carroll's Vanities*, and transfixed when she said yes, she'd like to have me call her and take her to supper some night after the show opened. I buffered myself financially by going without lunch for several days and negotiating a loan from Lois, and bought a seat in the front row of the balcony. Raptly observing the revue from that vantage point, I was distressed to find that distinguishing Sandra from the other "most beautiful girls in the world," what with stage make-up, identical headdresses, and physical similarity right down to and including the array of white breasts that were displayed in the "tableau" scenes, was practically impossible; in fact, I have never been quite sure that I was staring at the right girl. After the final curtain I went nervously around to the stage entrance. Several other escorts were waiting there, among them a genial but wrinkled old bird in a tuxedo who looked me over, offered me a cigarette, and inquired, "Is this your first offense?"

I took Sandra to a cozy little place on 46th Street recommended by Lois, where she ate what I felt was an astonishing amount of food in view of her trim physique; it also pushed my budget for the evening a notch awry, since my plan was to awaken her love and gratitude by conveying her all the way home to Jackson Heights in a taxi. I recovered by under-tipping the waiter disgracefully, but I began to realize on the trip across the river that Sandra had never expected to be taken home any other way, so that aphrodisiac effects were not likely to follow. She did hold my hand, but nestled into a corner of the cab and went beautifully to sleep. At the door of her mother's home in Queens I was rewarded with a perfunctory kiss, and then had to blunder around the deserted streets looking for the subway station, where I spent my next-to-last nickel on the long ride back to Brooklyn.

Having decided that postperformance dates were not going to work out, I met Sandra a couple of times for mild afternoon entertainments such as movies or riding on top of an open-air Fifth Avenue bus (cost: ten cents), but the romance never bloomed. One day I went around to pick her up at an address off Broadway which she identified as that of her agent. I waited there for half an hour or so, and was about to give up when she appeared—on the arm of a giant of a man in a long camel-hair coat whose heavy face seemed horribly familiar. It was, to be sure, Bela Lugosi, and Sandra explained to me, over tea and cake at the automat, that he was a very special friend and had been very kind. When I reported this to John the next day, he was indignant. "Halliday," he snorted, "that bitch is two-timing you! You've got to drop her right away!" I was not sure this analysis was fair to Sandra, considering the gossamer character of our relationship; but I was sure that I had gotten well out of my league, and I never called her again.

Another impediment to the good intentions John and I had adopted about going to the so-called legitimate theater was that both movies and burlesque were cheaper. I had been surprised and pleased at the abundance of nearly naked girls in *Earl Carroll's Vanities*, and was skeptical when John averred that this was nothing: there was more to be seen for less at Minsky's burlesque theaters. Sure enough, you could get good seats for matinee performances at the 42nd Street houses for fifty cents; and every now and then an emissary appeared on the Columbia campus to hand out special coupons admitting the bearer to the Apollo, on West 125th Street, for a quarter.

I suppose that burlesque was near its all-time high in that era before Thomas E. Dewey had undertaken the purification of New York. John and I were delighted by the formula: lewd but often hilarious skits, acted by slapstick virtuosos like Phil Silvers and Bert Lahr, interspersed with elaborately staged spectacles featuring the entire chorus in glittering costumes that invariably exposed their breasts, and finally (every fifteen minutes or so) the stunning phenomenon of the strip-tease.

The accessible abundance of New York burlesque probably had something to do with the fact that the winning proposal for our Columbia class motto turned out to be "The Perfect Thirty-Six." Supporting this proud legend, we cut afternoon classes in large numbers when the free coupons were distributed to troop up to the Apollo for what John aptly described as "basically, a tit show." The Apollo, though situated inside Harlem's southern boundary, was an all-white show in those years; it was, I believe, part of the Minsky circuit. John and I soon concluded that, with the possible exception of the Brooklyn Minsky's (where teen-aged dancers of dubious talent but very convincing measurements were sometimes tried out as strippers), the Apollo offered the best burlesque in New York. This was surely due in part to enthusiastic audience participation: for with the house more than half full of Columbia students averaging perhaps twenty years old, the atmosphere was quite different from that of the Times Square theaters. Down there, even an unusually good strip act often elicited only scattered clapping or a few drunken comments from an audience largely comprising dispirited, middle-aged patrons. At the Apollo, by contrast, great waves of student applause swept the strippers into multiple encores. There supposedly were certain legal restrictions on the amount of bodily movement they could indulge in once their breasts were bare, but with several hundred voices clamoring for more and the orchestra conductor swooping obligingly into another reprise of "I'm Sure of Everything But You" or "Orchids in the Moonlight," some of the stars let themselves go in stirringly ingenious displays of erotic dancing. "Incredible!" I said in John's ear one afternoon while a gifted young woman was somehow making one breast revolve clockwise and the other counter-clockwise. "Celestial spheres!" he replied, putting it all into the context of the Ptolemaic system, which we had been studying in Contemporary Civilization.

It was likewise during our freshman year that we first got to know the Savoy Ballroom, up at Lenox Avenue and 140th Street. Though its clientele was predominantly black, this grand emporium of jazz and dance did not discourage visitors from the paler world below 125th Street, and we found it a lively and exciting place to go. The big bands that habitually played there were always top-notch—Chick Webb, Duke Ellington, Fletcher Henderson, Jimmy Lunceford—and some of the vocalists had names that soon were to become famous, like Ella Fitzgerald and Billie Holiday. At our college dances, not yet transformed by what white band-leaders such as Benny Goodman would learn while playing with black musicians, the prevalent mode was still that of Guy Lombardo and his imitators: smooth, saccharine, dum-de-dum music to which we danced cheek-to-cheek, an occasional dip or twirl supplying most of the meager variety at our command. At the Savoy it was another story: the sheer musical impact of the swinging, antiphonal arrangements just about knocked us out. We listened with joyful astonishment, and we watched the same way as handsome black couples danced in a syncopated chore-ography no less inventive than the music itself. What we were witnessing, of course, was an early phase of the jitterbug phenomenon that was to catch up the entire country as World War II came on.

John and I both loved dancing, but we never were very successful at learning to jitterbug, much as we admired what we saw at the Savoy. About all we managed to achieve was a hop-jump step, easy to do if you had the energy, called the Shag. I suppose we shied away from appear-ing awkward in public, and besides, we didn't think it likely that we could import this acrobatic, spin-your-partner dancing to Columbia without being viewed as freaks. And there was another consideration: conventional dancing gave a perfect excuse for getting physically close to pretty girls in a romantic atmosphere, and we were not about to give that up for the yo-yo bedazzlements of jitterbug, however exhilarating they might be.

JOHN AND I confided almost everything to each other, but we were reticent on the subject of just how far we had progressed in our efforts to become sexual veterans. We resisted the male tendency to hyperbolize, feeling that to lie to your best friend was on a level with kicking your mother downstairs. The alternative was a vague suggestiveness that allowed us each to suppose that the other was doing pretty well. Although we seldom reported on particular encounters, we talked often about sexual techniques in general. Taking a classical approach, John checked a copy of Ovid's *Ars amatoria* out of the library, and we went to work on it with our high-school Latin, but the result was closer to confusion than illumination. We studied the diagrams in the textbook for the "hygiene" course required of Columbia freshmen, but found this, too, less than satisfactory—and somehow not correspondent with what we discovered firsthand in the back seat of a taxi with an excitable college girl. We discussed the exact location and function of the clitoris with the fervor of a couple of nineteenth-century explorers arguing about the true source of the Nile, and we speculated at length about the nature of the female orgasm, and how to induce it. Pragmatism, we decided, was the only way to go.

It is notorious, in this connection, that many young men in our society worry about penis size. With my tardy experience, I was perhaps more concerned than usual on this point, and asked John what he thought "average" was. He said he didn't really know and had never taken a measurement, but had always assumed that he was "at least average." Still mulling it over, I happened upon a book at the Brooklyn Public Library that gave the findings of a survey of 1,000 American men picked at random. The surprising extremes were three inches and thirteen inches, erect, so I figured the average was eight. John, startled, said he was pretty sure he couldn't measure up to that; but we'd better be more scientific about it. We both went home, measured carefully at the right moment, and then conferred by phone. We were somewhat disturbed by the results of our experiment, but at least pleased by the discovery that there was a negligible difference between us. We decided that if ever queried on this sensitive matter, we would nonchalantly reply, "Oh, about fifteen, I guess"—not mentioning centimeters.

One thing John and I learned about sex was repeatedly confirmed: we had a distinct tendency to be attracted to the same girls. A memorable instance was that of Garnette Snedeker, a languorously buxom beauty from Savannah with a deliciously slurred accent and seductive grace on the dance floor, whose conversation quickly dispelled any notion that she was a dimwitted southern belle. We were both dazzled by her, and since

Garnette Sneddeker, 1937. "...a languorously buxom beauty from Savannah...." Columbiana Library

we had met her simultaneously at a Barnard dance, we agreed that neither one of us had priority. For a few weeks we vied for her time and favor, but then John solemnly informed me that he and Garnette were "absolutely in love," and that further attentions from me might threaten our friendship. I backed off, assuaging my feelings with the thought that I was rather comparable to Sydney Carton in *A Tale of Two Cities* ("This is a far, far better thing that I do . . ."); I was a bit disillusioned when, finally, John's wooing of Garnette was unsuccessful.

NOTWITHSTANDING THE LARGE chunks of time that John and I spent on socializing and sex, we both were fairly attentive to our academic work, and finished the spring semester in 1933 with respectable grades. In June, John went off to his old prep school at South Kent, Connecticut, to get his diploma (which had been held up until he completed the year at Columbia because of his having skipped the last year at South Kent). That formality taken care of, he worked at odd jobs for the school for a few weeks, and on June 29 wrote me the first of many letters I was to get from him over the next ten years. He was having a swell time, he said, working and swimming and playing tennis ("I am practically certain the other side of the court is there, where it's always been, but damned if I can find it!"). He hoped I was having a grand summer.

My family's summer plans included a month up in Michigan, where my grandparents had built a cottage near Traverse City among an inspiring conglomeration of sand dunes, pine trees, and clear blue lakes. One of the loveliest of these was Crystal Lake, half a mile from the cottage. Its beach was controlled by a group called the Congregational Summer Assembly, a cluster of ministers, deacons, ushers, and their families, and although there were plenty of lively, tanned, and healthy young people who disported themselves there, on the whole the scene was reminiscent of a Norman Rockwell genre painting. Strange as it seems in these days of maximum exposure, in 1933 very few beaches east of California permitted even the male torso to be bared, so that when I appeared topless in my brand new swimming trunks I was greeted by censorious stares and a few incredulous gasps. I enjoyed it, of course, though Lois tried to convince me that the elders had called an emergency meeting with a view to ejecting me from the assembly grounds.

We had been there just a few days when a letter came from John, who was now back in New York:

I'm darn sorry you're not to be in town. . . . I have had a violent attack of voluntary inertia (laziness to you) since my return and have done practically nothing but attend operas, shows, movies, parties, have dates, read, roller skate, etc. . . . Reading "The Forsyte Saga"—it's splendid, of course. . . . Vaguely considering membership in the West Side Tennis Club, in Forest Hills. . . .

Be a good little rat and leave the women alone—no, on second thought, get interested in some new ones. Send me address and picture if they're good—tit for tat, brother!

I sent him a fairly rapturous account of the facilities and pleasures of Crystal Lake, to which he replied:

I paid tribute to your description of the resort with a sigh. . . .
Think of all those women with nothing better to look at (can you take
it?) than your Tarzanic torso. Boy, what a quiver of anticipation runs
through the assembled femininity when E. Milton approaches (as nearly
nude as possible, of course) to select his companion for the evening!
What raptures for the happy maiden (temporarily happy and
momentarily a maiden) to whom he beckons nonchalantly!

As for this veteran of a hard winter and the *!*X Comp. Lit.
exam, while you bask among blythe breasts and curvesome contours
(copy, Paris Nights), I have been so womanless that I was reduced,
about a week ago, to seducing a friend of the family's. That is, almost—
at the crucial moment I quit (after all, she's dam' near thirty).

. . . Play tennis constantly—belong out at West Side and am being
coached by George Agutter, author of Spalding's book on tennis and
one of the best pros in the country. He's changed my grips and swing
completely and I can't hit the side of a barn—says it will take me a year
to get decent. Rub noses with the great—Vines, Lott, Stoefen, Sutter,
Mrs. Moody, etc. I'm having a marvelous time, even tho' I'm rotten.

. . . My best to all your family, 'specially your charming sister—send
me a picture of her smiling and you handstanding, will you?

John
P.S. Don't miss "Twenty Years A-Growing"—it's delightful, poetic Irish
prose.

BACK AT COLUMBIA in September, we felt good to no longer be the
neophytes on campus. We knew the ropes now, or thought we did, and
planned a whole series of triumphs. After submitting writing samples,
John and I were both accepted for a course in advanced composition
taught by Mark Van Doren, whose reputation as a teacher, poet, and critic
we had become aware of the year before. I signed up for geology as my

required science course, convinced that it would be more interesting and easier than physics, and elected a reading course in German fiction and drama that I was sure would be, as we used to say, duck soup. John had worked out a similarly charming schedule, and was further excited by the fact that he was going to live in a campus dormitory instead of at home, evoking vistas of new social freedoms. I was envious of this, since I was still commuting by subway from Brooklyn Heights, but I figured that having John at the center of campus action in John Jay Hall would benefit me one way or another. And on top of everything else, we were determined to get into more extracurricular activities, beginning with a tryout for the college glee club.

Neither John nor I possessed any notable musical ability. My parents had obliged me to take several years of violin lessons, but I never evolved out of the scratch-and-screech category, and chucked the whole thing when I discovered, while still in high school, that the mandolin was strung and fingered the same way and was a lot more fun. John, despite his enthusiasm for dancing and popular songs, could carry a tune only so far before he was likely to veer unawares into an alien key. But the social attractions of the glee club were strong. There were concerts in conjunction with big dances; there were trips to other cities; there were bound to be (or so we imagined) admiring girls hanging around. By some unaccountable error we both survived the initial cut after the tryouts were held in the crypt of the Columbia chapel, a place with resonant acoustics that probably made us sound better than we were. My parents were as elated as I was by this, and proudly put up money for the necessary white tie and tails, which I bought immediately in order to be ready for the next formal dance, glee club or no glee club. Meanwhile, rehearsals began, and John and I ran into trouble right away. We couldn't even lend each other proximate comfort, since he was a baritone and I was a bass, and we sat in different sections. The fact was that neither of us could read music respectably, and we couldn't seem to learn to, even though my mother, who played the piano and sang beautifully, tried patiently to coach us. I partially solved the problem by making friends with the best singer in the bass section and always taking my place right beside him. When we sang a new song, I attended very carefully to the sounds he was making, and after a few run-throughs was able to mimic him closely enough so that when the assistant director came along to listen, I could fake it passably. I had, by luck, good voice quality for a bass, and before long could roll out (for example) the hearty bass part to "My Bonnie Lass" as if I knew what I was doing: "My bonnie lass she smil-eth, When she my love be-guile-eth; fa la la, la la, la la, la la la, *la* la, la la *laaaa*-la!" To this day I have no idea how the air to that old ditty goes.

John didn't make out so well, and came a cropper, I believe, during rehearsals for an elaborate choral treatment of the funeral rites for Beowulf as imagined by some modern musicologist. It was one of those distressing compositions, full of dire chants, moans, and dissonant wailings, later so wickedly parodied in *A Funny Thing Happened on the Way to the Forum*; but as John and I found out, you had to hit the dissonance as written rather than extempore. He left the glee club at that point, not feeling too bad about it (it took too much time anyhow, he said), while I hung nervously on, expecting the same fate from one mournful low C to another. Somehow I managed to stay on the glee club roster, although I learned to my dismay that when it came to concert trips, only a select cadre got to go on the jaunts to Philadelphia, Boston, or Washington, and I was not among the chosen. Still, when Columbia astonished the college sports world by being invited to the Rose Bowl to play Stanford on New Year's Day 1934, and even more astonishingly won the game, the whole glee club took part in the joyous festivities. They included an appearance on the Paul Whiteman radio show in the middle of January, entailing the delectable obligation to skip classes for a couple of rehearsals at Radio City, and finally the live performance itself, when we all belted out lusty renditions of "Roar, Lion, Roar!" and the Columbia alma mater, "Stand, Columbia!" while our friends and relatives gathered admiringly around loudspeakers tuned in to WEAF. (Lois swore loyally that through all the razzle-dazzle she could definitely hear my voice, at least on the longer notes.)

It was a heady season in New York anyhow, for early in December 1933, the complete repeal of the Volstead Act took effect, and to many on the campus this seemed to insure a brave new world of wine, women, and song. An old copy of Columbia's daily newspaper, the *Spectator*, which I recently dug out of a file, carries the headline UNDERGRADUATES PRE-PARE TO CELEBRATE DEATH OF PROHIBITION, over a story based on campus interviews. ("The Faculty," wrote the reporter dryly, "does not intend to celebrate the event.") As for John and me, we got into the mood early after our afternoon classes on December 5, sauntering over to a tea dance at the Casa Italiana on Amsterdam Avenue. There we met and danced with a pretty girl named Claire Sasser, who struck us as perfectly suited for the occasion: petite, smart, and jumping with sexy energy. The three of us had an invigorating time on the dance floor, already intoxicated with anticipation, and we agreed to meet at ten o'clock that evening in the lobby of John Jay Hall, ready for a salutatory visit to Times Square. John and I had strategically avoided any reference to dinner, since our funds were low and we wanted to save all we could for the celebration. I can't now remember whether we had dinner at the grill in John Jay Hall or went down for a free meal from Mrs. Berryman; but since dinner at John Jay cost sixty cents, I suspect it was the latter. Anyway, we passed the time until ten o'clock, and then showed up in the dormitory lobby, confidently awaiting the appearance of our brunette bombshell. Half an hour came and went without sign of Claire. It seemed incredible that any bright girl would pass up the opportunity to spend this great evening with a pair like us, and we waited, though increasingly less sure of ourselves, until eleven o'clock: no Claire. With our feathers considerably ruffled, we then headed for the 116th Street subway station, assuring each other sourly that a woman would have been a burden on such an expedition anyhow. There was no denying, however, that our enthusiasm was now quite wilted, and by the time we reached Broadway we had agreed to just stop in at a local pub for our first legal beer. Even that proved anticlimactic: we had to hike down to 110th Street to find an oasis, for the university had managed to impose its own local prohibition north of that line.

The next day in Brooklyn Heights the phone rang, and my mother called me to say John was on the wire. "Milt," he said, "go out and buy a copy of the *Journal*, and then call me back. You're not going to believe this!" I hurried over to Montague Street and got the paper. There on an inside page was a big photograph taken the evening before in some bistro off Times Square. Amid the revelry sat a bewhiskered old codger with a look of astonished joy on his face and a rollicking girl on his lap. He was, the caption explained, Theodore A. Metz—the reverend composer of "There'll Be a Hot Time in the Old Town Tonight." The girl, of course, was Claire—*our* Claire.

Old Timer ∻ Sings Hot Time Song ∻ In New Era

Theodore A. Metz, 85-year-old com- | Sasser at the Wivel Restaurant's repeal
poser of "Hot Time in the Old Town To- | celebration. Picture by Evening Journal
night," sings his famous song to Claire | Staff Photographer.

Claire Sasser, December 5, 1933.
"Amid the revelry sat a bewhiskered
old codger with a look of astonished
joy on his face and a rollicking girl on
his lap." New York Public Library

IT HAD BEEN a stimulating semester academically as well. The English
composition course with Mark Van Doren was a new kind of experience
altogether. In a way the wonder of his teaching method was that he did
not prepare. He read the essays we wrote, of course, and put comments
on them that always went right to the heart of the matter, but he came
to class without lecture notes, without a brief case, without anything but
a couple of books tucked under his arm from which he had decided to
read to us that day. He believed unalterably that good writing and good
reading could not be divorced. "I've been reading Gibbon's *Decline and
Fall*," he would say, opening the book. "This is what he has to say about
the emperor Septimius Severus." And in his peculiarly plangent voice,
which naturally bespoke the Illinois prairie where he was raised yet mys-
teriously seemed to resonate with universal overtones, he would read us
a few paragraphs, glancing up from time to time from under his slightly
peaked eyebrows, or stopping after a sentence to make some remark that
Gibbon's prose had evoked. "Notice how he balances that sentence," he
might say, and read it again. "It's a typical eighteenth-century construction,
yet what an unexpected phrase 'the inevitable mischiefs of freedom' is,
isn't it?" And he would pause, to see if any of us had anything to say, for

Mark Van Doren, about 1938.
"The English composition course
with Mark Van Doren was a new
kind of experience altogether."
Columbiana Library

the class was small and much more of a symposium than a lecture. The indelible impression he made was of a man actually thinking and learning and expressing his thoughts as they came to him, rather than of a scholar who has done his work and made his notes and tiredly condescends to recapitulate them for his students. It was extraordinarily exciting, and John and I often came out of that classroom, when the hour was over, in what can only be described as a state of inebriation. We began to love Mark Van Doren.

Although we worked hard for Van Doren, in other respects John and I did a certain amount of backsliding in the spring semester. I began to realize, for instance, that living in John Jay Hall instead of at home gave John some freedoms that he was inclined to abuse. Quite often, going up to his room after one of my midmorning classes, I'd find him fast asleep and hung over, having been out on a late-night beer binge with friends like Dana Crandall or Steve Aylward. This led him to abandon temporarily such time-consuming habits as shaving and bathing. Also, he had a tendency to spend more on girls than on mundane needs like lunch and dinner, so that he was constantly running down his health and out of allowance money. Periodically, he would launch a reform movement: I would find him spruce and clean and up in time to make his morning classes, having breakfast in the John Jay Grill and working out a new schedule or budget for himself. "Look, Milt," he'd say, "scrambled eggs, toast, and coffee for a quarter—you can't beat that! And I worked on assignments for five hours last night!"

My own neglect of proper academic concerns was due mostly to a longing I had developed to somehow get involved in the exotic world of the theater. In particular, I yearned to learn to tap dance—an urge that could be blamed to some extent on Ginger Rogers and Fred Astaire, for John and I had just seen their first film, *Flying Down to Rio*. But how to go about it? I got a book at the library that purported to teach the art; it didn't. One day Lois showed me a tiny ad in the classified section of the *Times*, offering group lessons for a very modest price. I went up to the specified address, an old brownstone in the East Fifties, and was immediately convinced that nothing would come of it. The rooms of the building were dingy and badly lighted, and the lady who took my three dollars (for six lessons) looked like an escapee from a carnival.

Things perked up, however, when the teacher appeared. Larry Vail was an archetype of the Broadway hoofer: about five-and-a-half-feet tall in his rather high-heeled shoes, neatly built, dark hair modishly cut and slicked down with expensive pomade, a pale, symmetrical face that was handsome the way a store-window mannequin's is handsome. He wore snug trousers that rose high at the waist and were suspended by colorful braces; his tapered shirt fitted him perfectly and had initials on the pocket, although it had not necessarily been changed very recently. His accent was pure New York, his talk full of slang straight out of *Variety*. To the class, a motley dozen that included middle-aged housewives, a couple of slender youths, and one tough and irascible old lady, Larry explained at the start that he was simply between Broadway musicals, and that he might have to fit class hours in with rehearsals as soon as his agent came through with his next show.

From the first lesson, Larry took special interest in me—mostly, it turned out, because I struck him as such an unlikely prospect as a tap dancer. He and the piano player, whose name was Al, were particularly impressed by my feet, which inevitably received a lot of attention in view of the nature of the class. Even for 6'2" and 185 pounds, my feet were indeed on the large side. By the time I went off to Andover at seventeen I wore a twelve, and in those days good shoes in that size were hard to find. Then my feet grew a little more, so that my proper size was 12½—

a size impossible to get except (as I later discovered) in the United States Army. (It's still impossible: even L.L. Bean, so accommodating in most ways, always offers men's shoes "Whole and half sizes, 7 to 13; no size 12½." Obviously, if you are crude enough to have feet *that* big, you'll not be sensitive to a misfit of a half size one way or the other.) The question was, would I be able to move those feet with the quick pedestrian skill called for by even the simplest tap-dance routine? I was agile and eager, and I managed well enough, much to the surprise of Larry and Al, who would exchange disbelieving grins after I had executed a time-step without missing a tap. (This was O.K. with me, but I was slightly piqued when I demonstrated my new-found talent to the rhythm of a dance record in John's dormitory room: "Halliday," he said, "you're twice as big as Astaire, and damn near a tenth as good.")

When we had finished a few lessons, Larry asked me to go out for coffee and pie with him and Al after class. We went to Bickford's and sat around for an hour, exchanging scraps of autobiography. Larry was full of intriguing and usually melancholy tales of the theater. The one I best remember had to do with Ginger Rogers, who, he insisted, had been his girl friend when he tried out for *Girl Crazy*, the last big musical he'd been in. "Then this guy Astaire comes along," Larry related morosely. "So he's already a star; so Ginger gets to rehearse with him for a couple of numbers. So she cuts me out. She goes with the big time, she leaves me flat. Hell, I taught her how to dance!"

One night we went to Al's small apartment on the Upper West Side for "a party" at which, he assured me, a beautiful girl would appear. Sure enough, a charming, dark-haired beauty showed up soon, but in company with a swarthy, handsome young man of about Larry's age. After pleasantries and a drink or two, Larry announced that he and I and Al were going to Bickford's for coffee, but would be back. I was puzzled, but went along, and we three had a typical apple-pie-and-anecdotes session for an hour. When we got back, the pretty girl was sitting on the couch, snuffling into her handkerchief, and the swarthy young man was across the room, chain smoking as he paced sullenly back and forth. This baffled me, and after they left, awhile later, I asked Al what it was all about. His explanation was simple: "They fucked while we were out," he said. I found this, in context, considerably upsetting, and told John about it the next day. "*Post*

Winann Vaughan, about 1935. "... a
marvelous girl whose acquaintance was to be
important for both me and John." Courtesy
Barbara Thomas

coitus triste," he said eruditely. And he quoted Donne, whom he had been
reading: "Ah, cannot we, as well as cocks and lions, jocund be, after such
pleasures?" Although I was still without personal knowledge on this score,
I found it very disagreeable to think that we could not. John assured me
that it was the experience of generations.

It was around this time that we met, at a tea dance, a marvelous girl
whose acquaintance was to be important for both me and John. Winann
Vaughan was a tall, leggy blonde with a face strong and animated rather
than merely pretty. She lived with her aunt, who had some connection
with Columbia University, on Claremont Avenue, just a block away from
Riverside Drive on one side and Broadway on the other. Among her
attractions was the fact that she was not just another college girl, but was
a talented artist, taking courses over in Brooklyn at Pratt Institute. Another
attraction for me—and a relief—was that for some reason not quite clear
we mutually felt more inclined toward warm conversation and friendship
than sexual flirtation. Winann was a great dancer, willing and able to follow
a strong lead through the most tortuous gyrations, and on several occasions
John and I took her to a college dance together, all three of us confident
of a good time unburdened by the chivalrous obligations owed to a more
conventional "date." I retain a vivid image of Winann and John, touring
madly around the floor at a formal dance that winter, Winann in a silvery

skirt that flared delightfully as she whirled to the intricate counterpoint of Gershwin's "Mine," and John very dashing in his tail suit, impressively correct until you took in his shoes, which were what we used to call white bucks. These white suedes had become a great fad that year, much to the distress of the proprietor at the campus shoe-shine stand, but I believe it was John who first had the nerve to combine them with white tie and tails. I had a pair of white bucks myself, but they looked like a couple of gunboats from the Great White Fleet when I donned them with my tail suit, and I declined John's invitation to join him in this blow for sartorial freedom. The innovation did draw a lot of attention to John's dancing, which he was proud of and which was generally regarded as daringly inventive. According to Winann, it was great fun trying to anticipate what John would do next, especially since he did not feel compelled to follow the beat of the orchestra at any given moment. "John dances to a different drummer," she observed.

Among other reasons, I enjoyed going out with Winann because our adventures were usually unplanned. One early spring evening in 1934, for instance, she and I and John and two or three others had a few beers at the Gold Rail, a favored campus hangout at Broadway and 110th Street, and got to talking about the wonders of Rockefeller Center, parts of which were still abuilding. On impulse, we hopped on the subway and went down to 50th Street. The proud towers loomed into the night, and to our joy we found that one ground-floor entrance was open and unguarded. We all cavorted in, up ramps and half-finished stairways, until we were five or six stories above the street, the spooky skeleton of the building enclosing us in a surreal maze of planks and girders, lighted only by dim and widely spaced bare bulbs. At that moment an alarmed watchman came clattering up shining a big flashlight, and with shrieks half of laughter and half of fear, we scampered down and out onto the street again. Somehow it struck us as a cardinal event, and we had to go and celebrate with more beer.

Winann's home was an interesting place to visit. Her cousin, Elspeth Davies, was a soft-spoken, beautiful girl, a star student and (as it seemed to me) prematurely mature. She was about our age or a big younger, but was not entirely of our group, often appearing to regard our shenanigans with aloof amusement, tolerant but not altogether approving. She usually wore her long light hair in braids that she wound around her head, which with her large clear eyes gave her an air of another century. I admired her greatly but tried not to show it too much, since my reveries of approaching her more closely always ended in scenes of imagined rejection: it was as if, I thought, like Anne Boleyn, she wore a necklace inscribed *"noli me tangere."* John, too, was subject to Elspeth's elusive appeal; in the following year, after I had transferred to the University of Michigan, he pursued her ardently but, in the end, without avail. Between Elspeth and Winann, both of us found reasons to go now and then to Claremont Avenue, in the spring of our sophomore year, where an aura of refinement always hovered, emanating from the shelves of beautiful books, and accented appropriately by a patriarchal grandfather—a retired sea captain—who habitually sat near a big window, quietly meditating or peering out across the trees of the Columbia campus with an old pair of binoculars.

The campus itself that spring was jumping with activity, much of it political and sparked by what was happening in Nazi Germany. There was a riot when the German ambassador made a speech denouncing critics of the Hitler regime; John Strachey, the British socialist, came and lacerated local feelings with the statement that the New Deal was nothing but "Social Fascism"; the editor of the *Columbia Spectator* stirred many of us with a piece assailing the trend toward war and declaring, "There is only one way to fight war and that is by refusing to fight." (I thought of that not long ago when I was on Morningside Heights and noticed, outside the Butler Library, a bronze plaque given to the university by the federal government in gratitude for having trained some 23,000 Naval Reserve officers during World War II.) Meanwhile, however, preparations were accelerating for the biggest and best Varsity Show ever, or so those of us who were in it persuaded ourselves.

The Columbia Varsity Show went back a good many years, and had its own corps of distinguished alumni including Richard Rodgers and Lorenz Hart, who had composed music and words for *Fly With Me*, the 1920 production. Doubtless the classmates of that famous pair were as unaware of their stellar quality as we were, in 1934, of the future eminence of Herman Wouk, who wrote the book and lyrics for our show, *Laugh*

It Off. Though no threat to *The Caine Mutiny* in his ultimate bibliography, it was an amusing mélange of skits supposedly revealing life on the Columbia scene, or, as the opening choral number promised:

> We'll show you Columbia,
> The classrooms where they encumber ya
> With a lot of useless knowledge,
> Forgotten after college—
> It's just a waste of time,
> But it's Cultsha!

The skit I most fondly recall featured Mae West—smashingly impersonated by a student named Martin Manulis, who later became a Hollywood producer—coming up to Barnard to give the commencement address. This took the form of a sultry aria exhorting the graduates to ignore conventional wisdom and strike out on more daring ventures. It was called, naturally, "Go West, Young Girl, Go West!" and for years afterward, over cakes and ale, John and I had a boisterous tendency to reprise some of the lyrics:

> The wages of virtue are deplorable—
> Virtue is its own reward.
> The wages of sin are more adorable;
> You'll find the wayside
> Has its gay* side.
>
> So when you're in the arms of someone you love,
> And he lets you know what he's thinking of,
> Don't go intellectual, don't go Park Avenue:
> Go West, young girl, go West!

Manulis was an excellent mimic with just the right amount of caricature, and his lavish costume, outbosoming the real Mae West but not by much, was designed to emphasize the outrageous bumps and grinds with which he punctuated his delivery. It was the hit of the production, eliciting many

---

*This may have been a pun, but in that era probably was not.

encores when the show went on at the Astor Hotel for three performances in April.

A traditional role in the Varsity Show was played by the Pony Ballet, a travesty of the sort of high-kicking chorus line for which Radio City Music Hall's Rockettes have become the paradigm. Since our cast was all male, the joke was to select, for the ballet, tall, hairy, heavily built young men, array them in silk stockings, tutus, wigs, and falsified brassieres, and make them prance with as much elegance and musical precision as possible. Paul Winkopp, the dance director, was a semipro who took his assignment seriously and worked us hard; he perceived that the closer we came to the real thing, the funnier it would be. John and our good friend Dana Crandall tried out along with me, but Winkopp decided that John was too short and Dana too thin, and they were relegated to the singing chorus. I found the Pony Ballet exhilarating—I don't think it ever occurred to me that there was any homosexual angle to the experience—but what was more exciting was that Winkopp needed a trio of tap dancers for a spot in a "sailors on Riverside Drive" number, and he picked me for one of them. This required a hurried change of costume from drag to bell-bottoms in the middle of the performance, and back again for the finale; but this seemed the stuff that show biz dreams are made on, and I did it with enthusiasm. I got Larry Vail and Al a couple of tickets for the show, and they beamed proudly at me when we went for a drink after the final curtain.

WHAT WITH VARSITY Show rehearsals, girl chasing, and fine spring weather that encouraged loafing, I had fallen considerably behind in my studies, and John was at least as delinquent. Over coffee one May afternoon at the Columbia Chemists drugstore on Amsterdam Avenue, we compiled lists of the books we still had to read before exams began two or three weeks later. It was appalling. John's big problem was English 64, an eighteenth-century literature course he was taking from Van Doren in addition to advanced composition: he was in debt for about twenty books, as well as a long paper on Locke's *Human Understanding*. I was dawdling through the reading list for "English Literature to 1500," hung up some-where between Gower and Lydgate; and in my German literature course I had not even attended class for many weeks.

My neglect of German had been deliberate, however. The rule at

Columbia was that if you maintained a B in a course, you were not penalized for being absent from class. My teacher was a benign but boring pedagogue, a German of the old school who had secured tenure at Columbia and was not inclined to exert himself at his profession. His notion of the correct way to conduct the course was to choose a list of books, make out a schedule of reading assignments, and then sit drowsily at the front of the room while the students, one by one, worked their way with excruciating pain through oral translations of paragraphs in *Frau Sorge* or *Mario und der Zauberer*. I found it unbearable, and since I had the reading list to go by, reckoned that I could keep up well enough without having to endure class meetings. This worked excellently for the first half of the semester, and I wrote a B+ midterm with little trouble. The old prof, not unreasonably, resented my attitude, as he indicated one day when, after an absence of a month, I dropped in to check on how far the class had progressed with Goethe's *Faust*, the big opus for the remainder of the term. "Ah," he remarked acidly to the class that day, "Ve haf a fisitor this mornink!"

The boom fell during exam week in June. I was strolling along 116th Street on a Tuesday, feeling pretty good about how I'd handled the geology final that morning and contemplating lunch with John, when I encountered a member of my German class headed in the opposite direction. From him I learned that the exam schedule had been changed: the final was to be held that very afternoon. Since I had counted on a whole day and a half to read the rest of *Faust*, this news flooded me with panic. I decided to throw myself on the mercy of Dr. Herbert Hawkes, the renowned dean of Columbia College, who was reputed to be crusty but kindly. In his office half an hour later, I explained my problem, ending with a plea for a special examination at some later time. To my dismay, a frown appeared between his heavy brows.

"The fact is," he said, "that you are simply not prepared for the examination, the time of which it was entirely your obligation to keep track of—isn't that so?"

"Yes, sir," I said feebly.

"Well then," said the Dean, with the air of an imperial mandarin ordering a prophylactic beheading, "I think it's clear that you'd better take an F in the course."

I shuffled toward John Jay Hall in a cloud of shame and despair, but even before I got up to John's dormitory room my emotions were beginning to shift. Goddamn, I thought, the old sonofabitch didn't have to be so righteous about it—it reminded me of my father's behavior when, a long time before, I had snitched a chocolate rabbit from Lois and then confessed to it. The analogy raised my adrenalin to a higher level, and as I knocked on John's door I was ready to fight.

John was completely supportive. "Hell, Milt," he said, "they can't keep you from taking the exam. It starts at 2, and it's only 12:30 now; you've got an hour and a half. I'll go and get you a good translation of *Faust* at the library, and you can work like hell till exam time."

I had my textbook edition of the play with me as well as my German dictionary, and I settled down fiercely at John's desk. He was back in a few minutes with the disturbing news that not a single copy of *Faust* in translation was available.

"Well," I said, "it's a big class. You get out of here so I can concentrate, and I'll wait till 3 o'clock to go to the exam. I've got nothing to lose."

The proctors looked at me, in fact, as if I had lost my wits when I walked into the big gymnasium where the exam was held, an hour after it had begun; but there was nothing they could do about it. And I had been lucky: of five or six key passages from *Faust* which were presented for translation, I had worked on three during my cram session in John's room. When the final grades were posted the next week, I came off with a C in the course—nothing to be proud of, but immeasurably better than an F. I resisted the impulse to go and tell Dean Hawkes about it.

Poor John did not emerge so easily from his academic gulch. Despite several all-night bouts of feverish reading, he was still many volumes in arrears by the day of his eighteenth-century exam, and though he did surprisingly well on the final, he added a note to Van Doren in his blue-book, apologizing for his sins. Mark, who cared much less about academic procedure than the actual reading and understanding of good books, felt that he had no choice but to give John a failing grade—ruefully, I am sure, for by this time they were friends as well as teacher and student.

The school year was over. John was miserable on account of his flunk, and impoverished because, he said, of stock market reversals suffered by his stepfather. My own situation at home had been worsening as the year wore on, the trouble being friction with my father over such fundamentals as religion, sex, and what he saw on my part as laziness and weak ambition. To my great irritation he took the liberty, behind my back, of consulting Van Doren about my idle ways. Mark told him that he did not think I was really lazy, but was perhaps prone to be somewhat "too sanguine"—a choice of words that allowed both Dad and me to think we had won the argument.

On the religious question, the healthy skepticism fostered by a liberal education was reinforcing a few things I had learned studying the Bible at Andover. It was a jolt to discover that Matthew, Mark, Luke, and John, whom I had always pictured hanging out with Jesus on the beach at Galilee, were all four of later generations and had never even laid eyes on the Master. How much credibility, I asked Dad, would stories about George Washington have if all of them were told or written by characters who never knew him, and there were practically no other records? In Lionel Trilling's course at Columbia I had read the sketch by Anatole France depicting Pontius Pilate as an old man trying—unsuccessfully—to recall anybody answering to the description of Jesus, and I got Father to read it. He did not like it, but he did pride himself on being reasonable and logical about all things including religion, and my nagging assault upset his mental equilibrium.

The generation gap with my father quaked from a fault to a fissure over Maugham's *Of Human Bondage*, which I had recently read on John's recommendation. The novel expressed so many youthful doubts, hopes, and dilemmas so truly, I thought, that reading it might make Dad understand me better than any number of tense discussions, especially since Somerset Maugham was exactly Dad's age. I asked him if he would read it, and he agreed so cheerfully that I had high hopes. A few nights later he came into my room, took *Of Human Bondage* off my shelf, and went back to his leather armchair in the living room where he sat every evening, usually going through the *Brooklyn Daily Eagle* or the *Christian Herald*, or sometimes reading Dickens aloud to my mother. I left my door open and sat at my desk trying to study, but actually listening attentively. From the other room I could faintly hear him puffing on his cigar and turning the pages. After about forty minutes, there suddenly came a report like a rifle shot; it was the sound of a book being not merely closed but slammed shut. I went out. *Of Human Bondage* was lying on his sidetable, and he was staring stonily at the wall.

"What's the matter?" I said.

"The book isn't true," he said. "It isn't realistic."

"Gee," I said, "that's what I thought was so great about it—it's really true to life."

"Nonsense!" Dad said. "Any young man as promiscuous as the hero of this book would be certain to get a venereal disease!"

That seemed to end the critique, so I picked up the book and went back to my room, feeling hurt and disappointed. As nearly as I could make out, the breaking point for Dad had come when Philip, the hero of Maugham's novel, had compounded his illicit lechery by going to bed with a *second* woman.

It was nevertheless my father who came up with a possible solution for what seemed to be a formidable family problem. He showed me a comparison he had made between my projected college expenses for a third year at Columbia, and for a year at the University of Michigan: even with travel costs figured in, Michigan came out ahead. "The only big thing on the debit side," he said, "would be your meals. If you could get a meal job, which I don't think would be difficult, I could handle everything else."

It was a tempting proposal. I did not want to leave Columbia; I had enjoyed myself there, knew I was getting a good education, and was looking forward to a great junior year with John and Van Doren, whose famous Shakespeare course we were planning to take; and there was Winann and her circle of interesting girl friends—a social nucleus, John and I both thought, certain to put us into highly desirable romantic and erotic orbits. On the other hand, I felt a desperate urge to get away from my family, and Dad would not hear of my taking a room in a Columbia dormitory. And Michigan had its own attractions: said to be the best of the big midwestern universities, situated in a pleasant town, proud of its many extracurricular events, and—I felt stirred at the very thought—with a student body including about five thousand coeds, many of them surely beautiful.

In those uncrowded academic days it was easy to transfer from one university to another, and I delayed my decision until well along in the summer, although I did take the precaution of having my transcript sent from Columbia to Michigan. The summer drifted hotly by, ending with a whole month up at Crystal Lake. From there, in the middle of August,

Halliday and girl friend, Crystal Lake, Michigan, 1934. Inscribed on the back of this photo, which was sent to John: "If you look closely, you'll notice that we are standing in some poison ivy. We discovered this the next day."

I wrote John that I was pretty sure I was going to Ann Arbor in September. His reply, which came a week later, digressed immediately to more practical matters:

Dear Milt,

God bless your little obscene heart, I've got a job! (16 point caps on that) And it's a honey, my boy, it's a honey—typing and editing for a woman author [pen name Clinton Dangerfield] who lives over on Staten Island. Evidently she got my name, along with that of five others, from the Appointments Office [at Columbia] . . . and I got the job on account of I'm so bright and such a good typist (?). The job really is a peach—it pays 50¢ a thousand words for either first draft or fair copy and she pays me a cool buck an hour for editing, and it's darn interesting work. I've set to work at some stories myself under the impetus. She writes for the pulps, and is quite decent along her line,

besides being a very delightful person to know and to work for. She is
a Savannah woman (but pleasant and reasonable, for a' that) of
excellent family and uncertain age, and has been writing these stories
(Westerns, crime, detective, mystery, love, etc.) since the famous
mother of Hector foaled (a euphemism, kid, a little twisted by my
constant references to horses, drat the beasts). She talks all her stuff
into a dictaphone, can get out a record of 1000 words in ten minutes,
and I take them from that, typing as I listen to earpieces. You'd never
believe how much I've improved in speed and accuracy . . . get about
1500 words an hour out. . . . It's a wonder, frankly, and may run into
real money if I'm able to turn out plots and stuff as well as she thinks I
can. God knows, I'll probably be a famous fifth-rate Western writer
shining from the pages of Argosy and Range Romances, and every
Goddam thing I believe and hope for will be ground to the proverbial
dust under the economic treadmill. Meanwhile, it's marvellous to be
working—you wouldn't believe how swell it is. I only got the job a
week ago Monday, and by about Wednesday of next week I'll have all
my debts paid, including the long-lived ten bucks to the long-suffering
dean, and will be about to get my poor carcass some clothes and other
sundries. Who knows? I may even have a date! Saw Crandall day before
yesterday and we talked for hours. . . . We're going out Monday night, I
think, though God knows with what—it was really pathetic to see us
racking our brains for just one woman, not to speak of two. Frankly,
I'm going to date the rather luscious lamppost on our corner if
something doesn't turn up soon. . . .

  By the way, you hydrophobia skunk, you're not going to Michigan
next year. . . . As soon as you come back, Tom and Steve (the bastard)
and Dana and Bill (from whom I had a card) are going to sit on you
and beat you about the head and shoulders until you give up the
thought. What the hell will New York women do if you're in Ann
Arbor? Damn nice of you to say you'll see me in September, but we

want to see you through the long freezing, constipated winter, though God knows why—you read *Time* and steal our bitches. Frankly, old man (he rasped with large, juicy tears in his bloodshot eyes) we think you're peachy—hey hey!

...I wish you'd been here when McGovern came down. We all got drunk as hell one Saturday night, two weeks ago, up at the college, and I blush to tell it, Berryman passed out dead as several volumes of the Anatomy of Melancholy after being as sick as almost any English painting you can think of (God, I'm a shark at similes, this evening, aren't I, said he dodging). God I was sick!!! And it was hell (I seem to be swearing a hell of a goddam f—— screwy lot this time), frankly, I woke up the next morning with a brown taste you could practically wrap around your arm, and staggered home, went to bed and didn't emerge for days. Never again.

I've really got to sign off, tired as you are, and go to bed. Please write as soon as you can let go of those breasts long enough, and don't spill any milk on this letter, either—keep your women out of your friendships, my boy, they don't mix. God bless you, Bainbridge and (gulp) make you happy....

Ipswich, and other such.

Despite John's cheerful browbeating I stuck to my plan, and early in September 1934, I was in Ann Arbor, looking for a good rooming house and waiting for the fall semester to start. It was exciting: I was completely on my own; the big open campus with its towering elms looked just the way a college campus ought to look; there seemed to be pretty girls all over the place. There would be plenty to tell John about.

TWO

Ann Arbor / New York,
1934–35

the long sweet days of Fall
the long sweet days of youths striving together
Friends so intense the world seems to hold no other
Henry remembers all
— Dream Song 306

Accustomed as we now are to the audiovisual age, it is sometimes hard to remember what a rare occurrence a long-distance phone call was in the thirties. Not only were such calls regarded as expensive, but they carried an aura of very serious events. When the operator said, "Hold on, please, long distance is calling," we waited apprehensively for news of illness or perhaps even death in the family.

What we did in those days was write lots of letters. Once I had settled in at Ann Arbor, I often spent the last hour before going to bed writing to members of my family or to friends. It was a satisfying way to evaluate the happenings of the day or the week, so that life did not slip by without due notice; and first-class postage was only three cents.

I wrote John a long letter soon after finding a suitable rooming house, a clean, well-lighted place near the campus, run by a lady of German extraction who settled on $3.50 a week for what struck me as a marvelous corner room on the second floor—comfortable bed with a down quilt; nice curtains on the windows; roomy desk with a bookshelf; and above all, entirely my own domain. Having explained why I had not been able to come to New York before going to Ann Arbor (my father had decided that since I was already in Michigan I'd better stay there), I filled John in on the circumstances of my new life that I thought might entertain him.

I had found a meal job almost immediately at the Delta Delta Delta

(Tri Delt) sorority, washing dishes three times a day. The food was excellent and ample, and the other members of the staff were pleasant company: two student waiters and a freshman scullion named Chuck, all ruled with majestic calm by Mrs. Lawton, the black cook, who saw to it that we ate very well and were not abused by the housemother. This was a most refined *dame d'un certain âge* who made a point of critiquing our performances when she visited the kitchen each day to dictate the menus. "You must pare them thinner, thinner; potatoes cost money," she would admonish Chuck, who would be doggedly trying to stay on schedule; when she had evanesced back into the polite part of the house, Mrs. Lawton would make amendments: "Just kind of round 'em off, honey; then they'll *look* like they've been pared real thin."

Convinced as John and I both were that I had taken a downward academic step in transferring from Columbia to Michigan, I was shocked to discover when I visited the registrar's office that they had me pegged as a second-semester sophomore instead of a junior. The trouble, it developed, was Columbia's Contemporary Civilization course, for which (an assistant registrar loftily informed me) Michigan had no counterpart and consequently was unable to give credit. I asked her if I could go to the heads of the various departments concerned to see if any of them would endorse my appeal for some credit, to which she grudgingly replied that I could try if I liked, but she did not think I'd have any success. My mother had sent me the CC syllabus along with my other books, and I took it around to the departments of history, political science, economics, and philosophy, where it was examined with much interest. All of the department heads were very pleasant about it, and I carried back to the registrar's office signed notes entitling me to a total of eighteen hours of credit for the work covered in CC. Since my Columbia transcript showed only sixteen credit hours for that work, this threw the assistant registrar into consternation; she indignantly declared that I *certainly* could not get *more* credit than Columbia had given me. "I demurely acceded to this," I told John, "and walked out of there a full-fledged junior."

A more lasting shock at Michigan was the football team. I had assured John that Big Ten football was a quite different game from the Ivy League variety, and that I was sure to see some titanic struggles. Indeed, the campus hoopla that harbingered each contest was exciting, what with bonfire "pep" rallies, Michigan's huge marching band, besweatered coed cheerleaders jumping up and down, and rumors of wild fraternity parties planned for after the game. I had never seen a football stadium like Michigan's—it held 100,000 spectators—and I went eagerly down there with my friend Chuck on a crisp Saturday afternoon in September to watch, as I confidently supposed, an easy rout of Michigan State, by tradition Michigan's first victim each autumn. To our horror, the Michigan State players, though visibly smaller, began to run through, around, and away from Michigan's hulking warriors from the first kickoff, and by halftime they were uncatchably ahead. The Michigan bleachers sat silent and disbelieving while the Michigan State crowd roared, and down on the field the Michigan co-captains, one of whom was named Jerry Ford, stumbled about in a kind of befuddled torpor (from which, in the unkind view of Lyndon Johnson, Ford never fully recovered). It was the start of a disastrous season.

MY CORRESPONDENCE WITH John led off from his side with a rather scurrilous missive dated September 17, 1934 (but with a scribbled superscript: "Curse it, I forgot to mail this"):

You're the worst sort of rat, the anus-sniffing sort, I'm sure. No insult intended. Scum! Why the hell did you decide to go to Michigan? Damn you to hell and equally lugubrious places. . . .

Your phrase, "inspiration of the opposite sex in classrooms" practically gives me constipation. Orgasm upon orgasm! I think it was a Michigan professor who defines a virgin as a girl between the ages of five and six. . . . I seem to be very insulting for no known reason—think as small as possible about it.

. . . I haven't yet met McGovern's woman—I intend to set the Smooth forces of Columbia on her posthaste. Tom is too political for words; he needs some chase to heat his rapidly congealing blood. Miss Garnette ("Soap in y'eyes") Snedeker is as unkind as ever—I am frankly brokenhearted. However, as I remarked to somebody at the college the other day, the hunting season is on. I just thought of a somewhat amusing resolution: "Well, the Class of 1938 (don't you feel aged, Milt? I have a superb moustache and feel ninety) enters Barnard today: out of some three hundred of them there should be, minimum estimate, ten Honeys. I hereby resolve, in the name of the Magnificent Hole-finder (Amen, amen), to become acquainted with all of those ten and to lay as many of the individuals as possible, taking precaution not to multiply the species, hey hey!" (You're right—not very funny.)

I really am damn sorry you aren't coming here this year—it will be distinctly lousy not to have you around. However, thank God there's someone to write to who knows what the hell it's all about (pat phrase—I haven't the foggiest what it means) and can talk his letters. I hate most letters because people write 'em, in fact (to the shame of the race let it be said) they compose 'em—you and I and Aylward and McGovern . . . may not write good letters in any Goddam conventional sense, but at least we talk 'em, which is the point. (What is the point—that sentence is so Proustian that I've quite forgotten what the point is; skip it.)

What courses are you taking and why? I don't know yet whether I'll be back at the college—certainly not with a full course, but maybe with four or six points. I've been making a good bit of money (said he smugly) but the family is broke as hell and I've been turning it all in, so haven't been able to save anything to buy clothes I need so damn bad, or for tuition or anything. This job is swell—I am doing regular collaboration now—she pours the rough narrative into the dictaphone and I take it out, edit it, revise, turn it into fair copy and market it. We split 50/50, which is swell. . . . she says she is perfectly well satisfied with me (as well she may be—in spite of this typing, I have developed into a peachy typist—turning out almost 13,000 words typewritten from the dictaphone, ten rolls, yesterday in seven hours; and, conceited as it may sound, I can use the poor language approximately nineteen times better than she can, and have an excellent eye for plot and structural weakness and implausibility. So I am practically perfect for her, and she can write plots like nobody's business and has some ninety years' experience, so she is perfect for me, although she bores me to tears. And by God, I'm not going to stay at this any longer than I have to—it's so damn criminal to use a simple word when another word is the right one, and to cut all decent description and correct adjectival work in favor of the vilest blanket words) (I find all this is one parenthesis), [but] she my boss has to give . . . her former collaborator another trial, so I don't know how the hell long my job will last.

Will read the Powys this week, though busy as hell. [This refers to *Impassioned Clay*, by Llewelyn Powys, which I had recommended to him as a fine testament of agnostic hedonism.] . . . We moved up here Friday and are scarcely settled yet. A seven-room apartment on the fifth floor of 115th Street between Amsterdam and Morningside. Very convenient [he meant for himself; the place was just opposite the Columbia campus], fairly awful apartment, but dirt-cheap—which is why. And I have a swell place to work, and room to have fellows in, if they can face the four flights of stairs. Ought to be a damn interesting year. Sounds silly as hell, but we can have a hell of a good time writing because I absolutely won't keep a diary but I love to write letters. . . . Now for God's sake don't go off on one of your silent sprees and retire into your den for weeks—write and tell me who is which. . . . Have a good time, fellow—your letter was funny as hell (said he with honest admiration). A*dor*ingly (whoops!)

John

[P.S.] Jesus Christ do I feel small! I wrote the preceding three pages the day after I got your letter, either two or three weeks ago and put them beautifully in my pocket, and Goddam if I didn't forget them.

. . . Tom is frankly awful and you're not back, and everything stinks. Steve and Dana are in the pink and we've had a peachy drunk, but no women. God save their nipples, I haven't had a date in so near four months that I am about to shrivel (or however you spell it) up and die. . . . How the hell are the women out there, guy? Remember, no raping! Congrats on the meal job—Dana hasn't got one yet and will probably starve before he does—it's really tough.

. . . Aylward takes the cake for his latest: he and Crandall had been arguing for hours, quite drunk. So he rushes to the door, flings it open and shouts, "You win a potfull of shit, but *you win!*"

. . . Haven't seen Van Doren yet, but will soon. . . . It frankly is a hell of a time till Christmas—but try and get away once you're in our fell clutches, heh, heh. . . . Oh yes, I finally got some clothes. You know I have hell being fitted, I take 40 shoulders and 37 through the body, I'm so damn thin. I finally found a belted Harris Tweed for next to nothing though, and that does nicely. . . . Got a topcoat—dark grey Harris Tweed—and all of it exceedingly cheap, as it had to be. Work coming along, not back at college of course, but in close touch—swell fun. Now write me, you worm, and tell me things. . . .

The plain fact of the matter was that I was having very little luck with girls in Ann Arbor that fall, and this was all the more irritating because there were so many comely ones on all sides. I found, however, that most of these beauties, uniformly arrayed in pastel cashmere sweaters, woolen skirts, and saddle shoes, were rather aloof, and given to behavior fit for a princess at a cattle show. I was also informed by one of my male classmates that if a coed's sweater displayed a fraternity pin, as many of them did, the message was that she was taken—i.e., engaged, at least temporarily, to a Michigan fraternity man. Even more distressing than this was that campus dances, which I had enjoyed so much at Columbia, were conducted very differently at Michigan. There were big dances every Saturday night at the Michigan Union and the Michigan League (respectively the male and female student activity centers), but no stags were allowed: you took one girl, and the only chance you had to dance with anyone else was by swapping with another couple—which few did. This seemed to me so inhibiting that I wrote a letter of complaint to the *Michigan Daily*, the campus paper. It was published, but caused not the slightest ripple in the local mores.

In desperation, I took to sitting down near any good-looking coed in the reading room of the big library and, if I got so much as a not unfriendly glance, passing her a note expressing admiration and a desire to know her name and phone number. After a couple of fruitless tries, I did get a note passed back from a ravishing brunette which read, "I am Cynthia Forbes. I go with Bill Starbuck"—or some such name; I forget what, but I knew it at the time as that of one of Michigan's star basketball players.

Back in New York, John was having his own social problems, as I learned from a letter written about the middle of October:

Everything is splendid at this end (go on, you sneak—I heard you sneer the rear end). Steve and Dana and I get drunk periodically. The other night we were down at the Gold Rail and began to make up limericks—we were there some four hours and emerged with about twenty entirely original masterpieces, viz:

There was a young man from Peru

Who openly screwed a kangaroo—

He said, this copulation

Would impregnate the nation

So, by God, it's wasted on you!

[There follow six other exempla, each worse than the one before, which the reader will be spared.] Etc. far into the night. We insulted everyone from the Dean up and down, particularly down, and were almost thrown out two or three times, declaiming in a loud voice—they're getting to know us very well down at the Gold Rail these days, refuse us more than five beers and two cocktails.

Meanwhile and elsewise, I'm studying. The goodam woman I work for has had nothing to do for about ten days and I'm strapped as a fool for money. I'm still doing 64 [the course he had flunked] and other reading. . . .

. . . Crandall and Steve and Ken Orr and I went up to the New College dance a week ago tomorrow. And thence dates all our glory! . . . They did these goddam square dances, while we sat in a corner and sneered. Then they couldn't stand all this charm in the corner, so they played dance music and did we dance. I was rather in fact hellish lousy, on account of lack of practise (I'm really marvellous, said he simpering)—but I got better and Dana and I picked out the only two passable women. They were Virginia Bennett. (full stop).

This is explicated in a three-page novella the gist of which was that John and Crandall were both strongly attracted to Virginia, and she to both of them, and that despite John's efforts to keep it platonic for Crandall's sake, "the simple fact is, that we were damn strongly attracted to each other." Almost before I had had time to worry about this difficult involvement of John's, another letter relieved my mind: "Virginia is past history, incidentally—I lost interest when she began to confess seven times during a neck that she loved me; she's called several times, but I don't think there'll be any serious consequences."

To this romantic splurge from John I had been able to reply more or less in kind at the end of October:

I had noticed on the very first day of classes a little blonde in my philosophy class. . . . She had (and has) one of the most perfectly formed bodies I have ever seen . . . slim waist . . . beautiful pair of hips, lovely legs, and last, but anything but least—you're right: the most marvellous breasts in the world. . . .

I went on in this erectile vein to describe how I had managed to spirit Hedda (for that was her name) up to my room, where her behavior had aroused hopes worthy of Andrew Marvell—to which John replied appropriately:

She must be a marvel! I lost approximately twenty pounds during the letter—you're graphic as hell in your eulogy of Hedda (in other times they would have called it a lay, old man—but in these decadent latter days I suppose we mustn't, not yet, anyway). I'm wild to see the woman, but for Christ's sake don't bring her East, because after all these years I'd hate to rat on you, and I've developed into the goddamest woman-thief on the campus. . . . have been to every dance . . . neck furiously with anyone worthy—Dana and I crashed the Junior Formal Saturday and I played with four that I remember and am charged with two others . . . was very drunk. . . .

I had a birthday a couple of weeks ago—Berryman is now twenty, and less consumed with a sense of serene importance than bewildered by the futility and insignificance of his past achievement. . . .

I've been reading a lot—all sorts of things, from Mencken's "Prejudices" to "Moby Dick," which is splendid. I confess to an abysmal ignorance of Melville until now—the man writes a splendid casual prose, which can drop at a moment's notice to the blankest realism imaginable (on as flat a level of reporting as O'Hara's Appointment in Samarra, which has created such an unjustified furor the last month or so—it is drab, filthy, uninspired pornography) or rise to brief glory and long, impassionedly colored, rich prose. Melville is a mystic of the first water and a naval fatalist, to coin a phrase, but he is definitely American, which saves him from the weak soppiness of the worst of the Irish. By the way, my fury at Irish sentimentality broke into meters recently and I wrote this (the rose represents of course rank sentimentality, all the bad poetry, etc.):

Recently the shamrock said to the rose:
    "For all I'm mystical, thou and I

Are much alike, my friend; the snows
>Have melted my reality."

The rose returned in long disdain:
>"A casual likeness, I confess;
But thou *pretendst*—and there's thy bane!—
>While I quite frankly deliquesce."

I've been writing a good deal of verse—it has improved steadily, I believe, since I clubbed my way out of the morass of adolescent love-verse which cluttered the summer, and took hold of the fairly good earth to prevent further gloomy flights. This late verse is decidedly intellectual—the nearest I've come to lyricism for the past month is this double-quatrain, which I find upon after-analysis to combine mystic-phrasing with a perfectly orthodox Shakespearean theme:

I lurk within the keening wind
>That blows from desert places,
Despoil the spots where earth is thinned
>To sand and bury the oases.

I anger when the wind is harried
>By an unyielding hand—
I summon Time and wait his arid
>Subtle breath to gut the land.

(The two imperfect rimes are intentional—in so tight and monotonous a form as the 4–3–4–4 quatrains tends to be, four strong rimes seem to me too "set".)

I've been experimenting with rime a good deal—amazing things can be done with the couplets of uneven length: here are a couple from the beginning of a portrait:

eye
cold and dry
as an old drab
on a slab:
brows furrowed
where bank-notes burrowed
folding the skin
grasping and thin. . . .

And I've been working with the sonnet again. Although it's primarily an intellectual form (as naturally from the Italian—Michelangelo, Dante, etc.), I think its possibilities as a lyric and particularly as a narrative form have not been realized. You have, of course, seen narrative sonnet sequences. . . . But to my knowledge, and Van Doren corroborates me, there are no single sonnets which even pretend to the narrative. . . . In any case, I hope there are no others, for then I shall have invented a form! I wrote the first one about a week ago and have done three others since . . . III is the most unusual . . . the octet is a soliloquy of a condemned man . . . and the sestet is objective narration of his hanging (incidentally, this sonnet is the work of an atheist! I want to talk to you—my beliefs are at a deadlock, I don't know what I believe or think). . . . If, which I sincerely doubt, I should ever gain a real power over poetic expression and diction, this narrative sonnet form should be an interesting one to work in. . . .

Winnie is in the pink—sends her love. Listen, you're coming home Christmas, aren't you? God you'd better—we'll come out and string you up by the testes! . . . we're going to have one big long very besotted debauch. . . .

God bless your little soul and keep you free of crabs and

fandangoes and syphilis—kiss Hedda fifty million times for me and think of your old pal when you fondle that bosom, you lecher!

John

For Christ's sake, send snapshots
of Hedda—I'm having fits!!

What's her last name,
cagey? Probably
Pznocskywncg.

By the time this opus arrived in Ann Arbor I was mired in a slough of despond, for Hedda had played the vixen, or so it seemed to me. After elaborate preparations that even included the purchase of a small radio, I had again lured her up to my room, convinced that a Great Event was destined to occur that evening. Auspiciously (as I thought), it was my twenty-first birthday. All went well until I unobtrusively tried to remove her underpants, at which point she sprang from the bed, her eyes flashing like lights on a police car, denounced me as an arrogant lecher "like all the others," and disappeared through the door and down the stairs.* I was so dejected that I didn't even answer John's letter until he prompted me with a postcard at the start of December, whereupon I got off this rather gloomy message:

Of course, Hedda turned out to be the Biggest Bitch of All Time. She gave me a few days of humiliating misery; now I'm relieved to have it all over with. That, too, I'll save for vacation; suffice it now to say that if she didn't have an exceptionally desirable body she would have no friends among the sex masculine. . . .

I was much impressed with your poetry. The Shamrock and the Rose is gorgeous; and I think there's a hell of a lot in your idea of the narrative sonnet. . . .

*She did apologize later—thirty years later.

John answered this, as we used to say in the days when it meant something, by return mail:

Friday [December 7, 1934]

Damn glad to hear from you—I was growing mildly apoplectic with the fear that you weren't coming home Christmas. In fact, last night over beer Steve and Dana and Ken and I projected a pilgrimage to the hinterland (snobbish for Michigan) in quest of you. God, I'll be glad to see you; when the hell will you be in? We want to greet you appropriately, with phallic symbols in our hats, bitches under each arm and liquor on the beastly hip. . . .

I'm terribly sorry about your despondency (hihat—vile word—for the dumps), especially Hedda, of whom I expected great things—in nine months. Biggest Bitch of All Time is some title, by the way. . . . Am still footloose, with a rapish gleam in my eye: Ken and I are going on a double Saturday, the girls are staying together, we've both necked them madly, there's a couch in the livingroom and one in the little annex . . . more later.

. . . My pal! Everybody else except Van Doren sneers at my verse— hell with 'em! When I'm famous . . . famous last words. Written some more but too lazy to copy it—will bore you to death when you come. . . .

. . . Making damn little meanwhile—life is still grim and I feel very dull. For Christ's sake write something gay—somebody has got to be happy! Will call your family this evening. . . . More anon. *Write!*

J

By this time the Michigan campus was beginning to close down for the holidays, and there was only one last incident that I thought worthy of reporting to John. I had stayed late at the Tri Delt house to give the sinks a scrubbing on the final day of classes. I was just starting down the back stairs to hang wet rags in the basement, when from the landing above I heard shrieks and giggles, and down the stairs leaped two long-haired girls, one entirely naked and the other wearing only panties and pursuing the first one with a big towel that she was snapping at her bottom. Engrossed in their game, they were almost on top of me before they saw me, standing (I suppose) open-mouthed with my armful of rags, whereupon with even louder shrieks and giggles they both leaped back up the stairs and disappeared, leaving me with a kaleidoscopic vision of flying limbs and breasts which has never quite faded from memory.

ONE OF THE wonderful things about going home for Christmas from Ann Arbor was the way you got there, if you lived in New York. Every night about 8 P.M., after a long annunciatory whistle, a crack New York Central train pulled into the railroad station down the hill by the Huron River and chuffed impatiently for three or four minutes while the pullman porters put down their steel footstools for mounting and dismounting passengers, and the conductors checked their Hamilton watches and urged all aboard. It was the Wolverine, so called after the unpleasant animal mystifyingly chosen to represent the state of Michigan, but belying the name in both its speed and its amenities. It made the run to New York City in about thirteen hours, arriving comfortably around nine in the morning. You could have an ice-cold martini in the club car, possibly striking up an acquaintance with an adventuress, make your way through the rocketing coaches to the deluxe diner for a splendid repast served on a rich, white tablecloth by the most skillful waiters in the world, and then go back to your Pullman section, which meanwhile had miraculously metamorphosed into upper and lower berths behind whose heavy green curtains there seemed to lurk the promise of intrigue. In the night the train would drowse you to sleep with the steady click of the rails and the gentle sway of the car, and if you woke up briefly, disturbed by the fact that it had stopped moving, you could peer out through the curtains' crack and glimpse a snowy little town somewhere in Canada or western New York, wreathed in great puffs of steam from the locomotive. If you asked the porter to wake you when the Wolverine left Albany, you could shave and dress and have coffee and a roll in the diner just before you got to

Grand Central Station. You felt like a character in F. Scott Fitzgerald, and all the holiday wonders of Manhattan were waiting for you besides.

The truth is that on my first trip back to New York on the Wolverine, I lacked funds for a berth and had to sit up in a coach all night. But the car was full of other homegoing students, and when several of us went to the diner for breakfast in the morning we could not have been much happier.

I phoned John within an hour of walking through the door of my parents' apartment in Brooklyn Heights. We met at the Gold Rail for a beer that afternoon and planned our social calendar for the holidays. Both of us had heavy remnants of academic work hanging over us, but we were cheerfully convinced that we could get it all done and still be the stellar playboys of Morningside Heights and probably Broadway too.

Winann called me a couple of days later and said that one of her best friends, Dorothy Rockwell, was home from Smith College and together they were giving a Christmas party. "There's a man shortage," she said, "and you and John are invited." I accepted with humble thanks, but it turned out that John's mother had theater tickets for the family on the party night. I did stop by the Berryman's new apartment on 115th Street— the first time I had been there—where I imbibed a scotch on the rocks to sharpen my wits for the party, and then proceeded to the scene of the action alone. Dorothy was a bosomy blonde, and there were four or five other attractive college girls there, including a slim brunette, Jane Atherton, who misheard my name when we were introduced and decided it was Hemingway, which she called me thenceforth. They all seemed very pretty and brainy and sexy, and I felt that life was opening out. Dorothy, I learned, was the daughter of a prominent theologian who was a respected acquaintance of my father. She was so alluring that I immediately began to hope she would live up to the popular notion of ministers' children as black sheep—an image to which I aspired myself but so far had only meagerly attained.

In this hope I was not much disappointed. Dottie, as she was known, was certainly the most avant-garde young woman I had met, left wing in her politics despite an impeccably bourgeois background, and liberated in her moral views. Most of us were that, of course, or thought we were; but Dottie, I inferred when we went out for a drink a few days later, had the courage of our convictions. There were hints of romantic involvements which had gone well beyond the pale, or at least had escaped the pale cast of thought that had turned awry several of my own erotic enterprises. I was quite dazzled, and resolved that I must woo this modern Cytherea as ardently and shrewdly as possible.

She was, like me, majoring in English, and I thought a good gambit would be taking her to a performance of *Romeo and Juliet,* in which Katharine Cornell was then starring on Broadway (rather nervily, since the famous actress could not have been under thirty-five at the time). My sister Dorothy had given me tickets to several plays for Christmas, including this one; but they were second-balcony seats, which did not strike me as classy enough for the campaign I had in mind. Scrimping, I exchanged them for good orchestra seats, and one night between Christmas and New Year's, with ostensible aplomb, I escorted Dottie down the aisle of the Martin Beck Theater.

Both of us were in an amorous mood that the love-drenched ambiance of *Romeo and Juliet* only inflated. We had our overcoats in our laps, and by the middle of the first act, with Juliet's nurse babbling lasciviously of dugs and teats and "falling backward," there was so much mutual groping going on beneath the coats, accompanied by so much impassioned panting, that two matrons seated in front of us turned to glare indignantly. I am not certain whether we lasted out the entire play, but at any rate, when we left the theater, and I proposed a drink somewhere, Dottie revealed that a friend of hers, a dance teacher at Arthur Murray's, had offered the use of his Upper West Side apartment; we could go there for a drink.

We taxied up and went into the dimly lit place. I was in a high state of excitement, telling myself that I must make my moves very carefully: timing was everything in these matters. My intestinal system, however, was not cooperating, and it was clear that before anything else, I had to go to the bathroom. When I emerged a few minutes later, prepared to resume my air of the cool Lothario, I was stunned to find Dottie lying back on the couch, smoking a cigarette and wearing nothing but a large bathrobe thrown across her shoulders. Panic seized me. I felt like an actor who had blacked out in the middle of a scene, and suddenly had no idea what his next line was supposed to be. Mechanically, as Dottie slipped out of the robe and arranged herself on the couch, I took off my clothes and lay down beside her. But all my ardor had waned in the face of this unexpected reversal of roles, and the more I pretended to passion the more obvious it became that nothing was going to happen to verify it. In this awkward situation my companion showed for the first time that she too was only just beyond the age of innocence: instead of offering resuscitative sympathy, she made some slightly scoffing remark and suggested that we should go somewhere and get something to eat. And so the evening ended lugubriously over scrambled eggs at a Child's restaurant on Broadway.

The rest of the Christmas vacation was fairly jolly. John and I spent hours quaffing beer, going to heavy Russian films, browsing in bookstores, and discussing Life—we decided, after much pondering, that Time is Change, and that a reliable social motto was "All Women are Bitches," which we later modified to "All Interesting Women are Bitches," a conclusion that made us decide to avoid dates for New Year's Eve. We also managed to waylay Mark Van Doren en route to his Hamilton Hall office and get him to join us for a cup of coffee. He quizzed me about Michigan, and I told him that the only teacher I had out there who seemed to me to be of Morningside Heights caliber was Warner G. Rice, my Renaissance lit professor. Rice was a tall, lean, somewhat grim-faced Milton scholar whose interests and knowledge obviously fanned out to much wider scope; he was also a tough teacher whose intolerance of nonsense in the classroom had not won him a large student following. I was much surprised to have Mark interrupt me with, "Oh, I know Warner Rice well. He and I were at the University of Illinois together—I think he got one master's degree in chemistry and another in English. He's the most learned man I know." This, plus my great enjoyment of Rice's classes, brought me into the small but loyal fold of his intense admirers, where I have remained ever since.

On New Year's Eve John and I split the cost of half a pint of Four Roses whiskey, drank all of it in a rather short time at his apartment—his mother and Uncle Jack having gone out for the evening—and headed for the Columbia faculty club in Butler Hall, where a big formal dance was in progress. Winann, who was to be there, had alerted us to this celebration, and several other girls we knew were going to be there too. Having quickly failed in an attempt to bluff our way past a crusty footman who accosted us in the foyer of Butler Hall—we were too obviously dressed wrong for the occasion—we went around to the back of the building, and to our delight found an unlocked window and a stairway leading to the second-floor ballroom. Stashing our coats and hats in a hallway, we sauntered onto the floor, spotted Winann and another girl we knew—I think it was Elspeth—and cut-in. The girls were amused, but we soon discovered that the chaperones, or patrons (or whatever they were) took a different view. An elderly gentleman in an old-fashioned tuxedo started making his way toward John as the orchestra reached the end of "Night and Day," but had just given him a preemptory tap on the shoulder when the music began again and John and his partner were swirling off to "You're Gonna Lose Your Gal." Winann and I were just as evasive, and the frustrated guardian had to blunder back to the sidelines amidst a good deal of hilarity; midnight was nearly upon us and everyone was working up to as much New Year's abandon as this sort of dance was able to generate. The clock struck twelve, the orchestra went into a ragged but enthusiastic imitation of Guy Lombardo's "Auld Lang Syne," and John and I decided that it was time to get out. We retrieved our coats and hats and were about to plunge down the stairway when John said, "Hell, let's go out the *front* way!" We milled back across the ballroom through the crowd of kissing and squealing couples, and out to the imposing marble staircase descending to the foyer. Without further consultation we both jumped sidesaddle onto the smooth marble balustrade—a trick we had long since perfected on the stairways of Hamilton Hall, the main classroom building—and crying "Happy New Year!" zoomed airborne past the startled and indignant face of the Butler Hall footman.

Out on 119th Street, feeling like Douglas Fairbanks in one of his big escape scenes, we pranced over to Broadway and tried to think of something that would keep up our level of elation. Only one thing, we decided, would do: we must find Mark Van Doren and personally convey our New Year's greetings to this great man. We looked up the phone number in an outdoor booth; John dialed and was answered by a woman who was not, she explained, Mrs. Van Doren, but a maid. Putting on a tone of deep import, John declared that it was imperative for us to see Professor Van Doren immediately. I doubt that anyone was fooled by this with the possible exception of John, but the maid did say that the Van Dorens had gone to a party at "Mr. White's house," on East 8th Street in the Village. We scanned the list of Whites in the phone book, found an E. B. White at what seemed to be the right address, and twenty minutes later were down there.

Our nerve, thus far sustained by whiskey and our smashing success at Butler Hall, quailed a bit as we stood on the doorstep, but after a moment of doubt I pushed the bell. The door was opened by a pleasant-looking woman who, however, did not appear to be in the bacchanalian mode that we had envisaged. I explained, after apologies, that we were students of Mark Van Doren, had been told he was here, and had come to wish him Happy New Year. Mrs. White gave us a big smile but said that unfortunately the Van Dorens had left a few minutes earlier. We must come in, though, and have a New Year's drink with her and her husband and their guests. What we found in the Whites' living room was a remarkably sober group of gentlemen in tweed suits and pipes, and ladies in sweaters and skirts, conversing cheerfully but calmly about books and politics. John and I felt ill at ease, the more so because we recognized some of the names we heard as those of New York literati: our bravado had disappeared and we could think of little to say. We finished our drinks, made polite salutations, and departed through gently falling snow for the Fourteenth Street subway station. Our mission of homage to Van Doren had not come off, but we still felt quite satisfied with our New Year's Eve as a whole.

JOHN AND I had parted after Christmas vacation with vows of quick correspondence, but it was near the end of January when I got this letter:

Wretch! I'm as ashamed of my silence as I hope you are of yours, said he stupidly.

God bless the blind lame and halt, I'm to be back in college this spring! Classes begin the 6th, next Wednesday—am I glad. This infernal indolence is getting into my roots and I am in great disrepute with the family for my sloth and procrastination—I blush to state that I have not yet completed the cursed and triplecursed English 64 reading. Going to take the course over, so why? But I must, and there's an end. . . .

Winnie tells me you have written Dottie—how is she and how are you with regard to her?? She seems to be a honey, but for christ's sake don't fall in love, man. It's hell. . . .

Hell with everything—I've made a lovely mess of twenty years. If I don't get to it, this spring, there's little hope. So pray for me . . . write me a hell of a harsh and typically fascinating letter to set me to work. I miss your bright and vacuous (heh heh) charm like hell. . . . All my love to the women you've ruined, and destruction to thee, villain!

John

It was true that Dottie Rockwell and I had started an exchange of letters. I persuaded myself that I was at least half in love with her, although I felt a nagging suspicion that what burned in me was more a desire to repair the humiliation I had suffered in our Christmas encounter than to win her love. But she was a talented and amusing correspondent, and letters began to transit between Ann Arbor and Northampton fairly often. I even sent her a romantic sonnet, not revealing, I fear, that it had been written as an assignment in my Renaissance lit course. It was fulsomely Elizabethan, with many thee's and thou's and lines like "Counting thy virtues while mine own decay," and I got praise for it from Professor Rice; I also sent John a copy. He replied with a sonnet of his own, nearly as imitative of Keats as I had been of Sir Philip Sidney; but there were touches of real feeling in it, and it certainly showed which of us was more likely to become the poet:

> When something less than you remains of you
> And I am likewise desolate in clay,
> I like to think (although I cannot say)
> That walks we had, and words, and things we knew
> Of foolishness and wisdom—all the crew
> That manned our double venture, will delay
> A while behind us, find a ship and stay
> Valiant as they served us, in conflict new.

> This is my hope. And yet this pales before
> The agony that I sustain when I
> Think on that final closing of the door,
> And that beyond I shall not hunger more
> To stand with you beneath a single sky—
> Great Death! We two at last alone to die!
> John
> *January 30, 1935*

I found that I was quite affected by this—so much so, in fact, that I was a little embarrassed at admitting it to John:

February 10

Dear John:

Before I become insulting let me say in all truth that I liked the sonnet: in fact (said the cynic sheepishly) I was rather moved thereby....

But...I am becoming the most wary, calculating bastard you've ever seen—I merely smile quizzically at Bierkamp's protestations of passion [Bierkamp was a coed I had been going out with], and sneer (without a great deal of enthusiasm, however) at Rockwell's cautious hints that *if* things broke right she *might* really fall for me....

I'm terribly glad to know you're back at college. Work like hell, have fun, and instill in V[an]D[oren] the fear that you'll have more poems in Untermeyer's next anthology than he.... Incidentally, his new book of verse seems to be getting decidedly better reviews than *The Transients* [a novel by Van Doren], doesn't it?...

Exams were hell, and I've gotten no marks as yet.... Rice has been kind enough to recommend me for the English honors course, which means that from now on I'll work frantically getting a liberal education which will prepare me for nothing.

...God, it's marvellous having this little radio out here.... There's a hell of a good orchestra playing "Flying Down to Rio"—remember that night we went to see it? While on the memories, wasn't that an incredibly wonderful New Year's Eve? They may come and go forever, and some may find us doing other magnificent things, like having mutual orgasms with Ginger Rogers or such; but I'm sure I'll never transcend that stupendous moment when we slid so blithely down the railing at the Faculty Club.

. . . Well old man, a joint resolution: we will work steadily and thoroughly, both on the books and on the women. . . . Tell me about them then; course numbers and bust measurements, respectively, for instance.

—*Milt*

As soon as he got my letter, John sat down and produced this effusion:

[February 14, 1935]

Dear Milt,

I'm bursting with good news—POP! Van Doren has changed that mark in English 64 to a B, I don't have to take it over, and the damn flunk is off my record! How's that? But believe me, the story behind the miracle is grim. . . . I had to grind it, beginning last Friday; . . . between then and 4 a.m. yesterday, when I finished, I read about sixteen books and wrote upwards of 15,000 words of criticism. Naturally, I only averaged about four hours of sleep a night, and I am practically a shade. However, there it is—I gave him yesterday noon the whole course, and Milt, it was 166 pages, something over 52,000 words! . . . I'm so proud that I can scarcely touch the ground. . . . Van Doren knows it was done mainly as a mark of esteem for him and to show *him* I wasn't as worthless as he may have supposed. . . . He is absolutely the justest person I have ever known, Milt, and that's only one of his majesties—he never wavers from the line he has set for himself, and it's the best line in America today. I absolutely reverence the man, besides liking him incredibly. . . . I'm switching into his English 20, the American Lit course. . . . Besides, I have Sociology with Casey (it's fascinating and completely bewildering), . . . Odell's drama course (he's a peach of an old fellow, very witty despite his being a perfect old-schooler . . .), Geology (the bastard! Steve is there with me, and we sweat . . .) and Solid Geometry with Dean Hawkes (who is a swell instructor and very funny, he gets all covered with chalk and pencils. . . .)

Was talking to Len Robinson, who is editor of the [Columbia] Review now, yesterday, and showed him some verse. He insisted on printing some, and made me feel like a fool for refusing, so I let him have "Delinquency has been my portion" and "Essential". It was no pose, my refusing—the Review prints so much shit, and since I've never had anything published, I'd rather the first were in something decent— but I'm glad enough now, since both of the poems are sincere, as skilful as I can make them, and sufficiently impersonal so that they won't bother me by being read (if anybody reads the Review, which I doubt.) . . .

I have been invited to the Sophomore Formal at Barnard this Saturday and am going! . . . you know, that's Garnette's class dance, and I know some hundred of them. . . . So I am fascinated by the prospect and intend to be so gorgeous that they'll all have fits, said he modestly. . . .

Your letter is even more exciting than usual (said he, finally ceasing to talk about himself). . . . our Junior Prom is next week . . . Dana and I have a solemn compact to crash it—hope we can and wish you were here. I have a copy of *The Transients*, said he irrelevantly, and it's a splendid piece of work. But I've looked through [Van Doren's] *A*

Winter Diary over in the Browsing Room and my boy, it has some of the best verse I've ever read. He's an absolutely marvellous poet. . . .

Luck in your marks—I wish to hell I were out there. Listen to me, you dog, you and I are going abroad the summer of '36. I don't care about the money, we can work across and bicycle through the Continent—but we've got to go, and we can, so make up your mind to it. . . .

Here's something that may amuse you—I did it four minutes ago:

ODE ON HALLIDAY'S BED

When joys (and other things) are laid
Aside, and debts have all been paid,
I like to think this bed will be
Reviled, my child, eternally.

For there are many righteous ladies
Who'd like to put all beds in Hades—
Especially one supporting joys
That bring to Bierkamp girls and boys.

However, friend, I don't agree
That double-duty beds will be
Polluted—nay, I will confide
I think they will be sanctified!

P.S. You may not know that [John Treville] Latouche wrote [the 1935] Varsity Show—it's called "Flair-Flair, the Idol of Paris"!! Don't know yet whether I'm going out this year—maybe I'll have time for chorus.— Caress your stein (Biermug, you mug!) in the properly improper places for me—

Enviously, *John*

Out in Ann Arbor, I was on such a busy schedule trying to keep up with new obligations in the English honors course, and with new girls I had recently met, that it was nearly time to go home for Spring Vacation before I answered John's letter:

. . . My silence was no indication of what I felt: I am so damn glad you're back in college that I could leap incredible distances with even more incredible ease. . . .

Well, I could sympathize with you and Steve and the Cretaceous period a little more if I weren't so very thoroughly entwined and befogged with Accrued Interest and Profit and Loss Statements. Which is to say that I (in one of those supremely noble pre-semester moments) decided to discipline myself by taking accounting. . . .

. . . WOMEN—Well, I must puff a bit. . . . It all started with the J-Hop Biermug took me to; since then the whole of Mosher-Jordan dormitory (450 gorgeous girls 450) has been in an uproar every night to determine who is gonna take Halliday to the Assembly Ball, who is gonna give him a ticket to the Junior Girls' Play, what sorority will be blessed with his princely presence this weekend, and so on indefinitely. . . .

But to stop shooting the shit, temporarily anyway, I *have* been having a stupendous time: several perfectly knock-out babes. . . . I'll tell you about it all when I get home, which isn't so long now, hurrah hurrah. . . .

Just waiting . . .

Milt

Spring vacation was not quite as wonderful as I had hoped. Rockwell had invited me up to Smith College for a big dance, and despite some exposure at Andover to the stock-exchange criteria governing the importation of out-of-town dates for such affairs, I foolishly supposed this might augur a rise in her affection for me. It was a disappointing business: I stayed in a fraternity house in Amherst with some friend of a friend who drove back and forth to Northampton in a persistent alcoholic cloud; the dance itself was unmemorable; and Dorothy showed no disposition to be more than categorically jolly and friendly. I met her roommate, who regarded me with what seemed to be an air of suspicion, visited the local Coke-and-coffee hangouts, and got better acquainted with Jane Atherton, who was quietly charming. In toto, I was relieved to head for New York for a few days of talk and movie going with John and a tea dance or two with Winann. I was even glad to see my family, and Lois took me to the new Cole Porter musical, *Anything Goes*, where she memorized all the lyrics to "You're the Top" before the final curtain.

THAT SPRING IN Ann Arbor, however, *was* a wonder. The weather was perfect for weeks, including dulcet showers that were a pleasure to walk in with a beautiful girl—and in the English honors course I had met two true beauties. Ah, Rosalie.... I described her enthusiastically in a letter to John: lovely blonde, 5′6″, 126 pounds perfectly distributed, but how she got admitted to the English honors course, I said, was a matter of some speculation. She was bright, all right—nobody doubted that—but her principal bent was not toward academic achievement. I could only surmise that the magical spell her presence cast over me had also overcome Professor Bennett Weaver, who ran the course. A Shelley specialist, he was highly transcendental, given to disparaging carnal love as against spiritual, and intoning "Oh wild West Wind, thou breath of Autumn's being" to his classes in a voice so deep and resonant that blackboards in neighboring classrooms vibrated in iambic pentameter. When I went in for an interview prior to acceptance as a member of the course, he peered at me over a nose that incongruously looked as if it had been broken in a brawl, and demanded to know what my special interests were. I cited literature, of course, and the theater, whereupon he confided that he originally had meant to be a professional actor. He had attended Carroll College, in Wisconsin, with Alfred Lunt, and the two of them had been stars in the dramatic society there. "Ah well," the professor mused, casting a melancholy gaze heavenward, "Alfred had the looks."

The other gorgeous member of Bennett Weaver's honors course was Rosalie's best friend, and a striking contrast: a dark brunette with large brown eyes, a musing expression, and a figure that moved John, when he

met her later, to quote Swinburne's line about "the deep division of pro-
digious breasts." There was also a fairly deep division in Jeanne Curtis's
interests, for she loved poetry and ideas, but was second not even to Rosalie
in her appreciation of campus high life. Together they cut a formidable
swath through the more lively Michigan fraternities, often double dating,
conspiring to defeat Dean Lloyd's proscriptions, and scatting off on weekend adventures such as a safari to the Kentucky Derby in Louisville. I
teetered on the edge of falling for both of them, and they kept me off
balance by going out with me just enough, and flattering me just enough,
to counteract my rage at the amount of time they spent with well-heeled
fraternity boys. My dates with Rosalie usually started with a visit to a
campus dugout called the Parrot, where a crap game was chronically in
progress in one of the booths. Rosalie, who carried her own dice in her
purse in case of need, invariably won two or three bucks after a few rolls,
either by some native skill or because her opponents were too distracted
to read the dice correctly. We would then hustle downtown for a dance
at the Moose Hall or a few beers at the Pretzel Bell, a famed Ann Arbor
oasis.

THREE
New York / Ann Arbor,
1935–36

I got *him* to review Tate's book of essays
& *Mark* to review *The Double Agent*. Olympus!
I have travelled in some high company since
but never so dizzily.

—"Olympus"

Between copious reading of Wordsworth and Shelley in
a hopeless effort to convince Bennett Weaver that I finally understood the
true meaning of Imagination, and tantalizing sport with Rosalie and
Jeanne, the spring wafted quickly by, and I was back in New York for the
summer. Once more I was despressingly unable to find summer work, so
time hung hot and heavy. John was enrolled in a couple of courses in a
push to ensure his graduation at the end of the following school year, but
we nevertheless managed to spend much time together. His family was
away for a good part of July and August, and so was mine, and I tended
to go up to his apartment and hover, reading Shakespeare and waiting
for John to reach a pause long enough for us to go out and play tennis
for an hour or so on the Columbia courts, or, more occasionally, trip out
to one of the Long Island beaches.

Our frequent companion in these diversions was Jane Atherton,
whom John had met at the start of the summer and immediately taken to
passionately. I was also growing very fond of Jane, who had a marvelously
cheerful and even temper, and was most pretty and witty besides. Her
mother had a sport roadster with a rumble seat, which at least once conveyed us to Jones Beach with me in the rear, a portable typewriter on my
lap, while John dictated to me, for he insisted he could not go unless he
finished a few pages on a paper he had due. Not much got written,

John Berryman, 1935—a snapshot taken by
Jane Atherton on the roof of her apartment
house near Riverside Drive. "Our frequent
companion was Jane...whom John had met
at the start of the summer and immediately
taken to passionately." Courtesy Jane
Atherton Roman

however, since we grew hilarious over the idea that every paragraph in
the paper should begin either, "Obviously,..." or "It is now clear...."

Then there was Radio City Music Hall. Astaire and Rogers were
already firmly installed in our pantheon, and when we heard that they
were opening there in *Top Hat* we headed for a matinée to adore them
and the Rockettes. Our euphoria was so great that we bought candy bars
at the end of the show in lieu of lunch, and sat down to revel in Fred and
Ginger's prestipeditation as they pursued each other through "Isn't It a
Lovely Day" and "Cheek to Cheek" one more time.

We three also spent a wonderful afternoon and evening in Brooklyn
Heights, taking a swim at the St. George Hotel ("The World's Largest
Salt Water Pool") and more or less destroying in the broiler at my parents'
apartment the filets mignon we had extravagantly purchased for dinner
along with a bottle of cheap red wine that John selected with exquisite
care. Afterward we went up and sat under the canopy on the roof, watching
the Staten Island ferries ply through the summer night in the harbor while
we made sparkling remarks. Jane called her mother and got permission to
spend the night (my sister Dorothy had arrived), and when we finally

Jane Atherton, 1935—a snapshot John took
to match the one of him on the previous
page. "Jane had a marvelously cheerful and
even temper, and was most pretty and witty
besides." Courtesy Jane Atherton Roman.

went to bed John said he must have a pair of pajamas. Not owning any
myself, I gave him a pair of my father's, which were much too big for
him. Festooned in these, John disappeared into the bedroom where Jane
had retired. He was gone for quite a while, during which I heard what
sounded like squeals of protest from Jane. Then he reappeared looking
aggrieved, the pajamas hanging on him like flags of defeat. "Well?" I said.
"She's a bitch, Milt," he said, and climbed into his bed.

The Van Dorens were up in their country place in Connecticut for
most of the summer, but every couple of days John would phone their
Manhattan number to see if by chance they had returned. One hot day in
July, Mark answered and said he'd be in town for the rest of the week,
whereupon John asked him to stop by for a drink. He said he would, and
the next afternoon John and I practiced making mint juleps "Maryland
style," as John defined them: he had decided this was the appropriate
cooling beverage to offer Mark. We had them pretty well perfected by the
time Mark arrived, and the three of us downed several more, for they were
indeed delicious and at least gave the illusion of mitigating the ferocious
heat. We all got rather tight, but were having a fine time discussing

Shakespeare's sonnets, which John and I had been systematically studying at the rate of one per day. We had found them more resistant to ready interpretation than we had expected, bogging down, in fact, on the precise import of the very first one. What did "Feed'st thy lights flame with selfe substantiall fewell" mean? What about "Within thine owne bud buriest thy content"? I had suggested, a week or so earlier, that it sounded like some kind of self-abuse; John had pounced on that and announced, "That's it, Milt! It's about masturbation!" Now, however, when we proposed this gloss, Mark looked dubious. "It's an argument against staying single, that's clear," he said. "But masturbation. . . . Well. . . . Maybe you're reading a bit into it."

Somehow that dissolved into a discussion of Edna St. Vincent Millay, and when Mark said he knew her personally, we of course wanted to know what she was like. "Edna St. Vincent Millay," Mark said, stumbling a little on the name, "is a bitch." This pleased us enormously, since it seemed a prime piece of evidence to support our conclusion about interesting women in general. After Mark had gone, making a somewhat precarious descent of the long stairway, John and I badly scrambled some eggs and composed a sophomoric limerick about the famous poet:

> As for Edna St. Vincent Millay
> There isn't a great deal to say.
> She started a trend,
> Laying words end to end,
> But her forte lay in laying Millay.

JULY FINALLY PERSPIRED away, but August was just as hot. Summer school came to an end and John went off to visit his family somewhere; Atherton was working at Altman's, or maybe it was Lord & Taylor; I was very much in the doldrums. Late in August, my spirits zoomed when I got this telegram from Sunapee, New Hampshire:

CAN YOU COME UP HERE ON THE FRIDAY NIGHT TRAIN
THIS WEEK WHEN ANN AND I NEED YOU DESPERATELY. . . .
LOVE—DOTTIE

(One of the delights provided by Western Union was that they so often garbled the message just enough to be funny; in this case I knew immediately that it should have read WINANN instead of WHEN ANN.) My feelings about Rockwell had been in a state of suspense tending toward atrophy, but the telegram revived them wonderfully. I wired back that I was on my way.

It was very relaxing in the cool New Hampshire woods with Lake Sunapee almost at the doorstep, and it was pleasant to have two smart, good-looking girls to hang out with. We slept late, ate and swam a lot, and dawdled about the cottage, reading Nero Wolfe detective novels with no great sense of urgency. Dorothy was mildly provocative—I especially remember how she would let her tiny kitten crawl up under her sweater between her breasts and surface at the neckline, purring away—but friendly enough, and I began to think we were getting on quite well. There was a certain amount of summer night life, the highlight of which was a dance with music by Jimmy Lunceford's orchestra—by all odds, in my opinion, the best dance band of the era. At the end of the evening Winann went off with someone else, and Dottie and I drove back in her father's sedan. It was a fine August night, and when she suggested that we park in a convenient spot and talk, I thought maybe my luck with her was about to change dramatically.

It was, too—only not in the direction I had anticipated. After allowing me a quasi-sexual kiss, she removed herself to arm's length and proceeded to explain, quite bluntly, that the prospect of a romantic future for us was so dim as to be invisible. I felt cast down and humiliated, but also angry at what seemed to me in retrospect to have been her misleading signals. We drove stiffly back to the cottage, and I returned to New York the next day, amply disillusioned.

Yet the cancellation of my fantasies about Rockwell did not protect me from being sorely affronted when, in mid-September, she carried on a vivacious flirtation with John at an end-of-summer party Atherton threw for all of us, and disappeared with him for an hour. Not only, I thought, was she thumbing her nose at me, but my best friend—whom I had not told about my rejection and disenchantment—was willfully flouting my feelings. I was too proud and too disturbed to discuss it with him, and tried to act bored when he remarked afterward that he thought Rockwell was getting quite interested in Steve Aylward. John sensed my tension, however, and sent me an admonishing letter in the form of an Audenesque poem that came a day or two after I returned to Michigan:

> Halliday,
>> Your roads are trampled by desires
>> Mixing mud with conflict. Clear,
>> Swift would be the passage for the State
>> Officials and the messengers of purpose.
>
>> Passionless and prey to any letter
>> From province or a friend, you seem
>> The many man, when none. Walk with me
>> Out of this elaborate, simply into the sun
>
>> And let the light like guns solve
>> Creditors, the framework of desire:
>> Cancel history, be altar for
>> The iron elate religion of the soul.
>
> Berryman

This struck me as sententiously obscure and failed to make me feel any better, and I did not answer it.

But the change of scene, back in Ann Arbor, was restorative. I enjoyed the eminence of being a senior, and I no longer had to work for my meals because my father, mightily pleased at my admission to the honors program, said he'd rather have me concentrate exclusively on my courses. As a gesture of cooperation I found a less expensive rooming house—$3.00 a week instead of $3.50—and prepared for a serious year. First, however, I wrote John on September 30, saying that, contrary to an earlier plan, I would not be able to come home for the Michigan–Columbia football game, and the celebration of his twenty-first birthday on October 25. I was low on cash, I said truthfully, and moreover had no desire to compete with Steve Aylward (or, I might have added but did not, John) for Dottie Rockwell's attention.

John wrote back a few days later:

Dear Milt,

I have so damn incomparably much to say that—trash and kindred fornications! First I'll toss to ye swine a few autobiographical details, then I'll answer your gorgeous and long-awaited letter. . . .

My course is the acne of Hell College. Three seminars—Senior Colloquium, [Irwin] Edman's Metaphysics, the last year of the Lit sequence—and three others: VD's wonderful Shakespeare, Weaver's Renaissance and Odell's Modern Drama. I average four hours sleep a night and meet myself coming and going. . . . You have never seen such a dull bastard as Berryman has become. . . . I did rouse myself last night, called Carson and wended (quite tight) my way to the open dance, but it wasn't so open that they'd let *me* in—are you in the dorm? says they, and I says no are you in the dorm? and they says yes, so what? and I says Aristotle says. . . . Well, when I collected the fragments, I'd taken Carson in a huff home and was in the grill, surrounded by my admirers. What a life!

This all sounds gay but it ain't, Klinker, it ain't. I be in a berry bad state—sleepless & gruffgruff.

Atherton broke like a bitch her date with me the night you left and went off with Ralph (spit!) I spent the goddamest evening of my career, sick with all the adolescent hopelessness, jealousy, rage, self-pity, love, yearning, etc. But the next morning we fixed it up (impossible to relate these things, isn't it? Eh, Klinker?) and I drove up with them [Atherton and her mother]. Smith is gorgeous . . . was in her room and in Rockwell's, Dottie not there. No rape, though. I wrote [Atherton] every day for a week, then got sick and less frequently since. God damn her, she's got to marry me whether she loves me or not—she *must* but she doesn't. . . . My other little objets d'amour were as nothing, Halliday—I love this Atherton with my eyes and my guts and my blood and my brains and my soul, whether I have one or not.

Something else has come up. . . . [Joseph Wood] Krutch gave me

Thursday four novels to review [for the *Nation*]. . . . He may not print
the reviews, but it's a swell chance anyway—thru VD, of course. . . . I
feel a little small but unawed . . . will let you know what happens. . . .

The game yesterday was lousy, but I see you got beaten—maybe
even *we* can . . . heh heh! Incidentally, Atherton writes me special to say
they're bombarding you to come. . . . For Christ's sake don't let
anything stop you if you humanly can!

. . . Wrote Rockwell some time ago & got a reasonably amusing
return which I haven't ackn. Jane writes wonderfully—your letters and
hers are all that keep me head up, me hearty.

Sorry as hell to stop, but I've still got two Dialogues, Dinsmore's
Dante, a hunk of damnable Wordsworth (I've discovered that part of
his name was omitted, it's Words worth Shit), and a play to read
tonight, believe it or not.

Write when you have time and I'll do the same. . . .

Castrate Klinker, the Balls of the Caribbean

As the weekend of John's twenty-first birthday (October 25, 1935)
drew closer, I did get a barrage of letters urging me to change my mind
and show up in New York. Atherton wrote persuasively; Rockwell wrote
with surprising warmth; even Steve Aylward wrote, protesting (a bit too
much, I thought) that nothing could delight him more than to step aside
as Rockwell's escort if only I would come and fill that office. I did not
change my mind, however, and John seemed to understand, as he indicated
in a letter written just three days before his birthday:

I really have no goddam business writing you, but I will briefly—no
bed before 3 a m for five days. Sorry as hell you're not coming, but
underneath it all I think you wise. . . . The Van Dorens, Edman,
Weaver, Winann, Elspeth, Steve, [Robert] Giroux, Dana, Rockwell and

Atherton . . . and Mrs. Atherton—these will be here, and maybe more. It ought to be gay, although I hate like hell being twentyone.

I've somewhat begun on a career, though—I got the proofs of my review of Cabell, Sackler and Jensen (called Types of Pedantry) from the Nation this morning, and am still joyous about it. . . . I've reviewed Auden's and Isherwood's new fantastic play "The Dog Beneath the Skin" for the [Columbia] Review—it's excellent. They're also printing the Elegy on [Hart] Crane. . . .

. . . I'm still in love with Atherton but my disposition is sourer and sourer and I've given her frigid hell for five or six letters. God strafe me—my friends put up with a lot: me. . . .

On October 25, when Mrs. Berryman gave the big champagne party to honor John's majority, I sent a telegram of what I deemed witty congratulations, timing it to arrive when I thought the party would be in full swing. As it happened, all the guests had gone by the time it got there—all, that is, except Atherton and Rockwell and Steve Aylward. As John described it in his next letter:

When your telegram came Friday night, just the four of us were here—and [Steve] knows goddam well you're my best friend, but we all went out in the hall and when I started down the stairs he rushed past and grabbed the telegram from the messenger and while I was signing for it he tore it open and read it to the three of us. *Yours* to *me* read by him! . . . I took it from his hand and went in the door. Rockwell followed, then the door was pushed shut. He and Atherton were out there alone. Not that there's anything criminal in that, but he'd been making passes at her since she came over with me. And . . . he sat in the hall outside my apartment with the girl I love at my party on my birthday. A friend isn't made of stuff like that. . . .

This, however, was merely the overture to a Wagnerian opera. John recounted it in eight anguished pages written on the Sunday after the birthday celebration—a rambling and somewhat incoherent narrative that probably benefits from excerpting:

Halliday, you are the only person who exists truly and strongly for me at this moment, now. Let me tell it as quietly and absolutely justly as I can.

... Atherton and I had been on ambiguous terms, but when I went over to her apartment for her about ten [Saturday P.M.] all the sickness had gone and we were very best friends. Aylward was there with Rockwell, and Beekman with Winann. We were going to a formal in John Jay. We all bounced around and were very gay and drank some, then we all decided to leave and ran all the way across campus to the dance.... I'd brought a pint of Corn that Bob [John's brother] had given me for my birthday, and Aylward knew it.... So when we were leaving Atherton's apartment, he said give it to me and I'll carry it. So I did. Well... I danced two numbers with Jane, then Beekman cut and I danced a number with Rockwell, then somebody cut and I cut Atherton, and during the first number Aylward cut. It was a little before eleven then. I didn't see either Aylward or Atherton again until five minutes of two o'clock. I danced a bit with Winann after being cut, then we went to look for the others to go down in the Grill. You can do a lot of looking and dying in three hours, Halliday. I didn't dance again, I just waited in the dance, wandering around looking to see if they'd come back, or went down and walked up and down the Grill... or went through the ground floors of all three dorms or walked in the Quadrangle and came back into the dance with my heart jumping to see them, but they were never there.... Halfway thru the last group of numbers, they came in. Atherton was very drunk and Aylward looked sneaking and dishevelled (I'm not putting this in, he really did). They both saw me at once apparently, and danced around close, talking. Finally . . . I went over and said may I break. . . . Looking at her smiling vaguely at me and reeling, I think if I'd looked at Aylward I'd have crashed him and killed him if I could. But I was empty, hollow, by that time, and I was terribly glad to see her at all—I thought she might have been run over or raped or god knows what. . . . I asked Jane where she'd been so long, and she looked dully at me and said something about fire-escapes, so in a white heat I called to Aylward who was walking away looking like the common dirty treacherous son of a bitch he is, and without looking I asked where they'd been. He said the Alpha Delt house. . . . Almost every fellow in the house is an enemy of mine! Christ, Halliday, her drunk in that house! . . . [After Jane had been walked home] I went home and smoked an hour, then undressed and went to bed but didn't sleep. I thought and hurt and cursed and wanted to cry and was sick, until ten this morning, when I got up. I can't stand this any more, Halliday, sitting here pretending to talk to you—everything is gone out of me. . . . Please write at once. . . .

In the same morning mail with this came letters from Dottie and from Jane. Dottie, at the moment, was entirely sympathetic with John. She couldn't, she said, get the picture of John's misery at the dance out of her mind. She was angry at Jane and Steve (although she had gone to a Philharmonic concert with Steve on the day after the disastrous dance), and thought John was "a double-dyed sucker" to still be in love with Jane; her only consolation was that for once in her life she herself was "on the *outside*" of such a bruising situation. Jane, although she did not say what she and Steve had been doing in the Alpha Delt house for three hours (later on, she explained that she had simply passed out from too much liquor), insisted that Steve was still completely loyal to John, and that John's resolve never to mention Steve's name again was silly. In any event, she said, she had decided after much earnest thought that she would not see John any more: she was not in love with him, and it would be cruel to keep him dangling. One thing that made her mad about Dottie, she said, was the way she tried to keep me on the string "with no prospect of her ever being in love with you or having you happy." Despite all this (she concluded), after Dottie had written to me they had finally discussed the dance episode dispassionately, Dottie had come to see the other side of the story, and that the whole thing was a tempest in a teapot.

Considerably flabbergasted, I sat down and wrote John a long and rather turgid letter intended to make him feel better. What it boiled down to was that he must remember that Jane had never been in love with him, and had said as much, and that consequently "values and obligations which loomed large for you simply did not exist for her." I was tougher on Steve: "If he was incapable (as he apparently was) of being guided by any perspicacity on his own part, he might at least have been guided by ordinary standards of conduct as practiced by intelligent people." While plucking this high note, I was not above reminding John that Steve's behavior had not been entirely unlike his own: "Remember that goddam brawl at Jane's house when Rockwell came down from Sunapee? . . . I've never told you right out—though I think you guessed—how utterly soulsick, and blindly, hopelessly infuriated I was that weekend on account of you and Dottie."

Before this epistle ever reached New York, things had taken a surprising turn for the better. Atherton and Rockwell, hearing one way or another that John was exceedingly distraught, began to worry for fear he might do himself in. According to Jane, they knew John's father had committed suicide—a fact he had never told me, although he and I had discussed the question of to be or not to be at some length in a philosophical context—and they decided that Jane should make an emergency trip back to New York to ward off any chance of such a tragedy. Meanwhile, John had talked to Van Doren and as a result was a great deal calmer by the time Jane got there, as he wrote me on November 1:

Your letter tells me again, in case I needed to know, that you're the swellest person and the damnest infinitely best friend that ever was or will be. Enough of this base flattery, Berryman. Unbelievably, the situation has mostly straightened out, but if it hadn't, I don't know what would have kept me alive but this. And Van Doren: he saw [in class] Wednesday that I wasn't well, and when he and Giroux were talking he told Bob to tell me that if I wanted to talk to him, VD, he'd like to. So I met Bob that afternoon and went over to Van Doren's office, where he and I talked for some three hours, the best talk I've ever had with anyone except for three or four of our classic conversations, Socrates. I told him what had happened . . . without any names . . . and somehow he managed to send me out of his office feeling absolutely straight and right with myself and outside, beyond it all. That sounds like incredible shit, but it's true. . . .

Well, Wednesday . . . I was surprised to find that Atherton was in town. . . . Went over to see her, and we talked. . . . It is more than ever clear to me that she does not love me and I doubt that she ever will, but I'm sure we can be good friends. . . .

You must know how goddam definitely I remember that brawl at Atherton's. . . . I am more sorry for that than for anything else in my life, Halliday. . . . I've come, I think, and mainly through you, to see something of what friendship is, and I can't conceive of my ever failing in any such way again. Van Doren and I agreed . . . that loyalty (trust, faith, fidelity, call it anything) is the most important thing there is— with treachery the most horrible, the most monstrous crime. . . . No lying of any kind, nothing that isn't clean and in the open and true, between us, Halliday.

. . . Let's have a hell of a fine Christmas holiday, Milt—with or without women, as the mood is, and let's talk and let's see Van Doren and let's breeze about like the fascinating, carefree bastards we really are. . . .

John

On November 7, my twenty-second birthday, I got a happy note from John wishing me joy and saying there was a copy of Stephen Spender's new book of poems awaiting me in New York. A fortnight later, when he wrote again, he was absolutely high on literature:

Saturday [November 16, 1935]

Dear Milt,

Christ! I've just read Richard II—listen: [and he quotes thirteen lines of Richard's great speech beginning "No matter where—of comfort no man speak"] How can a man write so? A few of the sonnets were beautiful . . . but in the ten plays I've read there's been nothing like this—a writing that can't be learned and can't be written, but it has been by some few great—a rhetoric that swells and transcends sound and was deathless when it began.

He goes on to quote passages from Gerard Manley Hopkins and from Donne:

I know damn well you know these, and devils are my witnesses that I am without leisure to copy thus, but zounds! and other loud ecstatic sounds. . . . The most important thing that is happening at present is that Van Doren and I are becoming real friends, I think. I am completely without awkwardness or constraint in his presence (which is something for me as you know) and we talk interminably about everything. . . .

I drove up to Northampton with Anne Atherton [Jane's mother] last Sunday, as you've doubtless heard. Had a fairly swell time and was witty and pleasant invariably (I hope—tell me what R and A said on this score), but I was shown clearly how goddam in love I am and how I've got to get out of it. . . . We went for a long walk alone in the wood there in the afternoon and once I offered to kiss her [Jane], but she said 'later' and I never spoke of it or gestured again, not even at leaving. She

knew I couldn't in selfrespect ask again, but not a move made she, also
knowing how I was being slowly murdered underneath it all—so
obviously nothing but cursed fucking blasted damned rotted ghastly
camaraderie of the chitchat variety remains. Hell and hell!!! But I bore
it well, as needs must, and wrote her a very tender letter, Christ only
knows how. . . . I've had an invitation from Elspeth and a Miss Perera to
a dinner-dance on December 27, and Elspeth says you should have one
by now—for God's sake, accept, and we'll have a wonderful time.
Formal and about forty people, Winann, Bobbie, Elspeth, etc., and *no*
Atherton or Rockwell.

I've mailed you out a copy of The [Columbia] Review—everyone
in sight says this is absolutely the best issue ever. Giroux [who had
become editor of the *Review*] modelled the format on Hound and Horn
and did all the work of makeup himself—it's swell, isn't it? And Elegy
[John's poem on Hart Crane] is well printed at last—what a hell of a
rumpus that little poem is creating, believe it or not—50 persons per
day ask what it means, and VD and I sit tight and won't tell. The damn
thing is crystal clear and unambiguous, I think honestly, assuming some
knowledge of Crane's life and work—they fail to understand their own
ignorance, the poem is simple enough. . . . Write soon . . . it's only a
month now [until Christmas vacation]. . . .

> *John*
> [P.S.] Letter from Rockwell will interest you.

The issue of the *Review* was indeed "swell" (our all-purpose superlative
in the mid-thirties), and I was pleased to see the Crane poem in print,
knowing that it had been rather snootily rejected by a couple of other
publications. I did feel some fellowship for readers who were puzzled,
however, since I was having difficulty myself with what I judged to be
John's unintentional ambiguity, caused in part by truncated syntax and a
liking for mysterious metaphors. (The poem begins: "Secure and white

John with Robert Giroux (on his right) and the staff of the *Columbia Review*, 1936. "I've mailed you out a copy of The Review—everyone in sight says this is absolutely the best issue ever." Columbiana Library

the shroud about the head / The imperceptible sea rests on his brow / And salt is where the lips. Question the dead / Does not disturb, is not insistent now.") I showed the poem to knowledgeable Jeanne Curtis, who looked at me with her beautiful brown eyes and said, "But Milt, what's this about the shroud? Hart Crane just plain jumped overboard, didn't he?"

As his postscript indicated, John had been indiscreet enough to enclose a letter Dottie wrote him shortly after his visit to the Smith campus. It irritated me sharply, not only because it was far more coquettish ("Dearest, dearest, dearest, dearest, de—Dear Berryman,") than any she ever sent me even before the summer epiphany at Sunapee, but also because she chose to make me the butt of some clever but unkindly humor. I was also in some doubt as to why John thought seeing her letter would be helpful to me, and I didn't write him for a couple of weeks.

He did not wait for an answer, sending me another lengthy message near the end of November that began, "Dear Milt, I'm no longer in love with Atherton," and went on for several pages to explain why. It had to do with a cocktail party Jane gave in New York for Bobby Winslow, her future husband, which John went to after an initial refusal, and found "goddam dull"—though he did allow that Winslow, whom he had not met before, was "a simply swell guy . . . very nice and honest and admirable. . . . " Jane got angry when John donned his coat and hat before the party was half over; he was persuaded to stay a while by delightful Winann, but was himself angry as well as bored. It was then that he decided he was cured of his lovesickness, and resolved only "to see her occasionally with perfect equanimity . . . I regard Atherton with sufficient indifference (I hope) to be rather friendly."

Veering to another track, he remarked that according to Jane, Rockwell was mad at him because he had sent me her letter, and I had then written "furiously" to Rockwell. "It looks to me, Milt," John wound up, "as if there's no help for us: we're going to fall in love with bitches, and we're going to be hurt, to the last syllable of recorded time. . . . I am approaching a basically promiscuous attitude, which is excellent. Went up to the New College teadance yesterday and ran into Jean Bennett, whom I rarely see—she confessed to a *burning passion* for me that has been flaming away since June. Hey hey. . . . "

ONE OF THE afflictions of the age bracket all of us were in just then was wisdom teeth; in my collection of letters from friends there are several doleful references to these tardy obtrusions. In my own case, however, they were not obtrusive enough, for X rays showed that both my lower wisdom teeth were lying completely horizontal, down under a sturdy roof of bone and gum. Unfortunately, I allowed a senior at the University of Michigan's School of Dentistry to persuade me that these sullen objects ought to be dug out, for fear of "trouble later on." And, he said, he was prepared to make me a wonderful deal: he himself would take them out for only ten dollars apiece—about one-fourth, he assured me, of what it would cost elsewhere. The moonlighting (and illegal) operation on the first one took place one night in an otherwise deserted clinic, lasted over two hours, nearly killed both me and the student, and left me with a jaw the size of a large balloon.

Just about then a letter came from John, apologizing for not writing sooner and explaining that he'd been "sick as hell—cold, terrible cough, earache, temperature, dizziness, continual headache. . . ." I was gratified to know that I had company in my misery, but the rest of his letter aroused such rage in me that I stopped worrying about my jaw:

Rockwell was down over the last weekend and stayed over until Thursday to get rid of a cold. I saw her Sunday afternoon and she wasn't angry in the least [about his sending me the letter she wrote him] . . . took her up to a dull party . . . that night. You were both right and wrong about 'her towards me': she does want to sleep with me (she told me so, at the same time saying it was impossible). . . . Then I went over Tuesday and proximity and no one around led to vague and amused necking—kisses, nothing else. Sorry to tell you about this, but I assure you it's not in the least important to any of us—merely want it on the record. . . . As for you, she reiterated her praises of you in all your aspects except sexual, but (I hate to tell you this) did not seem at all anxious to see you Christmas. . . . She had at least two dates with Aylward while she was down. . . .

Finally wrote my article for the new Review—comment on seven recent books of verse, three of them excellent. . . . I've got some wonderful Van Doren stories to tell thee . . . in fact, we're going to have the most joyful time ever, except it looks as if, if so be I be still alive and kicking against the pricks . . . I'll be working on three papers—5000 on Plato, at least 5000 on Shakespeare and some 3000 on Renaissance. Jesus, the grand old man he was before they cut his head off!

I was seething when I answered this, but grimly forced myself to compose a lighthearted version of my encounter with the dentist before letting John know how I felt:

First, about Rockwell. For Christ's sake, do go ahead and lay her. Let me go on record as being definitely in favor of all healthy copulation, reserving possible exceptions in particular cases which I can't think of now: this is not one of them. . . . I promise you that I shall take great offense if I see any signs of self-denial: any more of the deliberated 'Buddy' stuff. . . . My year of Rockwell draws to a close, and I feel more relief than regret at the going of it. . . .

See you soon. . . .

THE CHRISTMAS HOLIDAYS in 1935, though somewhat hampered by lacerated feelings on various sides, were reasonably pleasant. I took Jane to see Leslie Howard's performance of *Hamlet*, had some good talk with Winann, enjoyed Elspeth's dinner dance, and spent more time than usual with my family. The big event, however, was again New Year's Eve. Mrs. Van Doren, apparently touched by the aborted pilgrimage John and I had made to see Mark a year earlier, called each of us and invited us to a party at their house on Bleecker Street. We were excited by this prospect, but John was in a quandary: he had a long-standing date with Atherton for New Year's Eve. His mother, convinced that John was about to pass through an enchanted archway into the great world of letters, urged him to break the date with Jane, but this he refused to do. After consulting me, he phoned Dorothy Van Doren and explained the problem—and of course she instantly said, "That's fine—please bring her along."

Remembering the party at the Whites' in 1934, I thought we ought to wear slacks and sport jackets, but Mrs. Berryman would have none of that. So John and I got into white tie and tails, and when we picked up Jane for the trip to the Village found her resplendent in a long black dress and a regal red velvet cape. Sure that nothing now could take the wind out of our sails, we boarded the subway in order to preserve funds for a probable taxi later on, evoking stares on the way downtown which we chose to interpret as envious admiration. "Oh my!" Mrs. Van Doren cried in pleased surprise when she opened the door to us; and sure enough, nearly all the other guests were far more modestly attired.

Feeling a little awkward but not intimidated, we drank scotch a bit faster than we should have, and had a good try at chatting casually with literary lights who until then had been only names to us. Things went along very well until about ten minutes to midnight, when through the front door came Clifton Fadiman, his arms bulging with magnums of champagne. There followed a great ejaculation of corks and a filling of large highball glasses—the hell with champagne glasses, he said—and everyone was ordered to do bottoms-up on the stroke of twelve.

The effect was rapid and amazing. Like a little volcano of latent rowdiness, the party simply erupted: there was loud bawling of Auld Lang Syne in four-part disharmony; there were New Year's kisses that were far from perfunctory; there was the crash of breaking glass; there was an eminent professor of philosophy demonstrating the Big Apple in the middle of the living room. And there was a very beautiful blonde seated at the piano, ad-libbing dance tunes with less finesse than gusto while her hair, which had been piled atop her pretty head, came tumbling down the back of her low-cut green evening gown. After a while she said something fairly incoherent about her hairdo and headed for the stairs. Imagining that I was being ultra-nonchalant (for I was by now thoroughly drunk), I waited what I judged to be the right amount of time and went up after her.

I tapped on the bathroom door. She opened it, her hair still streaming down her back, and without a moment's hesitation threw herself into my arms. We kissed passionately, swaying around a good deal; then I picked her up and carried her down the hall to the bedroom where all the coats had been left on a big double bed. I managed to shove enough of them aside to deposit her on her back amidst the furs, and without further ado started pulling up her green silk dress. It slipped over her smooth white thighs with no trouble, and I then found to my engorged surprise that she had on no stitch of underwear. I fumbled around trying unsuccessfully to pull my trousers down, and then remembered that I was wearing suspenders. I was also wearing a brand new pair of so-called jockey shorts, and decided that the most effective approach would be to just pull them aside off one thigh. She took hold of me and poked me into her moist petals, murmuring "Please do, please do" in my ear; but then she let go, and the elastic on the jockey shorts pushed me enough out of alignment so that I slid off to one side. I had just rectified this when I heard heavy footsteps coming up the stairs. The door was wide open, and suddenly I had a vision of my head being bashed in with an empty champagne bottle. Dismounting quickly, I pulled a fur coat over the lady and got myself buttoned up. Whoever it was had gone into the bathroom, but by now frightened out of my lust, I went along the hall and up another flight of stairs which led to Mark Van Doren's study.

I sat down on a couch there and picked up a copy of Stephen Spender's recently published poems—the same book John had given me for my birthday. Dazedly, I leafed through it and found a poem that seemed to me mystically fitted to the occasion ("Here at the centre of the turning year. . . . I ask that all the years and years / Of future disappointment, like a snow / Chide me at one fall now"). I read the poem again and again until, I am sure, I fell asleep. How long I slept I do not know, but when I came to the house was silent, and I thought maybe I had dreamed the whole business. Where was everybody? I went carefully down the stairs, made a stop at the bathroom, noticed that all the bedroom doors were closed tight, and went on down into the living room.

There I found Jane and Mark, seated alone in front of a nicely burning fire, quietly conversing. Where was John, I asked. "He's asleep," Mark said. "I think he'll be asleep for quite a while. We were just thinking of getting something to eat; aren't you hungry?" I thought about that and said yes, I was. We three went into the kitchen, and Mark showed us how to make a kind of egg "sandwich" that ever after I have called "a Mark Van Doren." (You cut a disk out of a slice of bread with a shot glass; put the bread into melted butter in a frying pan and break an egg into the hole; turn it over after a couple of minutes, and you soon have the best part of an elegant breakfast.) That and a good cup of coffee revived me marvelously, and observing that it was nearly three o'clock in the morning, I suggested to Jane that we wake John and be on our way. Mark said no, he thought we'd better leave without John; he and Dorothy would send John home in the morning. I took Jane home in a taxi, grandly tipped the driver enough to give him a happy start on 1936, and caught the express to Brooklyn. When I called Mrs. Van Doren the next day to ask about John, she informed me that he had departed about noon, considerably the worse for wear (he had overgulped the champagne even more than I, and had thrown up), but stubbornly determined to travel about Manhattan while still in his tails and make formal New Year's calls.

JANUARY, A COLD MONTH at best, saw all of us glumly typing term papers, bracing ourselves for first-semester final exams, and complaining about the lethargy of our social life. John wrote that he was "in the hellish midst of it," and not having any erotic luck either:

God help us, Halliday, this running sore of chastity is all about us—for whereas we hear recounted prodigies of fornication, behold every woman in the country is a maid and none will spread, forsooth! Bored with my now-of-long-duration continence, I have made sundry sallies, to find virgins *everywhere*. Remedy there is none—I advise you to take up the milk-bottle.

Only a couple of days later, however, I received a short message sounding an altogether different tone:

Trumpets! I have just been appointed the Kellett Fellow to Clare College, *Cambridge* [England]. The Dean wrote me and I talked to him at length yesterday—formalities of nomination by the President and acceptance by Clare have yet to be concluded, but the thing is, incredibly, settled. They haven't chosen the other [i.e., alternate] man yet—so, incredibly, I was first.* This baseless legend that has been going the rounds (to wit: "B—— is bright") has borne big fruit. . . . I am speechless and greatly humbled. I disapprove their choice, but God bless them. More anon—tell no one, for the present. And cheers & cheers—equal joy and shooting stars attend thee, Milt.

This was a stunner, for the Kellett fellowship was just about the best one that any young man could hope for: two years at Cambridge on a

*John evidently never knew that his friend Bob Giroux, editor of the *Columbia Review* (and later John's publisher), had also been considered a prime contender for the Kellett fellowship, but had taken himself out of the running. This was because a discussion with Mark Van Doren had left Giroux with the mistaken impression that the fellowship carried with it some obligation to enter the teaching profession, which he did not wish to do; he also was left uninformed as to the generous financial terms of the award.

stipend ($2,000 a year) that in that time seemed like inexhaustible riches. In a reaction of a kind from which only saints are exempt, I wrote back enthusiastic congratulations to John, camouflaging my envy in dour remarks about my own prospects. He hurried back with a therapeutic clap on the back:

Hell, Halliday, you're the most able and charming person I know, and there are a thousand things panting for you to take them over!... your father's opinion is clearly wrong—in short, damn and hell!! Find out at once about all varieties of fellowship there and write Princeton, Harvard, here and Yale.... A fine time I'll have at Clare if you're withering!...

Exams start for me Saturday.... My fine headaches, due doubtless to my fine disposition, return in force at such times—they are bowling in the medulla oblongata this evening, heh heh.

Still staving off the fiend PUBLICITY: the Literary Digest, in person not as organ *qua* organ, called Tuesday & wanted a pitcher, which I did refuse as neatly as possible—said they were reprinting one of those goddam (my epithet) poems soon. I'll have to get over this mania if I'm to *get on* in the world. Curious—I'm getting to *hate* my name in print, but I save a lot of clippings... Mr. Freud?

Regardless of our moods, however, we had to get through the end-of-semester frenzy. John wrote early in February that he had garnered top grades on all his exams as well as his term papers: "Thus the first installment of this hell-year is completed to the joy of all (save possibly our Steve who is doubtless some annoyed at my magnificence...)." He had not really had time to go out, he said, but

Atherton called me Sunday night and I went over for a while—she wanted me to meet one Constance, a friend; and the omnipresent

Bobby was there. I was infinitely bored and left after an hour—they're trivial at best. For instance, they'd all seen Winterset, the Maxwell Anderson play, and asked me how I liked it. Oddly enough, I went down with Mother a week ago last night (and sat in glory in the square center of the second row—it was a kind of Kellett celebration), and I thought it miserable, so I said so. Well, that brought on an argument—except it requires some intelligence and a bit of knowledge to argue, so the argument was all on my side. Even Atherton, the most intelligent of the four . . . retreated into the stupid chatter and personal comment which passes for conversation. It really is a hell of a bad play—wretched as drama and unspeakable as poetic drama, confused, dull, cheap, overwritten and over-acted . . . its popularity and acclaim I attribute to the fact that people leave their minds at home when they go to the theatre, and read and see nothing but shit, so they have no standards of comparison. I have not gone dead-serious, Halliday, but I am pretty fed up with the spurious and the superficial (cf. Winterset and Atherton).

An up-beat phase had overtaken me when I answered this on February 15, 1936, the day after the big between-semesters dance at Michigan called the J-Hop. I had gone to it with delicious anticipation, for the two dance bands that were to alternate during this splendiferous affair were Jan Garber's and Jimmy Lunceford's. Garber played predictable, syrupy arrangements in the style of Guy Lombardo, and was supposedly the big attraction of the evening, whereas nobody I knew in Ann Arbor had ever heard of Lunceford. But as soon as the Garber musicians left the bandstand and their stacks of sheet music for a break, and the all-black Lunceford outfit—without a piece of written music in sight—started to pump out their surging swing arrangements, with wondrous antiphonies between the big brass section and the reeds punctuated by virtuoso riffs and solos from bass or piano, something interesting began to happen. Not only did the dancing immediately pick up new vigor and style—and damn the corsages—with a few daring couples trying elementary jitterbug steps, but a crowd began to gather around the bandstand just to watch and listen. This caused sore feelings on one side, since the kids squealed for more and more encores from Lunceford at the end of each set, while the Garber musicians stood around waiting for their turn in a state of considerable dudgeon.

I described this to John and then went on to his tough comments on Jane Atherton, of whom I had grown fond:

I honestly think you do her an injustice when you call her spurious, superficial, etc. I think you have a strenuous tendency to find in people what you would *like* to find. Consider the possibility that your judgment now may be no more accurate than when you thought she was quite the reverse of spurious and superficial. . . .

I wrote to Van Doren the other day; asked him to write to Harvard and Princeton [recommending me for a graduate fellowship]. . . . By the way, just when do you leave for Cambridge? Goddam it, what in hell am I going to do with you three-thousand-miles-of-salt-water away for two years?

. . . Have you ever read *The Way of All Flesh*? And do you know a tune called "It's Been So Long"? (No connection, except that I've just become acquainted with both.)

Toward the end of February there came a most gloomy letter from John, though it was aerated here and there by gusts of self-esteem. He had been sick for a fortnight—bronchitis and a bad ear infection—and had fallen horribly behind in his work; he didn't see how he could possibly graduate in June and thus would lose out on the Kellett fellowship. Moreover:

My sex life is disgusting without being, as it has been, puzzling. Pride somewhat piqued about this lovely Jean Bennett, so I went to

Jean Bennett, about 1936. "Pride somewhat piqued about this lovely Jean Bennett...." University of Minnesota Libraries

work with the all-but-no-time at my disposal, and she is now desperately in love with me—a stupid and selfish thing to do, because she's young and must not be seduced, and will grieve endlessly, unless I'm much mistaken, if I leave—one that loves forever, etc. She didn't have a chance, my record and position in the college being what it now is—I am extremely well known, incredibly, and even when disliked, respected. My double reputation renders me fascinating, of course—you know, rake and genius, that sort of thing.... shit, obviously, but it works as though it had validity.

... was too stupid to break up a long-planned family party night before last, so we all went down to At Home Abroad, which is very amusing.... [Beatrice] Lillie, whom I'd never seen before, is delightful.

Despite the frivolous sound of all this, I've been in bed mostly for something over two weeks and have done nothing except a bit of reading, much groaning, more medicining.... This is sickening and my ear is giving me hell—if it weren't for you I'd seriously contemplate what we've discussed. I'm a misfit of some kind, incapable of giving happiness either to myself or to anyone else.... Why wait? Sex drives me in a dozen abortive directions, and pretension and petty pride have corrupted the solid framework of any contentment. I am without reserve, either spiritual or physical, and could not survive any serious illness.... How necessary? Or if necessary, from whose point of view? Of morality I've little, as you know, but what I have seems to sustain this. Pragmatism, sleep. I've just finished *The Way of All Flesh*, which you mentioned, and I tend to agree with his conclusions more completely than I like to realize—taking pleasure as your criterion of virtue, and faith transcending reason (which struggle I am by no means done with—in fact, the dichotomy . . . is my chief problem): then, discard 'faith' and examine the standard resulting from 'pleasure', what results? Suicide. It seems more and more to justify any system. The question of it is profoundly bound up in the other works I've recently read—The Red and the Black, and Hamlet. The last I want to discuss with you—for the first time, I think I really know something about it.

. . . I'm very tired and beset—will write again when I can. Don't worry, by the way. I'll either work it out or I won't—and if I don't nothing much will have been lost. Look at the paragraph, near the very end [of *The Way of All Flesh*], on Theobald's death in sleep and on the phenomena of death. It's damnably true. But in my inconsistency I wish for you all the most fortunate phenomena of life.

—John

I did worry about John's suicidal brooding, but I had some confidence that the great attractions of Jean Bennett (whom I had met at Christmas time) would prevent him from doing anything drastic, and in any event I was so down in the dumps myself that I felt unable to offer him solace at the moment. Ironically, my depression was caused largely by a rite of passage that I had greatly longed for. I was in a campus drug store one afternoon, having a cup of coffee after my last class of the day, when I noticed a pretty girl sitting at the counter pretending to sip a soft drink but actually weeping quietly. She didn't quite look like a coed, and, as I later found out, she was only sixteen. I sat her down in one of the booths and heard her story: she had come to Ann Arbor to attend a fraternity dance with her boy friend, but they had had "a big fight" and now she had missed the last bus of the day that went back to Owosso, and she had no place to sleep. This sad tale aroused all my chivalry. I took her to dinner and to a movie, and then asked her—nervously—if she'd like to spend the night in my room. She said yes, that would be great—but could we get a little something to drink before we went there? Rather jarred, since I had mentally cast her in the role of injured innocence, I spent my next to last dollar on a pint of bourbon. Up in my room, she further surprised me by slugging the whiskey down straight as if it were root beer. We both got tight fast, and in short order we were naked in bed. I did have the presence of mind at that point to run to the bathroom and don a condom; when I came back the primal act I had so long anticipated took place very readily and very quickly. I was disappointed, especially since the girl evinced no symptoms of ecstasy—in fact, she was sound asleep almost before it was over.

The real downer, however, came the next morning when we were having breakfast at the bus-station restaurant. "So," she said, biting into a sausage, "whatever happened last night? We didn't *do* it, did we?" This threw me into a fit of melancholy from which I eventually escaped by deciding that I just wouldn't count that one: it was too, too far from my dreams.

In April John sent me the new issue of the *Columbia Review*, which gave cheerful evidence of his having emerged from his winter gloom. It was, indeed, a demonstration of how thoroughly he and Bob Giroux, with Mark Van Doren as mentor, dominated literary affairs on the Columbia campus in the spring of 1936. Boar's Head, the preeminent literary society, announced John's poem, "Trophy," as the first-prize winner in their annual contest; John was also cited as chairman of the Boar's Head Committee; Giroux was chief editor of the magazine; and together they had managed to get Van Doren to review a book of critical essays by R. P. Blackmur, *The Double Agent*, while Blackmur reviewed a book of Allen Tate's, *Reactionary Essays on Poetry and Ideas*. I was properly dazzled.

SUDDENLY IT WAS May—always a wonderful time in Ann Arbor after a typically snowy Michigan winter, with flowers, trees, and nubile girls burgeoning everywhere, and a nearly overwhelming slate of music festivals, plays, open-air song fests, and other enticing university concoctions. And it was, finally, glory time for the class of '36—if we could just deliver one last spurt of energy to carry us through senior theses, final examinations, farewell picnics, and beer parties. After an unusual gap in my correspondence with John, he brought me up to date on his own sprint to the finish line ("three term papers done, and three left . . . with classes and seminars and examinations and orals all in two weeks . . . first prize in the Boar's Head for "Trophy," and we had a very swell Reading—Blackmur, the wonderful critic I've talked to you about, came down and was guest of honor.")

And then in the first week in June came the last undergraduate note from John:

Just a word to let you know I am being graduated, in spite of all last-minute difficulties. A in Colloquium (11 A's & one B for the year—aren't I bright?) Hope you're finishing superbly. Had a special this morning announcing my election to Phi Beta Kappa; it's wonderful what a legend will do. I hope you make it—I'll feel silly as usual otherwise.

I did not quite make that, having been harpooned by a D in accounting, a course I should have eschewed; but I was graduated with honors in English. From Northampton came communiqués of other academic kudos: Jane also made Phi Beta Kappa, and Rockwell was graduated with Highest Honors. Steve Aylward surprised everyone except perhaps himself by becoming a novitiate at a monastery shortly after getting his diploma.

I had decided to take a year of postgraduate work in literature, but there was no way to do it without some kind of scholarship help, and my hopeful applications to Princeton and Harvard had netted zero, as I explained to John:

. . . at Harvard they sent me a letter saying that I had been recommended for one by their English department but merely placed on the waiting list by the fellowship committee: "We received no letter from Professor Mark Van Doren." Naturally that disturbed me considerably . . . since I had told them to expect a letter from VD; you can imagine what a hell of an impression not getting one must have made on them. I haven't the faintest notion what could have happened, because he wrote me stating definitely that he had written to Princeton and to Harvard. . . . Well, the thing's done now.

Reading that half a century later startles me: evidently it never crossed my mind to get on the telephone to Van Doren and to Harvard and straighten the matter out. Long-distance calls, as already noted, were reserved for news of disaster.

Michigan, however, came through with a scholarship, and I was not unhappy at the prospect of another year in Ann Arbor. I had grown accustomed to the place; I had even decided to stay for summer school and not go to New York until August. When Jane Atherton heard about this, she gave me a nice surprise by turning up for my commencement exercises along with my whole family. The weather was wonderful, and as I wrote John:

She and I had a mad and merry time out here being the center of
family tempests, riding bicycles, and crashing dances in true
Morningside Heights style. Wish to hell you could have been here too;
it would have been almost like a year ago when you, she, and I used to
play tennis and go to Long Beach, remember?

FOUR
Ann Arbor / Cambridge,
1936–37

> ...I kissed Jean
> & Mother & shook hands with old Halliday
> and I mounted to the *Britannic*'s topmost deck
> O a young American poet, not yet good,
> off to the strange Old World to pick their brains
> & visit by hook or crook with W. B. Yeats.
> —"Recovery"

In 1970, in the volume of poetry called *Love & Fame*, John recalled his departure from New York for Cambridge, thirty-four years earlier, with the lines quoted above. Historically speaking, there is a minor flaw here: I was not present. John had confused in memory his departure and his arrival home in 1938. I had hoped to see him off, but he wasn't sure when he was going, and meanwhile I was much engaged in Ann Arbor, as I explained to him in a June letter:

...Summer school started last night with the first dance, and the place is full of young and buxom if somewhat provincial schoolteachers who have spent all winter repressing naturally libidinous egos, and are now all a-panting for excitement and titillation.... I'm having a swell time, although I am practically penniless. I've cut loose from the paternal purse strings...have a meal job...[am working with] the play-production group.... Already I am a Young Communist in Katayev's delightful farce, "Squaring the Circle," and I fully expect to play the lead in "The Old Maid."... Incidentally, how are your social views these days?...you and I were never much concerned with

John and a shipboard friend, en route to Europe, 1936. "I mounted to the *Britannic*'s topmost deck...." University of Minnesota Libraries

economic and political matters, our view being generally obstructed by breasts and things: but of late, you must know, I have become a determined if rather unviolent socialist. In theory, at least, it answers most social problems....

My speaking role in *Squaring the Circle* was minimal, my main obligation being to look as much as possible like a young Communist in Moscow. This was not as easy as I had supposed: at the dress rehearsal Mr. Windt, the director, stopped us midway. "Halliday," he said, "I want you to see me later about costume and make-up. You look exactly like Abe Lincoln the Railsplitter."

The conversion to socialism grew in part out of my own reading, but was cultivated by two good friends, Paul Probert and Robert Campbell. Paul was a cousin of mine from Flint, where he had been watching with fascination the effort by the CIO to organize the automobile workers; this was to lead, later that year, to the famous sit-down strike. Paul could quote John Maynard Keynes with the enthusiasm that I accorded to Shakespeare,

Bhain Campbell, 1937. "Campbell...
was one of the best-looking young men I
have ever known."

and often did so over a mug of beer at the Pretzel Bell. Campbell reinforced
this with eloquent stories of his factory working experiences in Detroit.
Less logical than Paul, he had more flair, for he was a poet and looked
upon economic injustice with the fervor of a William Blake.

Campbell, whom I had first met at a university play audition, was
one of the best-looking young men I have ever known. By best-looking
I mean not just that he was extremely handsome, although that he was.
In his face there seemed to show such intelligent empathy, so open and
generous a mind, so clear a conviction that all things could be made
brighter and better if only the right thoughts were spoken in the right
words, that cynicism and indifference had a wonderful way of wilting in
his company. He was to become a fine and much loved teacher in the
short life that was allowed him, and his influence on John, to whom I would
introduce him two years later, was to be catalytic and lasting. Years after
Campbell's death at the age of twenty-nine—the very age at which his
poetic idol, Shelley, had died in 1822—John wrote what I think is his
best short story, "Wash Far Away," about their friendship. Centering on
a professor who is teaching "Lycidas" (as John did at Princeton in the
forties), the story poignantly juxtaposes Milton's grief over the loss of his

young friend Edward King, and his ruminations about poetry and death, against John's as evoked by his memories of Campbell.*

In the summer of 1936 Campbell and I gravitated toward each other with almost as much mutual pull as John and I had felt in our freshman year at Columbia. We both had small parts in an upcoming production of Maxwell Anderson's *Mary of Scotland*, and after rehearsals we would wander through the summer night talking of plays and poetry and politics and girls in a conversation that never quite seemed to end. It was Campbell who permanently changed my given name, for he declared that he could abide neither Ernest nor Milton. No, he said; he was going to call me Hal for Halliday, and that was that. All of my new friends, and many of my old (John being a notable exception) took it up, and I was not displeased, since I had long considered it overweening on the part of my father to make me his junior with two such juiceless monickers. In return, I agreed to call Campbell by his middle name, Bhain, which clearly befitted a poet far better than "Bob."

I fell in love with Sally Pierce voice-first. She was an Ann Arbor girl and the current star of the university theater, but had been away for a year; I had not seen her perform before. One June night I stepped into the cool dark of the Lydia Mendelssohn Theater to watch a dress rehearsal of Ibsen's *John Gabriel Borkman*. I was a few minutes late, and Sally (who played Ella Rentheim) was speaking as I sat down. Before I hit the seat I was already in thrall to the resonance of her voice; it carried beautifully even in the nearly empty auditorium, and seemed to have some sort of magic in it. For a while that summer I imagined that I had some special susceptibility to Sally's voice, but I found that many others were similarly affected; later, I heard Estelle Winwood, that *grande dame* of the American theater, who was in Ann Arbor as a guest star, say that it would be "tragic" if Sally failed to go on the stage professionally: "She has everything it takes, plus an absolutely sensational set of vocal cords." She had excellent off-stage attributes as well—a statuesque figure, a keen, well-furnished mind, a face striking and vivacious, though not "pretty" in the conventional mode. But her voice echoes in the chambers of my memory even now.

*"Wash Far Away" is included in *The Freedom of the Poet*, a collection of Berryman's prose writings published by Farrar, Straus & Giroux in 1976.

Sally Pierce, Ann Arbor, 1936. "She had excellent off-stage attributes as well. . . ."

Sally was Queen Elizabeth in *Mary of Scotland*, and I was thrilled to be cast in the same play with her, however modestly. Bhain Campbell, observing that I was smitten, urged me to ask her for a date, but I was too shy. One night, however, as I left rehearsal through the stage door, I heard Sally's unmistakable voice behind me saying, "What I need now is a *big* lemon Coke!" I turned to see what lucky guy she was speaking to, and was seized with a wild surmise: no one else was there. After the lemon Coke we went for a walk; I got my nerve up and put my arm around her waist. We walked that way for half a block, when she suddenly pulled me aside onto a shadowy lawn and turned her face up to me. Her kiss had a tender, cool, clinging quality that seemed to promise infinite bliss. I was a goner.

It was the first time I had really been in love. The summer went by in a dreamy daze of rehearsals and performances, quick embraces and kisses backstage when we thought nobody was looking, many lemon Cokes and thick milk shakes, midnight dips at a swimming hole euphemistically called Loch Alpine, and nearly all-night sessions of love and love talk on a big couch in Sally's home or, when it was too hot (and it was a very hot, dry summer) on a bedspread in her back yard. We were chronically short of sleep, and remonstrated with each other about our bad habits without any intention of changing them. While we were still rehearsing *Mary of Scotland* and I was helping her test her lines, we came to Elizabeth's speech to one of her courtiers: "You can sleep later, when we're old and the years are empty." "That's it," Sally said "—there's our cue for the summer!"

The only academic chore I had during that season of theatrical dalliance was to act as assistant to Professor Joe Lee Davis in his popular course in modern drama. Joe Lee was an extraordinarily amiable fellow with an easygoing southern air. He was well aware that Sally and I were doing Daphnis and Chloe that summer, and kindly made corresponding allowances. Even his tolerance must have been strained at the end of August, however, when I was supposed to administer the final examination for the course. Sally was scheduled to leave on a vacation trip with her family that day, and I was about to go to Crystal Lake for a week. Parting was such sweet sorrow that we spent all night at it: I finally stumbled up to my room at 5 A.M. I put my alarm clock three inches from my ear and set it for 8:15; the exam was to begin at nine. When I regained consciousness I could tell even before looking at the clock that it was late: the sun was high and already hot. It was ten o'clock, and I may have set some kind of track record crashing up to the campus, arriving at Angell Hall in a breathless swelter derived as much from horror as from exertion. To my unspeakable relief, I found the students all bent busily over their bluebooks while Joe Lee Davis, looking cool in a white linen suit, gave me a genial grin from the front of the room. "I guess you overslept," he said mildly after we had stepped into the hall. "I woke up at eight and smelled smoke—my hot-water heater was out of kilter. I fixed that, and then decided to come over here and see how the exam was going. Got here at 9:15 and found the students milling around in the hall. Let's go and have an iced coffee."

JOHN AND I HAD not written to each other since June. I heard through Jane Atherton that he had been working on a play—never finished—and was very busy with arrangements for his trip to England, which had been postponed to September; I hoped to catch him in New York just before he sailed. But during my short visit the telephone at the Berryman apartment repeatedly rang unanswered, Atherton and Rockwell were both in Europe, and I couldn't find anyone who knew where John was except that he hadn't yet left for Cambridge. When I got back to Ann Arbor early in

September, I was surprised to find a letter from him postmarked at Williamsburg, Ontario, on September 3:

Halliday, I have got to see you before I go. You are the most important of the three reasons why I haven't sailed long since—the others being my natural but incredible procrastination, and my health which is miserable—no germs, but endless fatigue, underweightness, nervousness, etc., etc. The doctors three prescribed rest, etc. So I'm up here in the wilderness . . . sleeping and reading. Wmsburg is the habitat of the Ontario Myth, one Herr Locke, who has performed no miracles upon me. Wherefore I'm going to Montreal tonight, thence probably to Quebec (j'avais une fois il y a longtemps grand désir à voir la Sanctuaire de Sainte Anne de Beaupré—et je l'ai encore), and will be back in New York next week. I have to be in residence at Clare on October 3rd, which means sailing the 20th, as I intend to take a freighter who will convey my books. *So you got to come East practically at once, and no excuses!!!* God only knows what will happen in the next two years and I want to see you. I estimate we have about two hundred hours of uninterrupted talking to do—which if we don't do now, we may have to do in Hell under rather difficult conditions. . . .

THE PRINCIPAL REASON for my not getting to New York to see John off was Sally. I had never before had the experience of coming back after an absence to a girl I was in love with, and it would have taken a mule train to get me away from her. There was also the exciting business of moving into an *apartment* with Bhain Campbell—the first time either of us had been master of an independent domicile. It was no great shakes, having been contrived as one of several in a red brick house of Civil War vintage, but to us it seemed like a department of heaven, and it cost twenty-eight dollars a month, furnished.

We seemed to be setting out on an *annus mirabilis*. Bhain and I were both slightly fazed, however, to find that as graduate students and candidates for the M.A. in English literature, we were expected to labor mightily and perform on a distinctly higher level than the undergraduates. Professor Reinhard, for instance, who conducted a Chaucer course open to seniors as well as graduates, required the bachelors of arts to put a big G at the top of each paper or bluebook, so that he could shift into tougher gear when he was grading their work; and in class we had to read Middle English as if it was our mother tongue, whereas undergrads were allowed a good deal of mumbling room. The fact that, as Bhain was fond of pointing out, neither Professor Reinhard nor anyone else really knew just how Chaucer pronounced his English, made no difference: Reinhard established the correct system by reading the entire Prologue of *The Canterbury Tales* aloud in class, and we took it from there.

With this sort of pressure on us, Bhain and I decided we'd better abandon the university theater for the time being and stick to our books. We did play small roles in Irwin Shaw's *Bury the Dead*, which was put on to strident acclaim in November, but that was it for the year. Meanwhile, Sally was tremendously involved in play production, both as an actress and a director, so we continued to hang out with the theater crowd in what time we could spare. My usual routine was to work diligently all evening, after Bhain and I had done the dinner dishes, and then go over to the theater about eleven o'clock to pick up Sally as she came out of a rehearsal. It was an excellent autumn, with many clear, crisp nights, the stars bright through the branches of trees whose leaves floated gently down as we scuffed happily along. The first fine, careless rapture of our summer seemed to have been recaptured by the change in the weather: we felt sure now that it would never end. Bhain, who if possible was more romantic about me and Sally than we were ourselves, composed a celebratory song:

> When rain and the angels shining slip
> Out of the springtime sky,
> We'll over the hedges wanton skip,
> Mad Hal, mad Sally, mad I.
>
> We'll loose the goats of an antique joy
> And whistle them through the town,

With planets bowl the towers of Troy,
In our wine of laughter drown.

Nor will helmed Roman gods, or flowers
Revoke our final sigh;
No man shall have felt our windy hours,
Mad Hal, mad Sally, mad I.

This seemed very nice, notwithstanding the melancholy tone of the last
stanza; but when I think of that fall in Ann Arbor I more readily associate
it with the lyrics, however inapplicable, of "A Fine Romance," as sung by
Ginger Rogers and Fred Astaire in *Swingtime*, which we had all just seen
with much enthusiasm.

When you keep house with someone, regardless of sex, you come to
know your housemate rather intricately. Bhain and I started out fond of
each other, and in many ways our friendship was bolstered by our living
together—but of course there was minor friction, usually over points that
seemed minuscule to one of us but important to the other. I was amused
to find that Bhain took very seriously the problem of cutting a grapefruit
precisely so that neither of us got more or less than half; he also spent
what struck me as an unconscionable amount of time in the bathroom
each morning trimming his elegant moustache. In turn, he regarded me
as something of a slob because I tended to take a shower only three or
four times a week, instead of daily; and he pointed out that I had the
proper relationship between urinating and washing my hands exactly re-
versed. "I always wash my hands *before* I take a pee," he explained, "not
after." "Come on, Bhain," I said, "everyone does it the other way. Your
way doesn't make sense." "Yes, it does!" he said indignantly. "Hell, my
cock's not dirty, my *hands* are dirty!" One thing we agreed on perfectly
was doing the dishes each night before going to bed so there wouldn't
be a mess in the morning, the only problem being that we always discussed
such fascinating topics while engaged in this task that the last couple of
pots and pans often got washed and dried three or four times: I'd wash
and rinse one and put it on the drainboard; Bhain would dry it and absently
put it down; I'd absently wash it again, and so on into the night.

Bhain enhanced his extreme good looks not only with meticulous grooming but with a wardrobe more expensive than he could afford and with manners that would have done credit to a captain of the queen's guard. This sometimes annoyed me, but it was eased by his good humor and a modicum of self-mockery that he could draw on when needed. ("I'm a bit of a dude, you know," he said to me once.) One night that fall he had a date with a new and very pretty girl he had met on the campus, and it was agreed that she and Sally would come to dinner, and then we'd all go to the dance at the Michigan Union. Everything went beautifully until the moment of departure. Bhain's date, feeling liberated by the after-dinner cognac we had purchased especially for the occasion, was sitting on the floor leaning against the big couch, and Bhain decided that the knightly thing was to bend over and pick her up. He was strong, but the girl weighed perhaps more than he had looked for, and as he lifted her off the floor there was a report like a champagne cork, stopping the conversation cold—until Sally let go an uncontrollable giggle, and we all joined in. Even Bhain joined in, but he had somewhat affronted his own dignity and he never dated the girl again.

ALTHOUGH I WAS remiss in writing to John, I naturally thought much about how things might be going for him in England, and finally got a letter off in the middle of October:

Graduate school turns out to be stiff like a great phallus, and all of us yearlings scurry frantically around at the beck and call of professors whom, last year when we were lordly seniors, we regarded as a trifle passé.... For example, there's a perfect bitch of a bibliography course ... where we have to go rooting around the dusty lower depths of the library stacks looking for things like the date of a pirated edition of *'Tis Pity She's a Whore* which appeared within three months after the authentic second edition....

... I honestly should be in the library now working on Chaucer; what prompted me to write at this inauspicious moment was a marvellous rendition of "In a Sentimental Mood" [a Duke Ellington

favorite of John's] on the radio. But I certainly will write again soon
and longer. Do thou likewise, omitting nothing of voyage (including
stateroom episodes, Beast), first impressions of England, etc etc.

Ship mail was slow, but John got this in time to send me an eloquent
reply on Clare College stationery on his twenty-second birthday, October
25, 1936:

Dear Milt,

Yesterday and today have been beautiful beyond any days I have
ever seen: full Autumn, but green, green lawns and parks, undiminished
glory of gardens, and the complex splendor of the leaves falling and
fallen. I've been on the river both days, yesterday in a punt and today
in a canoe—it's like a dream, drifting along the quiet Cam, under
ancient bridges and the shadows of stone and wood, into the clear
sunlight bordered with green, and the light that struck the shore along
the water!

No, I have not gone crazy nor precieux nor [Sir Thomas] Browne,
but my god Halliday you ought to see Cambridge now—and by all
report it's even more gorgeous in the Spring. I'm afraid a latent
Romanticism is seizing me and I shall turn out after all to be a
counterfeit Keats. Than which—horrors! However, there is some excuse
in that I be twenty-two today and feeling incurably sentimental—you
are all so damn far away and I'll be here such a comparatively long
time. If you don't come over next summer I shall infallibly die. Even
Beetle has lost his zip and looks definitely like a nostalgic horse's ass.
Ai, ai, que j'ai faim de mes amis! Et d'un ami surtout. Circonflexe.

What reams I have to tell you. Letter-writing I have found to be a
staggering problem (shifted attribution—'tis I who stagger while the
letter-writing stutters), and hopeless of solution: will write you every
few days until I get somewhat caught up—boat, etc. And do thou

likewise, worm! Tell me somewhat of your beloved: my chastity commenceth to bore me mightily, and no relief in sight. Christ, only to talk to a presentable girl would joy me hugely.

Now please please write and I will also—am hard as hell at work, even as thou—this too I will detail. . . .

OUR PROMISES WERE sincere, but John and I were both so busy that no further correspondence ensued for over a month. The novelty of being graduate students had waned considerably for me and Bhain, and we settled into a fairly dogged routine of classes and long reading and writing assignments, our chief diversions being conversation, handball, and food. We were determined not to eat out more than once a week, so we worked diligently at learning to cook, with Sally as our monitor. It was easier than we had expected—I have never forgotten our wonder, for example, that a good roast of beef or pork could be produced simply (as I put it in a letter to Lois) "by sticking it in the oven, leaving it there for an hour or so, and pulling it out. And I always thought there was some mystery to it!"

It's true that we were afflicted with mild anxiety when we had unusual guests for dinner. One of these was Professor Reinhard, who had unwittingly aroused our empathy. It had become apparent to us that he led a reclusive bachelor existence, removed from the current social scene by his absorption with medieval culture, his head chock-a-block full of information that almost nobody wanted to hear, his natural aloofness exacerbated by his conviction that life had been better in the fourteenth century. He took us by surprise one afternoon as we sat on the steps of Angell Hall looking up words like "swyven" in the glossary of our Chaucer text, the better to enjoy "The Miller's Tale," which we had just come to recognize as one of the best dirty stories ever told in English. Suddenly we were aware that Reinhard, on his way down the steps, had stopped just above us and was looking over our shoulders to see what we were up to. His pale blue eyes shifted just perceptibly from one of us to the other and back. "I believe that a man should keep his tools well lubricated," he said distinctly, and went on down the steps. When we had digested that, and convinced each other that he meant what we thought he meant, we decided to reward this unexpected wisdom with an invitation to dinner. Bhain wrote it out neatly on some blue note paper he had, and we handed it to him at the next class meeting.

Reinhard flushed, but accepted, and we consulted with Sally about an appropriate menu. She suggested roast beef with small oven-browned potatoes ("You can roast them right along with the beef"), Chianti, and cheese and fruit on the theory that a man like Reinhard would disdain a sweet dessert. As the date drew closer, Bhain said he thought we ought to try out the whole dinner on Sally beforehand so as to make sure there'd be no hitches on the occasion itself, and I agreed. I was coming back from the market, my arms loaded with paper sacks, on the cold, rainy day before the actual event, when I saw Reinhard approaching from the opposite direction. He was moving slowly along, pausing at every house to check the address against the sheet of blue paper in his hand. For a moment I panicked, sure that he had the date wrong and was about to ring our doorbell. Then I remembered Reinhard's reputation for punctiliousness, and realized he was doing the same thing we were: rehearsing his moves so that everything would go smoothly the following evening. I quickly tugged my rain hat down over my face and crossed the street until, having noted the right house, he headed back toward the campus. The dinner was a big success—both nights.

I WAS PLEASED but somewhat shamed, the first week in December, to get a long, thoughtful letter from John—without my yet having answered the note he sent on his birthday:

Memorial Court [Cambridge]
29 November 1936

Dear Milt,

For the two closest friends eastward of Eden, we are fine correspondents, aren't we not? . . . although I did scribble you something on or about my birthday, which I hope you got. . . .

I forget whether I was happy or otherwise when I wrote you the aforesaid note; one is as likely as the other for I've gone temperamentally up and down like a kite all fall, with more misery on the whole than else (mind not, the old old men say, my present style; it springeth with many qualifications from the late style of James . . .). The change into this appalling climate and my general un-wellness has a good deal to do with it, but mainly it's the effect of mental instability, fits of terrific gloom and loneliness and artistic despair alternating with irresponsible exultation. I find I depend to a really grotesque extent on a few friends, that I mainly detest the smug British, that I'm rather more in love with Jean than I thought, and that I'd give my left eye to see you. I've actually done a good bit, I suppose, but the general impression is one of horror and joy at the end of term which is practically here. . . . I'm both damned serious and for some reason frivolous, and above all nervous as hell, as I've been for the past two months. One of the main causes isn't far to seek, it's my enforced and galling chastity; none of the girls on the boat was worth sneering at really, of course I met no one in London (was there only three or something days), and I know almost no women here: there is a rigid etiquette which prevents town girls from having anything to do with undergraduates (seduction at the core) and I've not met any girls from Newnham or Girton, the two women's colleges, yet, nor have any desire to do so, from what I've seen: all the Englishwomen are horrible, dull and thick and healthy and big and graceless; the young American wife of a friend here, Kay Fraser, is the only passable one, but adultery isn't my line; and apparently this goes on for two years—it drives me really mad. It isn't merely lack of sexual satisfaction, God knows I've never had a hell of a lot of that, but not even kissing anyone is deadly, and I get a remarkable stimulation, as I think you do, from talking about anything at all to attractive women—well, there's none of it. I've been to no dances . . . and I suspect the dancing is miserable anyway. . . . Of course most of this is overstatement—I haven't the patience to think exactly what I mean and then to try and say it concisely—but the trouble is real enough and large enough and grim enough. (Time out while I scramble some eggs—signed out of Hall tonight and am getting hungry, four hours since tea.)

10:30 p m

I've been thinking while eating, and for the first time have the problem I think in reasonable shape. . . . suddenly (after a helter-skelter summer . . .) I found myself not merely with everything—place, friends, continuity of work which implies for me certain fixed aspects—broken off and put away, but with an entirely new and intrinsically difficult set of conditions, impressions pounding on a hardly recovered sensibility. . . . The results have been remarkable. I seem uncannily to have developed a supersensitive, "poetic" sensibility: the moon among bare branches in mist can move me to tears; I am constantly alert for dramatic possibilities, for tragedy; I suffer from love as I've not suffered before; I grow rankly sentimental about my friends; only my artistic sense remains fairly intact, due probably to the intense, tough sanity of the seventeenth century poets I've done the greater part of my reading in. I ponder by the fire for hours over tremendous problems of time and life and God, have been reading Revelations and Job and the New Testament and wondering whether I can accept honestly Christianity, as I should so passionately like to be able to. I am irascible and unstable in the extreme. In short, I present a perfect image of the young man gone mad.

Obviously, of course, I am sane as hell (you can depend upon it, if ever I feel I'm losing my mind I shall tell no one but go quietly into the next room and perform a secret final ceremony); I'm telling you all this because I didn't know it myself an hour ago, and it's a good thing to have the devils on paper, and because I assume that you're in something like the same state, for different reasons. . . . And if the political situation bothers you in Ann Arbor, what my blooming lad do you think it does to me in Cambridge? Everything is so goddam much nearer, in fact quite *present* to the mangled sense.... It is thought here that Germany and Russia will break relations over Spain and be shortly at war, with Italy and France and God knows who else shortly behind.

...I wish with painful constancy that we could work together for a year or so—we have simply got to, Milt, either next year or after I come back. And if you can't get over next summer, I shall die; if war's not on, you must.... Term is not officially over until the 5th [of December] (Cambridge is a residence university—you have to have spent so many nights during full term here before you can take a degree, so they're very strict; can't leave your court after ten, must be in always by midnight except with tutorial permission, and fines for coming in after ten; also cap & gown always after dark, and for visiting supervisors, for lectures, etc.—wonderful to go streaking along on your bike with square rakishly set and gown streaming through the narrow, dark streets).... I may go directly to Paris ... in any case, address me at American Express, Paris, and do so tout de suite or I shall crack to thee the head. I'll write soon again, to your home this time; hope, belatedly, you had a good birthday, and god bless you Milt—

John

I had been in a chiaroscuro of moods myself, but sat down and replied right away:

Yes, I got the letter you wrote me on your birthday; it's been lying on top of my desk ever since, the Clare Coll. Camb. coat of arms eyeing me with decorum and a suggestion of reproach. You were in a very happy mood when you wrote it; eulogizing Nature on the Cam. ... But I know what you mean when you say you've been up and down all fall; moi aussi. I guess we're manic depressives of the first water....

Verily, the winds came, and the rain descended; but along about November 7th, having arrived at the age of twenty-three, I got out Milton's sonnet ["How soon hath Time, the suttle theef of youth / Stoln on his wing my three and twentith yeer!"], and decided that I didn't have anything to worry about after all. And have you ever read a letter that Donne wrote as a young man; it's quoted in Izaak Walton's *Life* [of Donne], and sure sounds as if things looked grim to John at that point.

Well, I must get this in the mail tonight. . . . Have a swell time in Paris; write me as soon as you can; Merry Christmas, you old bastard. God, how I'm going to miss you New Year's Eve. . . . I'll call on your mother, of course.

Transatlantic mail was slower than usual at Christmas time, and I did not hear from John again until I had gone home for the holidays and come back. Then this buoyant epistle arrived:

London

22 Dec 1936

I've just seen a hell of a good play beautifully done, Halliday, and it's confirmed my plans for us—plans I've been thinking about all fall and longer: You and I, my boy, are going to produce (by the mingled mangled might of our masterful minds) the best damn plays the Western world has seen for three centuries. They're going to be unutterably tragic, because nothing exists in this hysterical time but tragedy, and when the stuff is too ghastly to do straight, we'll use irony—and they're going to be magnificent. . . .

Sorry for a scratch note, meant to write before leaving but have done nothing for ten days except loll at the Frasers' and (not a word to anyone) copulate. A young and gorgeous artist living in Cambridge with quite the best body (& the most accomplished) in the Empire; neither of us in love but mutually admiring & fun. She is also engaged, but he doesn't mind, nice chap who went down from St. John's last year, I met him Monday. More later. Love Jean more than ever—my sex is at last departmentalized. Stroking the breasts of someone you're fond of, and elaborations of intercourse, do *not* signify love, I've finally learned.

In town just for tonight—came down too late for visa & have got to get from the French Consulate to Victoria, visa complete, by 10:05 tomorrow morning. Bookstalls, tea, "The Witch of Edmonton" at the Old Vic, superbly mounted and played, now here, an anonymous 4/6 bed & breakfast house in Waterloo Rd. Arrive Paris after 5 in the afternoon. . . . Hope you're having a marvelous holiday—my best to your parents & Lois & Dot—may Priapus & Sophocles guard thee—

John

I sent him in return a summary of holiday doings in New York:

Ann Arbor
January 7, 1937

Vacation was very strange without you. That difference amplified several others until I wondered whether I was I. Jane, as you may know, is agreed to marry Bobby Winslow; Rockwell bears a queer and unknown relationship to one Nelson, besides other companions of her youth. Winann is the same. . . . Coming home with my traditional Christmas cold, I stayed there with it as an excuse for the entire first week; the family was pleased, and I found them all newly loveable. That is, I stayed away from Morningside; I did go to the theatre rather frequently and saw some good plays, of which later. On Christmas day I went up to see your family; but I was to stop in at Jean's for a few minutes first: eggnog party. She looked fresh and young and charming; but the place was full of dull people. . . . Jean and her sister Kay were all that interested me for the time; with Kay I danced and drank eggnog until we were quite joyous. By that time it was unaccountably eight o'clock, and I had to run to a performance of the D'Oyly Carte where the family waited testily. . . .

The next day, I think it was, I *did* get to your mother's, where I found her, her mother, Uncle Jack, Bob, and Jean; everyone, in short, except you. The accentuation of your absence made inevitable by this gathering was something for Beetle to ponder. . . . after much brilliant, spontaneous, and inspired conversation, mostly about you, I retired to the red leather chair of old fame and started reading your letters [to his mother]. . . . They are really swell letters, John, and worthy of a poet's first days in England.

. . . the letter from Yeats, certainly, merits a separate paragraph . . . [John had sent Yeats a letter and a complimentary poem, and the great poet had replied with a note of thanks]. . . . Did your Mother tell you about phoning Van Doren? But of course, she must have. And here of all places let me thank you for the beautiful copy of Yeats [his collected poems]. . . .

To resume the narrative: vacation dwindled on, and came to New Year's Eve. I wanted to cable you, but your mother didn't know exactly where you were, you elusive reveler. . . . I wandered up to Winann's, and together we wandered over to Jane's. . . . Some twenty-five people in one small apartment where was scarcely room for three. . . . Eventually I and Jean [Bennett] . . . escaped into the bedroom where Richard [Jane's brother] was playing good dance tunes on his victrola and swaying, slightly tight and passionate, around the room with his hands clamping the breasts (large and firm) of some young thing who belongs to our junior generation. We grow old, Brother John, we grow old. At sight of us they stopped fomenting, and we all four sat and

listened to various tunes of the older day such as Moonglow. . . . Finally
. . . left Jane's (Jane having departed to bed, at last convinced that she
had the flu, poor girl) and ran around upper New York to various
drunken parties, all equally unexciting. I think I got home at six a.m.,
very tired and very surfeited with life. Incidentally, I had called Van
Doren at midnight; he was out of town, as he had been all vacation. I
hope we weren't too much for him last year.

AS 1937 GATHERED MOMENTUM, my love affair with Sally Pierce
was heading for trouble. Sally was feeling a powerful mating urge that
rose, as it were, straight from her womb to her heart. She was fairly subtle
about it, never actually suggesting that we ought to get married, but airily
observing that the university theater was really the best future for her—
and how neatly that might fit in with the life of a college English teacher!
Or, as we danced close to each other at the Michigan Union on a Saturday
night, with the band playing Cole Porter's seductively wistful "Easy to
Love," she would sweetly intone the lyrics in my ear in her sexy contralto.
The hell of it was that I knew we *would* be grand at the game; it wasn't
that I couldn't see my future with her but that I could see it all too vividly,
and I wasn't ready for it. The malaise of the overworked graduate student
was upon me, and I was by no means sure that I wanted to become a
teacher; and along with that large doubt I was stirred to wanderlust by
John's reports of amorous conquests in exotic places. I was also subject
to the hubris engendered in most young men the first time they are truly
loved by a passionate and sensitive young woman: it seemed very clear to
me that Sally would love me to eternity. The painful irony of this was to
hit me a few months later, but in the meantime I chafed under the disparity
of Sally's readiness and my own unreadiness, and tried to think of reasons
why I should not love her.

My correspondence with John, about this time, had entered (literally)
a ships-that-pass-in-the-night phase; only a few days after mailing my letter
to him I received one written in Paris on January 2, 1937. It was a nice

illustration of the effect a first visit to that city can produce on a susceptible young American:

My friend, I feel magnificently filled! Poetry, poetry—I merely communicate to you my most profound emotion and it turns out to be iambic pentameter. . . . "Magnificently filled"—there is the inspiring period, conjuring up my days of starvation (verily, through a contretemps the night I arrived—I'll tell you one day in anatomical detail—I became penniless; for four days I ate not, neither did I smoke—and this past week it's been impossible to get enough to eat; came in at 10 tonight, discovered still hunger & went out to feast, whence I am returned, as I say, replete, even to the cigar.) . . .

Happy New Year, mon enfant! This incomparable letter of yours I found awaiting me . . . it doth cheer the antique cockles of my heart. . . .

Oh yes, about Paris . . . but it's late & I be sleepy—tomorrow, m'boy, will be, I predict, another day. More then—meantime, cherchez la [sic] clitoris!

Wed.—10 p.m. God damn it, Halliday, *il faut il faut il faut* that you come over in the Spring—this is fun, but when I think of how superbly (and as I write 'superbly' my whole body is moving into my face with uncontrollable joy)—how magnificently you and I could boil around Europe—. . . Good night, before I get maudlin (excellent Haut-Barac . . .) and outrage Anglosaxon convention by saying I love you— which I do. & so to Bed.

—Paris, my boy, is not a city: it is a process—

John

Since the only appropriate reply to this seemed to be an empathetic grunt, I waited for John's next letter, which was sure to include some

reactions to the news I'd sent him after Christmas vacation. It came early
in February:

Clare College
Cambridge
31 January 1937

Very glad indeed to have your letter; it is really fantastic, you know,
that we don't write each other more. . . .

I am, probably, unreasonably distressed about Atherton and her
imminent marriage. . . . Am ashamed of her and of all of us. Wrote her
yesterday, enclose the letter; I felt very strongly what I had to say and it
came naturally in verse, so I was glad to write it in verse. . . .

We've had a hell of a course with women, haven't we? . . . We both
feel the same thing, and wish we didn't: that copulation is an over-rated
pastime, and man was not made to *feel* alone. I was watching intently
the other afternoon the cat in the tea shop in Magdalene Street where I
often go (there are in it—an Aran expression—two very pretty,
vivacious girls of seventeen who fall in love with me by turns . . .) it is
beautifully marked and incredibly graceful in the most commonplace
actions, and I thought how much more beautiful than a woman is
almost any animal. Difficult, it's true, to appraise aesthetically a nude
woman, but think how wretched the proportions are. And how
monotonous! If I take the trouble to undress a woman, I should at least
be rewarded by fascinating markings of some kind or fur or
something—but all I get is a dull expanse of white, ineffectual skin, two
nipples more or less brown, a matt of hair, and two legs that coyly
open on an odorous and impatient portal. I am sacrificing truth to wit
now, but there's something in it all the same. At any rate, I begin to
understand Swift's disgust as I never have before (have been reading
him a lot this term . . . a gigantic, uncanny man, riddled with mortal

pride and terrible rage, and one of the central glories of English
literature—I invariably feel a desire to laugh when I begin talking like
this, but I am honest too.)

. . . Have seen little of my mistress since coming up this month;
principally bored, though I drop in every few days for an orgy. . . . a
painter studying Latin & anatomy (oh, in many ways!) here with a
tutor before going to London next year to read medicine; dark,
handsome, excellent body, particularly two perfect breasts; her main
attractions are convenience without complication, pivotal skill, physical
ingenuity (we arrive at the most complex and satisfying positions ever
contrived) and the delicious little noises of pleasure she makes while
being stroked or entered. . . . But limited, Halliday, limited, and I am
but mildly fond of her. . . . My love for Jean grows apace, as J B
Priestley says, and I am wildly anxious to marry her . . . she is a lovely
and able and generous girl and I adore her and think of her
constantly. . . .

But with all due respect, how could you find her sister anything
but common and shop-girl and dull as hell? Round, true, but Halliday,
Halliday, she is nothing—Jean is inexplicable in that family. It's a pity I
don't know Sally—please tell her that I am automatically very fond of
her. . . . What really matters it that you and Jean and I, with or without
some wife of yours, must live together until the end of time. . . .

I think you should in every way possible counteract for a time your
training in the body beautiful—it will stand you in vile stead, if
undiluted, sometime or other . . . what in god's name is eight bodies
beautiful against the way our minds work when we talk, you and I, or
against [Donne's] Elegie XVI (which go *immediately* and read, if you
read it but five minutes since), or against the single immaculate moment
of finding what you want, writing? . . . About Paris I have definitely rare
stories to tell thee. . . . We shall be in Paris together, and I don't want to
anticipate your vile young enthusiasm. . . . I am, you may have gathered,

God's misfit as a traveller; ghoulishly inefficient about details and tickets
and visas and trains and money and hotels. . . . always spend four times
the maximum amount I can afford, and am very unhappy about the
whole thing. With you it would be different, but alone it resembles
Canto XXXIV of the Inferno. . . .

Don't yet know about Easter vac; I shall stay here for some time
after the end of the full term and do some quiet work (social hell has
set in, engagements and engagements—even today, Sunday, has been
riddled by breakfast with the Dean, two hours' table tennis at the Club
in the afternoon . . . tea with Mollison, Hall, coffee after Hall with
Ramsey, Kitchin and a faffing, pale, plump, hyphenated ass from
Trinity, then an hour or so of Paul Robeson records, . . . dashing back
to this court just before midnight, when one *must* be in, on fear of
suspension. . . . The summer is a perfect enigma, will doubtless be
penniless by then and deported for non-payment of town bills; I owe
(no whisper to a soul) some forty pounds for books here. . . . The books
I do not in the least regret and think I never shall. I have excellent
authority, remember Walton: "Mr. *Donnes* estate was the greatest part
spent in many and chargeable Travels, Books and dear-bought
Experience. . . ." And so is mine, and the greatest of these is Books.
(Do you remember, by the way, a discussion we once had of
modernization or retention of old texts? Well, I recant. I am now
become a pedantic fiend for being able to read things as they were
written or first printed, and the more so since the period I am buried in
at present is the seventeenth century; marvellously complicated and
emphatic page they turned out, infinitely subtle punctuation and
capitalization and italicization. . . .) Books *and* books. But I have
bought none foolishly and few really dear ones. . . . have got together a
wonderfully useful set of books, none of which I intend ever to sell. . . .

I know well the letter of Donne's you referred to last month—the
dispiriting thing is that he had *already* written all the songs and

sonnets, and what have *we* done? . . . It grows late and ghastly late, 2:25 a m, to wit, and I've been at this letter off and on all day . . . and I am very tired, and I have a rendezvous with a dentist at ten-thirty tomorrow, and a bleak morning it will be . . . and time is money, no, time is change (same thing) and there isn't enough wit left in me to keep a whippoorwill alive—a small *wizened* whippoorwill, mind you, with practically no teeth and many debts and a sour, silent look, altogether a contemptible bird, but could I keep it alive? No, and again No, I say, and canker eat it.

I am in a sorry fatigue—I have been staring madly at the "to wit" up there and thinking in Danish "to wit or not to wit, a mo*men*tous question." I have also been thinking about the inquiry you put to me about ethics and aesthetics, and after all this time the answer has suddenly come to me. The answer is: Phallus. Look closely at Phallus, then look intently at Phallus, then look intensely at Phallus—and Phallus will inform you. If Phallus does not inform you,

> goe and catch a Lincoln car
> get with childe a looping jade
> examine closely where you are
> and never never be afraid, or J M Barrie will

get you and cut you into little fat luscious pieces and feed you to A A Milne and you will be *very* unhappy and so I hope will A A Milne. The rest should long since have been silence. From this time forth I never will speak bird.

> loveydovey ibbydibby toodles

[signed] *Scratch*

Despite its dollops of jocularity, this Berryman letter perplexed and annoyed me for several reasons, and I was not helped by a rather pompous note that came a few days later, enclosing a carbon-copy of a letter to his mother, in which John declared that henceforth he would regard correspondence as a literary exercise: "Letters can form a style, while doing the work of information to best advantage, or they can set habits of extravagance and triviality." When I finally calmed down enough to answer him, late in February, I decided to skip over his remarks on sex—which, between the passage on his British mistress and the one on the aesthetic deficiencies of a nude woman, struck me as oddly muddled—and comment on other irritants as coolly as I could:

> ...I must protest mildly against your going too purist in your
> epistolary style, as suggested by the letter to your Mother which you
> enclosed with your last to me. "Letters can form a style, while doing
> the work of information to best advantage...." Yea, Hornflogger; but
> don't you go using me for your old form-styling, or style-forming; nay,
> nor for a mere receptacle of information, neither....

> I was somewhat awed; withal, by that same letter to your Mother.
> ...certainly you are living in an intellectual world to which I voyage
> not often and timorously....your vision of Yeats [a hallucination John
> had reported] is the kind of thing which both of us would have
> recounted, three years ago, with curiosity and wonder; I still do. Such
> things are not part of my experience, and probably never will be. And I
> am not entirely sympathetic towards your creed of isolation for the
> individual so as to avoid the "fantasia and a population of clods." It is,
> I suppose, a good program for a genius; but although it may make
> possible marvellous poetry, it will do practically nothing towards
> alleviating the evils of "this unfortunate time." Poetry is written,
> presumably, to be read; it is, if it is to have any but solipsistic
> significance, essentially social in its nature.

I then went on to what I knew would be the most prickly point between us, the verse-letter he had written to Atherton about her forthcoming marriage. It was well done, with some fine Shakespearean turns of phrase, but it also included some appalling insults, accusing her of

Jane and Bobby Winslow in Cairo,
on a round-the-world wedding trip,
1937. "Yes, Atherton is married...."
Courtesy Jane Atherton Roman

insincerity in her love for Bobby Winslow ("that mild insipid man"), and
of having decided to marry him out of "despair" and "expediency." By
the time of my reply to John, the marriage had already taken place. I had
not been able to attend, but had sent what I thought was a nice wedding
present: a pair of marble bookends carved into stylized horses' heads, for
which Jane thanked me in an excited, scrawled note that was postmarked,
as it happened, at the very moment of her wedding: Four-thirty p.m. on
February 20, 1937, in New York City.

"Yes," I continued to John, "Atherton is married."

Did you really send her a copy of that poem? Excellent verse; but I hate
to think of how some of the lines may have lashed her soul. The thing
was set.... I cannot see what your writing to her in that way could
have achieved. At any rate, she was married in much glory, the
ceremony being performed with some difficulty [as reported by my
sister Lois] by Drs. Milliken and Rockwell in conjunction... [Dottie]
Rockwell was the MAID of honor. Yes, I felt very dubious about the
whole matter when I was home for Christmas; but apparently Jane has
developed a sincere affection for Winslow, who after all is steady and

honest if dull. And not really knowing him, I am not even sure about the latter . . .

My work this semester is stupefying.

. . . Master's dissertation (75–150 pp.) due on May first . . . Hopwood entry [for the University of Michigan's lucrative creative writing contest] of 150 pages to get ready before April 21st. Grave doubts are being excellently entertained as to whether the latter ever will be done. . . . I'm writing my thesis on Swift: his attitude towards science . . . not necessarily so dull as it sounds. . . .

For the rest, all is well enough. Sally and I, after a stormy two weeks, have settled to a steady, seaworthy relationship which promises to last at least until June. Life seems good if accumulatively complex and mysterious. . . . I'll try to write more regularly. . . . Don't let those visions get you down, brother, and say a prayer at night for Poor Tom the Pauper.

—Milt

FIVE
Cambridge / Ann Arbor / New York, 1937–38

I never expected to meet her again.
But Cambridge is a small place, & a few days later
she was almost out of Portugal Place wheeling her bike
as I was wheeling mine in. *She greeted me.*
With heartburn I asked her to tea. She smiled, & accepted.
                                                    —"Meeting"

John was, not surprisingly, annoyed by my letter, and a month went by without further correspondence. It was a month of hectic activity in Ann Arbor for me and Bhain Campbell. Besides our final push for our master's degrees at the end of the semester and our struggle to ready our entries for the Hopwood contest, both of us were distracted by our relationships with women—for Bhain had recently fallen completely for a beauteous creature named Florence Johnston, and could hardly get his mind off her long enough to write a line of poetry that didn't end up as a love lyric. On top of all this, our social life had turned busier than it had been all year. Bhain was gregarious and generous, and could not resist inviting people back to our apartment for a beer or for lunch—especially a growing corps of young socialists and Communists, with whom he was getting intricately involved. Then there were other poets, later to become more or less distinguished, like John Malcolm Brinnin and Kimon Friar, and there were new friends from the university theater circle—with which I was still connected by way of Sally and my own interest—like Arthur Miller and Norman Rosten.

Norman and Arthur had both come from Brooklyn to Ann Arbor with the idea of pursuing careers as writers. Bhain and I met Norman by accident one night early in the semester at a campus cafeteria where he sat down at the same table with us. His Brooklyn mien and accent made me homesick, and his enthusiasm for poetry—he had just written a master's thesis at N.Y.U. on Gerard Manley Hopkins—captivated Bhain. At the moment he was more interested in theater than in verse; in fact his enrollment at Michigan had been financed by an award from the Theatre Guild for a play he had written. Norman became a good friend very quickly, and through him we got well acquainted with Arthur Miller—tall, lean, dourly humorous, and thoroughly engrossed in becoming a successful playwright.

As spring came on that year, I discovered that Norman Rosten had taken up with Hedda, my *passion manquée* of three years earlier. I had seen little of her during the interval but now renewed the friendship, especially since a housemate of hers, Mary Grace Slattery, was going around with Arthur Miller, and the four made a lively and congenial quartet. Bhain informed me that according to what he heard, the two couples were "getting serious" but neither he nor I realized how serious until one wet night in April when we were at home, studying morosely for a Chaucer exam. There came a knock on the door, and when Bhain opened it, Hedda and Mary Grace were standing there, dripping with spring rain and both looking rather pale and nervous.

We asked them in, of course, and offered them a beer. But the conversation faltered, with many uncertain glances between the two girls, and finally Hedda asked if she could speak to me in the kitchen for a moment. Puzzled, I stepped out there with her. "Listen," she said. "This is kind of embarrassing, but we couldn't think of what else to do. You know I've been seeing a lot of Norman, and Mary has been seeing a lot of Art, and things are getting—well, things are getting kind of serious. The thing is, I'm still a virgin—which is probably no surprise to you—and Mary is, too. And Norman and Art want to go to bed with us; but we think *they* think we're women of the world, and we're afraid they'll be disillusioned if they find out we're so innocent. So we wondered if you and Bhain...."

I stared at her. "Jeesuz, Hedda," I said. "Jeesuz, I don't know...."

"But just as friends!" she said. "No complications; just as friends! You like me, and I know Bhain likes Mary; and you both like Norman and Art. We thought if you'd just—well, you know, show us how it's *done?* We just don't want to seem stupid about it when the time comes with *them*. We wouldn't *tell* them about it, of course."

Flabbergasted at this turn of the worm, I called Campbell out to the kitchen while Hedda went back to the living room with Mary Grace. I explained the situation as tersely as I could. He stared at me much as I had stared as Hedda. "Good God!" he said. "What an amazing proposition! But I don't think I . . . I mean, I'm attracted to Mary Grace, but. . . . How do *you* feel about it?" I could see his natural gallantry struggling with his sense of propriety: what would Sir Walter Raleigh have done?

"Jeesuz," I said, "I don't know. I've always wanted to lay Hedda, but . . . I'm not sure I could do it in this—well, in this cold-blooded way."

I had given him the word he was looking for. "That's it!" he said. "That's it! It's just too cold-blooded. It's just too deliberate. We'll have to turn them down; but how can we do it politely? Kindly?"

"You tell them," I said cravenly. "You'll do it much better than I could."

So Bhain told them—eloquently and sensitively, I thought, with nice regard for their pride and sympathy for their intention. I chimed in that I was sure their maiden condition would not be scorned by Norman and Art, who undoubtedly loved them—and were just conceivably less experienced themselves than they made out to be. The girls were a bit crestfallen, but we also sensed that they were relieved. They had made an adventurous pitch, and it hadn't worked, but they went off into the spring rain none the worse, and possibly better, for the fiasco. At any rate, Hedda married Norman, and Mary Grace married Arthur, a few years later.

BUSY AS I WAS, I still could not keep away from the Lydia Mendelssohn Theater. Sally was almost always there, for one thing, and the program for the spring included an unusually attractive set of musicals and plays. The annual Junior Girls' Play—an all-female counterpart to Columbia's Varsity Show—was that year directed by Sally and written (book and song lyrics) by Dorothy Gies, a close friend of hers and a good friend of mine. I spent more time at rehearsals of that show than I should have; and not long after that came a marvelous production of Shakespeare's *Henry the Eighth*—not precisely his best play, but, as Valentine Windt realized, one that begged for lavish sets, costumes, and pageantry. Bhain and I regretted not taking part in the festivity: it seemed that nearly everyone we knew

Clockwise from left: Arthur Miller, Norman Rosten, Mary Grace Slattery Miller, Hedda Rowinski Rosten, about 1940. "At any rate, Hedda married Norman, and Mary Grace married Arthur, a few years later." Courtesy Norman Rosten

was in the cast, including Sally as Queen Catherine, Norman Rosten as Cardinal Wolsey's secretary, and Arthur Miller as the Bishop of Rochester.

Bhain and I were not getting along as well together as we had earlier. This was partly due to the irritation of spending so many hours at our typewriters in the same room every day, but there was also friction over political philosophy. We were both liberals, both pleased with the overwhelming defeat of the Republicans and FDR's re-election the previous fall, both aroused to indignation by the pro-Fascist bleating of Father Coughlin on the radio, both incensed about Franco and Hitler and the Nazis. But Bhain had recently undergone a conversion: he had convinced himself that the ultimate solution to poverty, unemployment, war, injustice, and general unhappiness was Marxism. He went to Communist meetings in Detroit and Ann Arbor, and hung out more and more with Bart Breed, a buddy of ours who was so ardently devoted to the cause and such a lovable character that his persuasions were hard to resist. Bart came from rural upstate New York and spoke with a native American twang and a homespun rhetoric: you could not doubt his sincerity, and you knew that he was totally without guile. But I was of too skeptical a disposition, and had spent too many years mentally working my way out of the system of Christian religious beliefs in which I had been swaddled, to be won over by any secular panacea. I upset Bhain by saying that the theory of economic determinism made about as much sense as the theory of original sin, and I made Bart uneasy by comparing the Moscow purge trials, from which horrid reports were beginning to emanate at that time, to the Spanish Inquisition. We finally decided that if we were to get through the semester and finish our work, there would have to be a moratorium on political discussion in the apartment.

My romance with Sally, meanwhile, was veering off the primrose path into the bushes without my quite knowing it. As April moved in, I unilaterally cut back our dates to three a week, then two, because I was working something like fourteen hours a day on my master's thesis and my Hopwood entry. "You could at least come over late and take me home from rehearsals," she said, to which I replied that if we did that we'd roll around on the couch in her living room until two in the morning and neither of us would get enough sleep. I felt that I was being very noble about all this—subjecting both of us to salutary self-discipline, refusing to lead her on with unrealistic expectations, and saving most of my energy for my work. The only factors I failed to consider adequately were Sally's feelings, which she outwardly muted, and my own, which (as I was soon to discover) I had been perversely concealing from myself. Since I was so busy, Sally said, would I mind if Fred James walked her home from rehearsals now and then? They were both in the cast for Smetana's *Bartered Bride*, and he had been sort of following her around. Mind? Certainly not, I assured her, my vanity pricked to its zenith. I knew Fred—a somewhat gawky architectural student and a nice guy, but certainly no serious competition, I felt sure.

Along with these torrents of spring came a crusty letter from John, defending his behavior vis-à-vis Jane Atherton and giving a rather intoxicated view of his life at Cambridge:

None of your cavil. Don't you realize that I've nearly gone mad about eight times here, that I am continually hysterical except for hours of intense work, that I have been drinking a great deal, that I am unspeakably miserable for the most part, and that if I sat down to write automatically (as letter-writing mostly goes with me) I should appear insane, wildly tedious, infantile? I was slightly drunk when I began a letter to Mother last night and with controls down, drivel it was. I dislike being thought pretentious when I'm not, [or] rarely: style *can* form and inform my thought; and without it, God knows. . . .

You forget how slowly news reaches me; the marriage was not, to my knowledge, 'set' when I wrote that letter, and I really had a grotesque hope it might turn Atherton's mind. Of course I sent it; of course it did no good; and of course it is not good verse. See Donne, Elegies, for good verse in that kind. I do not think Jane's an admirable character. . . . Winslow is a staple in this unpleasant century, worth moral judgment only in example: individually we can avoid them. Aristocrats without blood or taste or personal tradition, without honour.

Nothing connected with Swift could sound dull except scholarship; I know little but I feel a hell of a lot; have read this term all his verse and scattered pamphlets and letters in a complete (except correspondence) 1856 edition I have. . . . Good luck with your Hopwood essays, on what are you writing? Delicious marks, my boy. Not sure I'll take a degree here, in any case no examinations until June 1938, unless practise ones this spring. Swift wrote marvellous verse, ain't?

Young poets all over the place. . . . I spent week before last drinking and reading poems by the hundreds with, among seven or so mad ones, Dylan Thomas, a young Welsh poet who is highly touted and actually has some merit. Your little remark on Paul Engle . . . [Here a lacuna]

. . . I am quite drunk and have lost the second page of this letter begun years ago . . . and the hell with it and you for not being here. Tuppence for the old guy. I've been ill, allowed up today and must go down tomorrow (energetic place, England, first by doctor, second by Tutor). . . . driving down to London, where we'll consider possibilities. Ireland in any case. All that now interests me is chasing shepherdesses up dark lanes. Whee for pious penis. It's time I left, nearly raped the wife of my best friend here yesterday, she willing we think. No harm done. Working on the fens to relieve the flooded natives gives chill and makes one if feverish frisky. Epigram. Flagellant tendencies to be investigated, also Emily. But the mouth, Halliday, the mouth; not Emily's, Rosanna's. Gorgeous it is, only instead of coming she sent me a lot of goddamed books. Books I've got, copulation I need. . . . My amazement to find she can act, I've seen her lovely but incompetent in several plays, then in act II of something Saturday she was superb, eerie: dominated despite suicide the last act, too. Cheers. Flowrs. Yips. Virgin I feel, but it can be got over. Hell with prejudice. Sick entirely sick with this place. . . . Must now write the little Jean and finish a letter to Mother I once began, her last seven are unanswered, plague me like the Holy Ghost. I meant to explain poetry and morality in this letter, have worked out my views, but that can wait (a sweeping gesture here). Remind me to get up in the morning. Good night to you my lord. . . .

John

Bhain and I managed to finish our master's theses and hand them in; by staying up all night once or twice we got our Hopwood entries typed up just in time to have them bound as required by the rules, and slipped them into the contest an hour or so before the deadline. (For the obligatory pseudonym I chose "John Mark," in covert tribute to Berryman and Van Doren.) Then we settled down to wait for the results while we studied restlessly for final exams.

On the morning of June 2, 1937, the postman never got a chance to ring twice. It was the day of the Hopwood Awards: we knew that if either of us was a winner, there'd be a special-delivery letter. Bhain whipped open the door at the first buzz, and we saw with a jolt of joy that there were *two* specials. Each message read simply: "You have won a Hopwood prize," along with the superfluous reminder that we should go to the auditorium at the Michigan Union that afternoon for the actual awards.

There we suffered through a meandering discourse by Christopher Morley, the guest lecturer, after which the prizes were handed out. Bhain won $800 in the "major poetry" division; I won $500 in "major essay." It sounds like not much nowadays, but in 1937 even $500 was enough to make you wonder deliriously how you were going to spend it all.

Several of our good friends had also won awards, and for two or three days we reveled in a mood of celebratory joy. Art Miller, who had entered the "minor drama" part of the contest—you could not enter both major and minor at once—won $250 for a play called "No Villain"; he had already won another minor the previous year for "Honors at Dawn." (The history of the Hopwood contest is replete with little ironies, some of which do not surface until years later when the contestants have achieved various degrees of fame. In 1938, the following year, Arthur entered the "major drama" contest but won nothing, while his friend Norman Rosten won two majors that year, one in drama and one in poetry.)

SALLY, LIKE EVERYONE else I knew, was excited and congratulatory about my Hopwood prize, and with final examinations behind us we had one evening that made me think everything was going to be all right. But then she dropped the bomb: she had a date with Fred James for Saturday night, and she refused to break it. He had been tremendously attentive, she explained—he was always at her beck and call; he sent her flowers; he was in love with her and wanted to marry her. And he was, as a matter of fact, "quite a wonderful person"; she wasn't in love with him, but felt attracted to him and had grown quite fond. Moreover—and this cut the deepest—she was no longer sure how she felt about me. I had been neglectful and evasive and sometimes rude; she was sure I did not really love her; she would go on seeing me if I wanted her to, but she was going to see Fred James as well.

This turnabout, of course, was a very old story, the theme of innumerable popular songs, many of them banal; but it was the first time I had gone through it. I felt as if I had been run over by a truck, outside and inside. My emotional anguish was so acute that it worked its way all through my body: I could neither eat nor sleep properly, my bones ached, there was an awful tightness in my throat, my heart thumped audibly in my ears. As I put it in a letter to John: "furious jealousy, self-accusation, and a horrible impression of having ruined my last year in college all jumbled miserably together in a macabre festival and roared and jangled inside my skull."

I did not know what to do, but the prospect of staying in Ann Arbor and competing with Fred James seemed intolerable; it was too much for my pride. I had enough money now to go abroad, in fact my father actually had made a reservation for me on the *Queen Mary* as soon as he heard about my Hopwood prize—but suddenly the thought of bounding around Europe with John, which had been an alluring fantasy all year, seemed flat and empty.

At this painful juncture I happened to encounter Jim Doll, the costume and set designer for the university theater, as I forlornly crossed the campus one afternoon. He was an old friend of Sally's—a tall, gangling, long-fingered homosexual with a cynical wit, who scoffed at every convention and broke as many as he thought he could get away with. I liked Jim, and knew he was one of the few people who was aware of my trouble with Sally, so I was pleased when he suggested a Coke and a chat at the Besty Ross, across from the campus.

He had a sensational job for the summer, he told me, as a stage designer at the University of Iowa. Why didn't I go out there with him—they had a brand new theater building, and a terrific visiting director, T. W. Stevens. If I really had enough talent to be a professional actor, T. W. would surely bring it out. It would be a great change of scene, and he was damn sure it would be good for me to get away from Ann Arbor for a while.

It took five whole minutes to persuade me. I had been packing to move out of the apartment anyhow, for Bhain and Bart Breed had gone off to New York to enlist in the Abraham Lincoln Brigade and fight the Fascists in Spain. (I was happy to hear, during the summer, that they turned Bhain down as unsuitable, for I was convinced he would be killed in some heroic but foolhardy action. Bart, who was a most nonviolent person, was rather surprised to realize that they actually wanted him to go over there and shoot people, and decided to abstain.) My faint hope that Sally would protest my going to Iowa turned out to be vain, and within a week I was on a streamliner heading west, listening to the miles between us click off behind me, and feeling (as I wrote John later) "a deep tint of indigo."

MY CORRESPONDENCE WITH John now went into a two-month slump for opposite reasons: I was too miserable to write, and he was too happy. My mother forwarded to Iowa City a short but alto-cirrus communication from him dated July 2:

Dear Milt,

How did the Hopwood go? Merry & profitable, I hope—but fear other, since you've not written. Also, are you exalted? M. A., I mean. Write & say, how is life and what chance of your becoming international.

Very busy I've been, with parties & May Week do's of all kinds, tennis, Shakespeare and a paper just finished (Wednesday, having been started on Friday—I slept little)—77 pages on character & role in the comedy heroines. A set & tic topic, but I expanded it—ask Mum to let you see it. Also, I am deeply & joyously in love with the most remarkable girl I've known, Beryl Eeman. Leave here tomorrow to see her do Rosaline in L[ove's] L[abour's] L[ost] on Lord Harder's estate in the South. Last performance, then in London with her parents, & on Monday we go to Germany for a month. It will be heaven—just work & B—we feel entirely married—You cannot conceive the depth & range of satisfaction possible in a perfect relationship. She is 21, an undergraduate here & a brilliant actress—hard, powerful mind, absolute honesty, *no* sentimentality, very complex wit and great physical beauty & grace. I speak very soberly indeed. The first rapture is so transformed now in both of us that no mist is left. God I wish you & she and I could be together. We will be, don't worry.

Beryl Eeman, Germany, 1937. "I am deeply & joyously in love with the most remarkable girl I've known, Beryl Eeman." The setting evidently is one of the spectacular amphitheaters built for massive Nazi rallies. University of Minnesota Libraries

Write me care of American Express, Heidelberg, & immediately. Forgive my foolishness two months ago. God bless you, Milt—

John

I tried to answer this, but could not get a page finished, and an ecstatic postcard from Heidelberg in the middle of July ("You cannot believe a place can be so lovely . . . heavenly hills & woods & river & shops & people & food & coffee & beer & the Schloss & plays & Beryl & Shakespeare . . . in short I have never been so happy . . . ") helped not at all. It was September, with that dismal summer finally over, before I pulled myself together and got a letter off explaining it all:

I am incapable of describing to you Iowa City. RAW is the word which characterizes everything about it: the place itself; the people; the food; the climate; the theatrical productions: everything. I knew the minute I set foot on that seedy campus that if I stayed I'd have one hell of a time; and for a few days I didn't think I could stick it out. But I phoned Sally and got no satisfaction. . . . I had wanted so desperately for her to urge me to come back; instead, of course, she urged me to stay. . . . Meanwhile I was quite unable to find any friend in Iowa, male or female, although I tried hard at intervals.

I was certainly overwrought when I wrote that, for although the University of Iowa in 1937 did not compare favorably with Michigan, it was not as bad as I made it sound. True, the new theater building was in the middle of what was then a mosquito-ridden marsh; you got to it via a rickety wooden causeway. True, I found only one restaurant—the Town & Gown—where the food seemed passable; true, the weather was unbelievably hot (the Town & Gown had the only air-conditioning in Iowa City, which remarkably improved the menu); true, none of the pretty girls on the campus seemed pretty to me because my mind was obsessed with memories of Sally. But "unable to find any friend" fails to explain several nostalgic letters I got from both males and females after I was back in New York, reminiscing about the fine times we'd had dancing at the Red Ball Tavern, outside of town; drinking bootleg gin (Iowa was dry) with 7-Up at big picnics down along the river; joking our way through rehearsals, and so on.

Ah well, misery is a highly subjective state; I had been miserable and I wanted John to know it. (My complaint about Iowa City might, in an ideal world, have forewarned him: he was himself to have an intensely miserable experience there some seventeen years later when he went to teach at the university.) My letter to him reeled on for nine single-spaced typewritten pages, with subsequent scenes in Ann Arbor, up at Crystal Lake, and in New York, during which I nearly won Sally back again, but in the dénouement was prevented by the sudden and furious arrival of Fred James, who now considered himself her betrothed. Sally thereupon climbed on the Wolverine and went back to Ann Arbor, and Fred James followed hard upon.

BY THIS TIME I had a job in New York—a rather odd one, and not at all what I had expected when I started looking. *Life* magazine, which had begun publication under the auspices of Time, Inc., the year before, was expanding its staff, and I had heard that the chances of editorial employment for a young man with my background were pretty good. On the September morning when I headed for Manhattan for an interview, however, I overtook Edwin Robert Rumball-Petre on the way to the subway in Brooklyn Heights. He was a good friend of my father's—an impressive Englishman, tall, heavyset, ruddy, with an intimidating two-tone spade beard. What I liked most about him was that although he claimed to be an ordained minister—between churches, as he put it—he was fond of advancing outrageous opinions on everything including religion. He had once admitted, or rather boasted, to me that the "Rumball" had been added by him when his genealogical research turned up a British nobleman of that name who had put a "bar sinister" on the Petre escutcheon back in the eighteenth century. Rumball-Petre considered himself primarily a writer and, stirred by his discovery of a vein of bluer blood, had concocted a book-length manuscript purporting to be the journal of an upper-class English lady contemporary with Dr. Johnson, Boswell, and that crowd, but more advanced in her views than any of them. He did it well, with fine attention to an equipoised eighteenth-century style, and persuaded Brentano's to publish it without any disclaimer as to its origin. Several reputable critics were taken in, much to Rumball-Petre's delight, but Christopher Morley challenged the journal's authenticity on the ground that this prescient lady never made *any* mistakes in her aesthetic judgments, choosing for her leisure reading only works that later became monuments of English and French literature.

Anyway, I overtook Rumball-Petre on Hicks Street that morning, and paused for a chat. I was looking for a writing job? This was providential, he said, for his assistant at the publicity bureau he ran for the Transatlantic Steamship Conference had just quit, and he would hire me immediately. What was the job? It consisted, he said, of writing interesting travel articles about Europe for publication in some sixty American newspapers every week. But I had never been to Europe, I said. No matter, said Rumball-Petre; in fact, that would be an advantage: "You won't have any prejudices." I protested feebly that I hoped for a job on *Life*, and that I had heard they paid pretty well. "Nonsense!" he said. "They won't pay you as well as I will. I'll pay you thirty dollars a week, and give you an hour and a half for lunch. Two weeks vacation. You'll enjoy the job."

I did enjoy the job for quite a while, although the thrill of seeing a story I'd written about the delights of (say) skijoring in Norway, or consuming *Schlagsahne* in Vienna, published in fifteen or twenty newspapers under the by-lines of the local travel editors, palled rapidly. What did not pall was Rumball-Petre's seismic energy and the enthusiasm with which he conducted the business not only of the Institute of Foreign Travel— for that was the august title of our little one-room publicity bureau—but that of his real preoccupation, Bibles of Yore.

Bibles of Yore was a second-hand book business which Rumball-Petre ran out of the same office in his spare time, dealing exclusively in antique sacred texts. It was the logistics of the enterprise that fascinated me. I soon learned that the scores of old Bibles, testaments, and psalters that were described and offered for sale in his handsome catalogues were not exactly on hand. What he did was to comb through hundreds of catalogues from British book dealers, pick out the most appropriate items, and list them in his own brochures. When some millionaire collector in Denver wanted to buy, let's say, a good, clean copy of the 1560 Breeches Bible (so-called because it describes Adam and Eve covering their nakedness with "breeches" instead of mere figleaves), Rumball-Petre would dash off a cable to the bookseller in London, and assure the millionaire by letter that his purchase was on the way, but might take a week or so because of the need to pack it carefully, insure it, and so forth. When the Bible arrived from England, Rumball-Petre would pounce on it, upwrap it, check it over quickly, and then with astonishing dispatch pack it up again in Bibles of Yore wrappings and send it off to Denver, together with an invoice for approximately five times what he had paid the bookstore in London. After getting to know him fairly well, I twitted him once or twice on this practice, but he showed no unease. "It's all for their good," he explained. "Most of these rich Americans are dismally ignorant, and a rare old Bible can only improve their education and their morals. My role as middleman is indispensable; otherwise they'd never know such things existed. Of course, I overprice them in a sense; but you see they judge the value of a thing by its cost, and I don't want them to undervalue these magnificent old books." My early inclination was to regard Bibles of Yore as something of a fraud, but I slowly recognized that Rumball-Petre was a genuine expert in the field, often consulted on biblical minutiae by

Edwin Robert Rumball-Petre,
1938. "I grew fond of him.
He was a lively old dog
conversationally, and took me
to lunch every fortnight at
Fraunces Tavern."

theological seminaries as well as rare-book dealers. I grew fond of him. He was a lively old dog conversationally, and took me to lunch every fortnight at Fraunces Tavern, around the corner from our office, where he would regale me not only with superb food but an inexhaustible store of autobiographical yarns most of which had a tantalizing aura of light censorship, as if certain intriguing details had been left discreetly untold.

MY LONG LOVER's complaint about Sally lay unopened in Cambridge while John and Beryl were traveling, and late in September he sent me a letter from Stratford-on-Avon calling me various names for not writing, and bringing me up to date on his own doings. Their stay in Germany had been "perfect" except for all the "flags & troops"; he had grown a beard that was "an object of universal admiration." Now he was seeing performances of Shakespeare every day and working "desperately" on the plays and on Shakespearean criticism; he was preparing for the Oldham Shakespeare competition at Cambridge—"deadly complex & subtle examinations, and on so broad a field obviously it's impossible to say one is 'prepared.'..." But there would be a first prize of some eighty pounds, and he was determined to have a go at it. After that, "I shall marry at the end of the year, but I've no certainty about how or where I'll live. I doubt

John in Germany, 1937. "My beard is an
object of universal admiration."
University of Minnesota Libraries

I could stick England permanently; fortunately B. doesn't mind. New
York, probably."

The next mail brought a sequel:

Cambridge
26 Sept [1937]

Back from Stratford something over an hour ago . . . and found
your letter. I did nothing but gasp for several minutes, then read it
through at dinner and have just finished. . . .

You poor devil. I'll write you at large about this and my
meanwhile doings, but next week: the Oldham papers are Saturday and
Monday and I've not a moment to spare now. . . . Beryl will be up to
stay several days with me, and not even that will interfere.

I am even more delighted about your winning the Hopwood than
furious with you for not letting me know. . . . I'd like to see especially
the Swift paper, if you've a copy. . . .

. . . So much to say now that I can choose nothing. Besides, I hit in the train on a most important point in *Lear* I.1 and want to work it out before I go down to bed. . . . I'm very anxious to edit *Lear* . . . no edition worth drains exists. . . .

One thing to say, then to work. I am happier than I have ever been before, at once more puzzled and more confident of my ability and my character. I wish these, and far more, for you.

John

Cheered as I was by this sunny message from John, I myself was by no means happier than I had ever been before. It was good to be earning a living and putting a little money into a savings account at the Seamen's Bank each week, but it was a strain to be under my father's roof again, and my social life was torpid. Stubbornly burning my torch for Sally, I made no effort to find another girl who might interest me seriously or even distract me from my unrequited obsession by sexual games. Most of my evenings were spent reading or listening to records—I was beginning to discover that Chopin as well as Fats Waller had done interesting things on the piano—or just wandering around Brooklyn Heights gazing moodily out at the harbor. There seemed to be nothing worth writing to John about, in contrast to his stimulating life in Cambridge as reported in a letter in mid-November:

I still can't write at length, being at last in a shocking nerves-cold-indigestion state waiting for Prize results. Either Harness [another Shakespeare competition] or Oldham or both will be posted by the Senate-House any day at all, and they are damnably important, and since my impassivity finally shattered under Beryl's anxiety, I've been wild.

Finished a few days ago a one-act play on Cleopatra and am revising; it will be produced here this term or next. Blank verse, 400-odd lines, three characters, fairly stylized; I think it excellent. No other news except Cambridge fog and the odd concert. . . .

The Oldham papers were difficult, I did far better than I expected even—question of someone being equally full & accurate and better organized, that's all. My occasional absolute confidence is what worries me: experience says man never got what he counted on. Brief and sad, but sufficient for the undertaking of things eternal.

I hope you're relatively happy and very successful. What dashed your plan of writing to me? Anon, anon, Sir—

John

To this I scraped together a reply, conveying the basic information about my job and Rumball-Petre, plus a few tidbits that I thought might interest him:

Brooklyn Heights
November 21, '37

Nothing at all dashed my plan of writing to you—it still flourishes. But I seem to do few of the things I *want* to do. . . . Rockwell, as you may have heard, has taken an apartment with a Smith girl named Parke: they live in the Village . . . R. is supposed to be engaged to [someone] out west somewhere, but she hasn't seen him since last summer, and is getting very restless. . . . Parke is a curious and loveable person with beautiful (really; have you noticed that we have actually reached an age where girls of our own generation are beginning to have droopy bosoms?) breasts, a passionate love for music, and a whimsical and stubborn disposition. . . . I miss Sally so much that I am a little sick all the time. It makes it very difficult for me to tell whether my desire to go back to the university, scholarship, and teaching, is an honest one or merely a branch of my longing to be back with Sally again. . . .

How did you come out with the Oldham papers? I hope very much that you won the prize; and if you didn't I'll be surprised. . . . I

am ashamed to say that I haven't yet been up to see your mother . . .
[Mrs. Berryman told me shortly after this that John had indeed won
the Oldham]. I wish you'd come back here soon. It's beginning to seem
overlong, your exile.

JUST BEFORE CHRISTMAS, I sent Sally a long, carefully pondered explanation of why she would be infinitely happier married to me than to
Fred James, and why she ought to welcome my return to Ann Arbor so
she could make the right choice after a fair and balanced comparison. Back
came a curt note, the main point of which was a piercing coup de grace:
"I happen actually to love Fred. I have made my bed of roses and am
quite content to lie in it, and all your fine logic can't lure me away." I
wish I could say that the trauma of this barbed shaft cured me forever of
attempting to *argue* a woman into love, but I have always suffered from
a witless faith in the power of reason in such a situation. Nevertheless,
my adrenalin finally rose to the occasion: I angrily canceled my plans to
return soon to Ann Arbor, and began to look around New York for balm
in the form of other attractive girls.

JOHN AND I SENT each other books for Christmas, but aside from that
our correspondence languished during the winter—which is to say that I
wrote him a couple of times, but got no replies. I kept him abreast of
local news: Van Doren had sent me a note suggesting that we get together;
I was through with Sally (or vice versa); Jane and Bobby Winslow had
just returned from Australia; I had a new electric phonograph and a lot
of new records; and "a buxom lass named Ellen Mayo (I believe you know
her) and I spent five hours at the Savoy the other night and sat down only
once. That was when, in the midst of an exuberant effort to imitate one
of the more primitive (not elementary) manoeuvers of a Harlem hot-boy,
we both suddenly hit bottoms on the floor. . . . Ellen is a fine girl; we love
to discuss Life & Literature while reclining, more or less, on a bar in some
unlikely metropolitan spot."

This at last evoked a reply from John:

Cambridge, 15 March 1938

Dear Halliday,

I owe you, at the last count, eighthundredsixty letters. But let that pass. I've not yet thanked you for the splendid first [edition] of Yeat's Shadowy Waters, which brings the number of my Yeats firsts to a large fifteen. But let that pass. I have answered no questions, I have sent no news. But let that pass. I have not commented on the two-volume revelation you sent in September. But let that pass. I am a small grey rat, some say. That, sir, I must deny. My card: eis schokoladen at two feet four inches. . . .

Nothing has happened this term except that I spent an entertaining afternoon last week having my beard reduced to malleable size. The neck muscles aren't what they were and I'd acquired a hunched look, God wot. British Barbers are a Good Thing; mine has spent the last few years tending Shaw's beard, is much better read than I am and shows a perfect shark on the terms of dramatic criticism, neo-Chekhovian, etc. We missed our calling, old boy. But I have a couple of Oxford songs and a flock of stories to console us through the long winter hours. . . .

Who is Rumball-Petre? He sounds an Egyptologist with at the least a glass eye. You'd like Geoffrey Heath who makes up extraordinary rhymes, Theo Redpath who is the mad genius destined to be Prime Minister or Dean of the Moral Science Faculty, Lynn Ludovyck who is Gordon's friend from Ceylon and a little coffee Gordon incarnate, Wendy Morrison who is a breezy American chastity at large, John Bateman who is ever so shy, Sir Frederick Whyte who is all English men at once, Irene Heller whose tiny Russian charm has levelled this venerable place, and a few others. You wouldn't like

Rylands who has golden hair, now alas very thin, and is the Duchess of King's, Robina Bookless who is ever so slinky, or any of the Clare dons who are all worms and incubator-worms, not got after the downright way of creation. But you might like dear *beautiful* Satterthwaite, New Haven's joy, Anne Whyte, English womanhood at its best, and the willows along the Backs. Dear me, what a thing travel is. Broadens the brainpan and castrates the accent.

Were you serious about perhaps coming over in June? Lovely Halliday! I reel with joy. But as usual my statistics are rather feeble. The Trip [Cambridge slang for the B.A. examinations] is in May, I know, and Full Term ends on June 10; I must stay up until then to keep term; never anything but festivity after the exams, why we have to stay only the Vice-Chancellor knows. Then I'm free to go where I like until degrees are given about two weeks later, when I must return for a day to take mine unless I want to pay five pounds for taking it in absente, which I don't. Then the first boat. That's all I know at present. . . . Write me what you think. It would be marvellous, Cambridge is gorgeous in June.

This is all slightly tentative, inasmuch as I'm trying to get an instructorship at Columbia for next year and a course in Summer Session; should I get the latter I may have to donate five pounds to this bloody firm anyway, in order to be back in time. . . . My plans with Beryl are pretty vague too at the moment.

I feel quite frivolous and completely fed up, for I've got to move into Thompson's Lane tomorrow; Mrs. Young [his landlady] is giving this house up. Monstrous amount of books and furniture, etc.; an entire bore. . . . I've been spending more time than I ought on chess, an intriguing game. We'll have hilarious talks for months on end, my son. . . .

I must say, Milt, I'm damn glad the Sally business is over. I don't doubt she was marvellous, but after so much trouble together you could never have lived together in peace, I'm convinced. I hope you're well through it now; profoundest sympathy. From this distance it necessarily assumed an heroic aspect which probably it didn't have.... Note on euphony: Sally Halliday is as bad as Beryl Berryman. Think nine times before giving our names away.

Expect to cross to Paris on Sunday after a day or so in town [London]. Perhaps two weeks there, then back here and to the Lakes for the rest of the vac.... My regards to your parents and sisters, Milt, and luck with your beastly job; may a windfall, etc.

John

This all sounded quite ebullient, although I wondered what had caused his plan to marry Beryl to waver. I answered him at the end of March:

Thank god you're really coming home in a few months. After a hard winter's search I seem to have emerged with as many male companions as I had when I entered: to wit none....

Jane and Bobby... are now ensconced in outrageous comfort in a penthouse of some ninety rooms complete with maid and two small Scotch terriers. Rockwell, Winann, and an Austrian gentleman named Fritz who has lately become (apparently) indispensable to The Old Gang, spend most of their time up there, as far as I can see—which admittedly may not be very far: Bobby, while friendly enough, seems in no way anxious to have me hovering around Jane.... But I am bound to say that Jane seems to be very happy indeed with him....

Well, I wasn't fooling when I spoke of whipping over in June... but for want of discipline and encouragement I fear I have not been salting away the farthings fast enough to make it.... I may get a windfall between now and then, in which case... I'll be in Scotland before you. Remind me to tell you about Maxine Sullivan.

Ellen Mayo and I and most of the others in our New York crowd were crazy about Maxine Sullivan that spring. We would push in to the bar at the Onyx Club on 52nd Street (much cheaper than going to a table) along with about a hundred other people, buy one drink, and stay long enough to hear her sing a couple of sets to the perfect accompaniments supplied by her husband, John Kirby, and his small but superb jazz ensemble. Her interpretation of "Loch Lomond," of course, soon became famous; but there were many other songs that she took possession of with her limpid, inimitable style, including "Annie Laurie," "The Folks Who Live on the Hill," "Brown Bird Singing," and a version of "Easy to Love" that had me quivering between nirvana over Maxine and nostalgia over Sally Pierce. Nobody else in that era was singing with Maxine's utter directness—her clear, rich voice, almost without tremolo, gently stroking each note with absolute but easy precision: no trick effects; no gestures; no grimaces—just radiant Maxine and the music, as she stood straight before the microphone, her long white gown effulgent in the spotlight.

While I was enjoying the watering places of Manhattan, John was rambling through those of England's Lake District, as he reported on April 16, 1938:

We've had glorious weather and the lakes are all they're said to be—even Eliot might forget his caution in this air.* We're staying (John Bateman came up with me from Cambridge a week ago, after B & I returned from Paris . . .) staying, I say, halfway up the west bank of Windermere. . . . Thursday we went up to Little Langdale by Hawkshead, stopping at a beautiful tarn called Highlow for a dip; walked up Wrynose Pass . . . went up the Carrs, a northern peak of the Coniston Range, some 2300 ft. Very deceptive mountain—six spurs, one after another, we thought the summit.

Yesterday . . . we left our bikes and tried Helvellyn. Most impressive

---

*I learned later that T. S. Eliot had just rejected a group of poems John sent him for *Criterion*, the British literary journal, with the comment that one or two of them were "almost" acceptable.

and exciting. Unfortunately we were late as usual and had to turn back when still several hundred feet short of the top, on Striding Edge. You and I'll finish it one day. Terrible push back up the pass, but then some four miles of superb coasting, never once having to pedal—a dream, worn as we were. The enclosed [a pencilled Auden-like sonnet] I wrote this morning.

Must stop, we're just going—will write from Cambridge.... Thank God I'll soon be back.

John

I had not even had time to swallow my envy over this before I got another message:

Cambridge, 18 April

Halliday, I love you. The letter I found here this afternoon is one of the old, marvellous letters and I exploded laughing as I've not done for months. Of course it's all gone now and I'm gloomy as hell and will doubtless write a bloody earnest letter but solemnly I thank you for putting on again the animal robe and issuing wit....

I'm pretty constantly depressed by politics... brutality again and again, insolence and disorder. A terrible crime someone once told me of keeps reconstructing itself before me, at the gayest moments I see it. Several refuges: If you can't look out without shuddering, you must look in; and if you don't like what you find, if it sickens you, you must go to work on it as best you can. Which is what I'm doing and will do. Bach can restore me for a bit, as a few minutes ago, but there must be a long-term arrangement. Discipline is the name I give it. My passion for chess, which I study continually, is one form. Writing is another, at once less and more satisfactory....

I sound a moral rat. I wish I were one, but the adjective is mine by

courtesy only; try 'tedious'. But I haven't your enthusiastic animalism
. . . and I've other worries as well: Bob [his brother], money, the
prospect for a livelihood, and my verse. Though, for the last, I was
enormously set up by the appearance of a poem on the train back this
afternoon, which I'll copy and send with this; it should make up for the
sonnet, which I believe is trash. A dull note, old boy, forgive me. I'm
glad about Mayo and whatever else is good to you. The nine gods fend
thee about with banknotes and luxury. . . .

John

The poem John had written that day and which he sent me a typed
copy of (see facsimile) was one of only about a dozen from his early years
that he considered good enough to include in his later published collec-
tions, where he called it "On the London Train." Its theme was the
universal and sometimes anguished need to find a mate—a shared concern
that from the start had been one of the strongest bonds between me and
John. As I said in the last letter I wrote him before he returned to America
three weeks later, I liked it very much, but was having some difficulty
with the last stanza. "Damn it," I wrote, "I'm probably dense as hell, but
I don't quite get the point of this frown-recompense idea, and I'd like to,
because the rest of the poem seems to me powerful and vivid." After John
got back I brought it up again; he said with some irritation that he thought
it was self-explanatory, and that if it wasn't, the poem was not a success.
But when twenty of his poems were included in the New Directions
anthology, *Five Young American Poets*, in 1940, he chose this one to
paraphrase in his introduction, as a way of illustrating essential differences
between poetry and prose. It was only then that I understood what the
problem was: John had the mistaken impression that shelled sea creatures
are asexual—"The sea-shell, undemonstrative, chaste . . . can puzzle its
Maker, can amaze the course of things. For the shell alone seems to be
exempt from the necessities of living creatures—under enormous difficulties, at their wits' end, to win a mate, to breed, to achieve security."
Notwithstanding this biological gaffe, I have always liked the poem.
    In that last letter I also brought John up to date on my own situation:

Despite the lonesome look
The man in the corner has,
Across the compartment,
Doubtless a dozen daze
Daily their eyes on him intent
And fancy him beside a brook,
Their arms with his laced,
Holding him fast.

While he for some virgin
Endures the endless night
Without rest and would go
On bare knees, eyes shut tight,
To Tomsk or San Diego
If she'd but let him in,
Bind his hurt knees, or say
'There is a doctor down the way'.

So it is and has been.
Summon an old lover's ghost,
He'll swear no man has lied
Who spoke of the painful and most
Embarrassing ordeal this side
Satisfaction. And the green
Difficulties later are
More than Zeus could bear.

Austere in a sheltered place
The sea-shell puzzles Destiny,
Who set us, man and beast
And bird, in extremity
To love and get a nest:
The frown on the great face
Is recompense, but little for
Who suffer on the shore.

John Berryman

On May 1st I finally gathered my sins about me and moved out of 2 Grace Court. I'm now living with three other young gentlemen at 122 E. 79th, just off Park and directly across from a Mr. Vincent Astor. We pay a total of $75 a month, which is not bad when divided by four.

The boys are all right. I find I can get along reasonably well with anyone who is reasonably—or tolerably—intelligent and good natured. They put up with me, too. But it's damn hard to do anything constructive when one of your roommates is laying some wench on your [convertible] bed, one is playing a certain phonograph record over and over, and the third is urging you to skid around the corner for a couple of beers. . . .

Anyway, I get along beautifully now with my family. . . . Lois [who had married in 1935] is on the very verge of having a baby. Quite true to herself, she seems to have enjoyed her pregnancy immensely, and shows no sign of fearing labor pains or such. . . . I meant to call on your Mother last Sunday, but was delayed in getting back from an out-of-town weekend. . . . I'll see her this week, however, and learn the glad tidings about your return. She tells me a letter or two from Beryl pleased her deeply.

Now, I hope you're coming back so soon that you have to answer this ten minutes after you get it in order to have your response arrive here before your own magnificent self.

SIX
New York / Ann Arbor / Detroit,
1938–40

This is what all men at one time have met,
An inexcusable error in the plot
Which nothing but day on day's work can set right.
Avoid being alone, keep in the light,
Rehearse the crises history can show,
Let her go, let her go.

—J.B. to E.M.H., 1939

About the middle of June, Mrs. Berryman phoned and
said that John was coming in on the *Ile de France* on June 21; she invited
me to go with her to meet him. We were both excited, and rather nervously
watched the passengers streaming off the big ship onto the pier, afraid
that somehow or other we might miss John. This fear grew as the stream
waned to a trickle, with no sign of the returning exile. "Could he possibly
have missed the boat?" his mother said—"You know how bad John can
be about that sort of thing." I said surely he would have cabled her if that
had happened. At that moment, far down the now almost deserted pier,
we saw a lone figure approaching slowly, ambling along with a rolled-up
umbrella in one hand and a book in the other, head tilted slightly to one
side, eyeglasses glinting at us between the shadow of a slouch hat and a
heavy growth of red beard. Mrs. Berryman grasped my arm tightly. "Can
that possibly be. . . ." The figure drew near. "I say," said John's voice,
"have you bean waiting long?"

IT WAS A STRANGE summer. There was a week or so during which the
simple joy of reunion kept me and John enthusiastically cheerful when we
were together, but I think we both sensed that a certain distance had
developed between us that had nothing to do with the geographical miles

John and his mother, shortly
after his return from England,
1938. " 'I say,' said John's
voice, 'have you bean waiting
long?' " Courtesy Eileen
Simpson

between England and America, and therefore had not been canceled by
his return. I felt that some part of John's personality—the outgoing, generous, humorous, self-mocking part, of which I had been so fond—had
either changed in England or had somehow been veneered by traits that
I found bothersome.

Prominent among them was his new accent, which of course had not
revealed itself in his letters, and which frankly astonished me. An upper-
class British accent, or perhaps any sort of British accent, is an intractable
thing, and I was already aware that few Britishers showed any inclination
to alter it upon taking up residence in the United States. (Rumball-Petre,
for instance, still rumbled along in his native pattern without an iota of
modification after some twenty years in this country.) But in less than two
years John had almost completely Anglicized his speech—that is, as far as
he was able. His ear was not precise, and he overdid some sounds and
underdid others without any consistent scheme, so that the result suggested
a high-school actor trying to imitate Noel Coward. All of this got under
my skin more than it should have, and I made the mistake of trying to
josh him out of it, which made him angry. "Goddamn it, I'm not putting
it on," he said. "It's become second nature. It's the only way I can speak.
Has it occurred to you, moreover, that it's the English language, and that
just possibly the English have a better idea than you do of how it should
be spoken?"

It did not help matters that John's material circumstances had changed
much for the worse with his return from England. There, with the ample
stipend of his fellowship and the generally easy conditions of the university

scene, he had lived very well: comfortable digs, good meat and drink, lots of wonderful books, several trips to the Continent, and the particularly luxurious ambiance of certain Cambridge social events. (This last was epitomized for me by an invitation John once showed me, the whole thing printed in beautiful type on a small, heavy, white card with the heading "Newnham College," which was Beryl's college at Cambridge: "Will you come and eat strawberries and drink hock, in the grounds of the Garden House Hotel, on June the seventh, from five to seven o'clock, to celebrate the twenty-first birthdays of Beryl Eeman and Marjorie Brown.") Back in New York, John found his family's situation no better than it had been during his Columbia days: Mr. Berryman—who did not seem to be around much in the summer of 1938; I believe he was sojourning at a family farm in Maryland—had experienced more downs than ups in the stock market, and Mrs. Berryman, though working very hard, was still stretching frayed ends to make them meet. John desperately needed employment, but despite strong recommendations from Mark Van Doren, nothing came through in the academic arena; and the job atmosphere in New York was still that of the Depression.

Not surprisingly, all this induced severe psychological depression in John; but unluckily it often evinced itself in rage and indignation which worked against him when he went for a job interview. Along with his fierce British accent and his beard, he was likely to take with him an attitude of contempt; I heard from a friend who worked at *Time* that when John applied there, he conveyed the feeling that although such work was beneath him, he might consider it if they made him a good enough offer. No offer was made. Meanwhile, John regarded with amused disdain the work I did for Rumball-Petre, and while I myself considered it mildly disreputable, this nevertheless hurt my feelings.

We made efforts to sustain our friendship, but they were not strikingly successful. We tried a few games of chess, but I had never been very good at it, and now John won so easily that neither of us enjoyed it. When John could afford it, we went to films at air-conditioned theaters—the weather was hot—and now and then we tried a tennis game up at Columbia, as we had of old. John would work out on the tennis ball some of the anger and frustration he had accumulated, belting it viciously into the net or clear across the court into the back fence, but winning few points.

The guys from East 79th Street: "Nick" Nichols, Halliday, and Bill Percival, with two charming companions, at Palisade Amusement Park, 1938. "I was by now quite enjoying my evenings and weekends with my apartment-mates. . . ."

On his side, he was perhaps right in his contention that I had made too many concessions to the mediocre in American life. I was by now quite enjoying my evenings and weekends with my apartment-mates on 79th Street, and I was unable to claim that the prevailing mood there was highly intellectual. All of us were college graduates in our early twenties; but Nick, the most charismatic of the ménage, was an ex star end at Colgate who now was doing well as a salesman of surgical instruments, and who tended to regard books as an adolescent problem, like acne, that he had finally overcome; Bill was a likable sports reporter with no vast respect for my M.A. in English; and Alden was an earnest textbook salesman who hoped that he was thereby working at least in the outskirts of the Elysian Fields. I took John home for a drink one evening in July and introduced him to the gang, but except for Alden, who was wide-eyed to encounter a living poet, the occasion was a dud. Nick and Bill agreed later that John was "a phony," and John expressed to me the opinion that all three of them were "hopeless clods."

Social life on 79th Street that summer was thus not something John wanted to share, although in an earlier day it would have delighted him. Three young nurses at Mount Sinai Hospital occupied the apartment above us, and there was a great deal of impromptu coming and going, and a great many gin and tonics and cases of beer.

Nick possessed a Ford roadster in which he and Bill and I often dashed around town, Nick at the wheel and one of us in the rumble seat. They liked to cruise up and down Third Avenue visiting a succession of Irish bars for beer, and sometimes getting involved in more or less cheerful altercations over such delicate matters as Bill's last name, which happened to be Percival. Nick was an expert driver even when full of beer, but he was so reckless that I often wondered if we'd ever get safely back to the apartment. One time we did not: he and I were returning from a party in Scarsdale very late, and as he came roaring around the corner of 125th Street and Broadway, into the gloomy forest of "el" pillars, we rammed hard into the rear end of a Sheffield's milk wagon that was stopped in the middle of the block. Quart bottles of milk flew through the air like bombs, bursting against the iron pylons; the poor horse was knocked over on his side along with the wagon, and could not get up; and the milkman, who luckily had been indoors making a delivery, came running out screaming imprecations. The front end of the roadster was a wreck, and I found that my head, which had crashed into the windshield, had a bleeding gash just beyond the hairline.

Nick was as cool as ever. "Take a look at this," he called to me from behind the car. An entire case of full quart bottles was jammed between the spare tire and the rumble seat, and the only possible way for it to have arrived there was to have flown from the wagon directly over our heads (for the top was down). "Lucky old Bill wasn't with us," said Nick, taking the cap off a quart of milk. "Here, have a drink. You'd better get to a doctor and have him look at your head." A police squad car had appeared, and one of the cops drove me down to St. Luke's Hospital, where I got stitched up in the emergency room. Nick subsequently convinced the law and the Sheffield company that the milk wagon's tail light had been out (which it may have been; I don't know), and collected enough from the company to fix his car. John, when he saw my wounded head and heard the explanation, took a sour moral view, declaring that I had fallen among reprobates, and ought to mend my ways before it was too late. This was so unlike the old John that I took offense, and we did not see each other for a week or so.

Late in July there occurred an explicit rift between me and John. Jeanne Curtis, my beautiful friend from undergraduate days in Ann Arbor, had come to New York for a visit in April, and we both had enjoyed it so much that we talked—a little vaguely—about getting married some day. It was only a quasi-romance, partly because she was still a virgin and skittish about sex, but it was sincere. In mid-summer she sent me a letter saying she would be in New York for one night, on her way to Europe: why didn't we go dancing or something? I had told John about Jeanne, and Jeanne about John, so I called him up, and he met us after dinner for a trip to the Savoy Ballroom, which Jeanne had never seen. John was much taken with her, and composed an instant rhapsody about her breasts while she was in the ladies' room; he also kept her out on the dance floor much longer than I thought was meet, considering that she was my date. Eventually we taxied down to the Wellington Hotel, where Jeanne was stay-ing, and I took her up in the elevator to her room while John waited in the lobby. A few minutes later, he and I walked down to 50th Street, where he descended into the West Side subway; I hiked on across town and took the Lexington Avenue local. Not long after, while John and I were having a ten-cent beer somewhere, he said there was something I ought to know about Jeanne: she had come on to him very steamily up at the Savoy, and in fact had set up a rendezvous with him at her hotel room for later that night. It hadn't come off, he explained, because by the time I left him at the subway he was feeling anticipatory guilt, and didn't think he should help Jeanne deceive me, but he thought I ought to know she was not to be trusted.

Instead of being grateful at his forbearance I was angry with both of them, and had actually written Jeanne an indignant letter before I remembered that her European itinerary was uncertain, and there was no way to get it to her. When she came back, a couple of weeks later, I saw her again and expressed the view that it seemed unlike her to have made a clandestine appointment with John behind my back. "But Milt," she said, "I didn't make any appointment with John. He came up to my room absolutely on his own." This naturally confused me, and I asked for an explanation. "Oh," she said, "he came to my hotel the morning of the day I was sailing, and banged on my door until I let him in." "I don't suppose you'd care to tell me what happened?" I said huffily. "Nothing at all happened," she said. "I was in the middle of packing, and I gave him a drink of cognac and told him to stop bothering me—although I must say he was pretty persistent."

None of this appeased me much with regard to John, and he and I had an unpleasant confrontation in which he apologized for his behavior but justified it, or at least explained it, on the ground that he was missing Beryl so painfully, and was suffering so from sexual deprivation, that Jeanne's attractions had overwhelmed his judgment.

Earlier in the summer I had introduced John to Bhain Campbell, my poet friend and old apartment-mate from Michigan. Bhain had taken his Hopwood prize money, paid off his debts, and gone to Europe for an extended pilgrimage in 1937, after he failed to be enlisted by the Abraham Lincoln Brigade to fight in Spain. Something of a strain had developed between us over his revolutionary enthusiasms, which had been reinforced by his travels—romantically, I thought: he wrote me that he had "wept in every capital of Europe," especially Moscow. I sent him what was undoubtedly a sarcastic reply, whereupon he scolded me for my bourgeois and conventional attitudes: "Neither will you, ever, so long as you live where you are, in your circumstances, think otherwise than you do." He had married Florence Johnston in January 1938, and in June they came to stay with her parents in Bronxville, and later, in a borrowed apartment, in midtown Manhattan. Bhain was more than ever dedicated to poetry, and was anxious to meet John, about whom I had told him a good deal. John was somewhat aloof and suspicious at first, but Bhain's contagious charm and good humor soon worked him into a more friendly posture. Since I was now slightly on the outs with both of them, though for quite different reasons, I was pleased to see the new friendship evolve: it seemed likely that they could find in each other intellectual satisfactions they could not get from me in my current mood, if ever. Bhain was taking a summer course at Columbia, where he and Florence would often meet John, to poke around the library or to beguile the afternoons in poetic discourse at some of the cafés along Upper Broadway where John and I had spent so much of our undergraduate youth. This went on until the end of the summer, when the Campbells—most reluctantly—went back to Michigan to see if Bhain could get some sort of job in Ann Arbor or Detroit.

In August I went to Crystal Lake for my two weeks' vacation, enlivening the trip back with my very first ride on a commercial airliner. (It carried sixteen passengers, and although the sky was cloudless, bobbed and bounced like a ping-pong ball all the way from Traverse City to Detroit.) When I got back to New York I found that John was out of town, and soon received an explanatory letter:

At the Allen Tates'
West Cornwall,
Connecticut
Thursday 25? August [1938]

Dear Milt,

I'm sorry I didn't write you at Pilgrim, but I forgot the address and wasn't well while you were away, in any case. I finally thought B[eryl] was coming and then she cabled she couldn't and things were worse if possible than before. Allen's invitation was in the nature of divine grace.

He went away fishing with his brother on Sunday, and Caroline [Gordon, Tate's wife] and I hold the fort; there are also Nancy, 13, a friend of hers, Bibi the world's extrovert dachshund, and the maid. Most beautiful weather and I have picked up a good deal. Driving a lot, which I enjoy, but mainly peace: drink, talk, swimming, reading. The first copy of Allen's novel *The Fathers* has come from Putnams and I'm reading that, also some Trollope. Mark and Dorothy [Van Doren] we see frequently, he is nearing the end of the *Shakespeare* [a book of critical essays], looks very tired. . . .

I have a fine poem to show you. The Herodotus pieces are not coming on as they ought, though . . . and a thing I thought finished apparently isn't. So Campbell said and I believe he's right. I saw a lot of them and we came to be very good friends. . . .

We do miss each other, don't we? Allen will be back early next week. . . . I may come back to the city. Depends on my family's being settled, etc. Write me here.

John

John was still jobless in September, but his demeanor improved with the assurance that Beryl was coming from England in October. Partly in anticipation of this event, Mrs. Berryman moved to a more commodious apartment on lower Park Avenue. It had a large back room with its own entry where John and Beryl could live more or less independently—although John's mother would still reign over the establishment.

I was not disappointed in Beryl Eeman. Her grave beauty, expressing itself in her luminous brown eyes, fine features and clear white skin, her dancer's figure and carriage, seemed exotic by comparison with that of American girls I admired. She wore little if any make-up, and dressed with decorous taste that made her look striking in ways I found hard to analyze but was no less affected by; and she spoke with such mellifluous precision that I began to forgive John for trying to reproduce her English.

With Beryl on the scene John and I got along better, and there were times when we felt ourselves back on our old footing of brotherly intimacy. Together we squired her around New York to see the famous sights, went to films and plays, and dawdled over many cups of coffee at the automat while we talked of what we'd seen and read and the work they were doing— for Beryl was hard at work on a play, as John was too. (John repeatedly began and failed to finish plays; I don't think he ever completed one to his full satisfaction.) I had time on my hands, for I had managed to persuade Rumball-Petre that I could do all the work he wanted from me in four hours a day—9 A.M. to 1 P.M.—instead of seven, and he munificently let me try it with no reduction in pay.

Having given up acting, and without the conviction that I could become a playwright, I was now attracted by the idea of being a drama critic. About once a week during the 1938–39 season I got a second-balcony ticket for an opening—often sitting up there in lone glory, for the people who bought balcony seats were not going to chance a new play before the reviews came out. I saw some excellent shows open, as well as some amazing lemons. One of the latter, which I had looked forward to hopefully and can never forget, was a dramatized biography of Sir Richard Steele called *Yr. Obedient Husband*, with Fredric March and his wife, Florence Eldridge, playing the leads. It was all deadwood, and they knew it; by the middle of the last act they were beginning to parody themselves. A few days later, when the show closed, there appeared in the *Times* an ad reprinting a well-known *New Yorker* cartoon—it shows a couple of circus aerialists, one of whom has just missed catching the other in midair and calls out, as his colleague plunges toward the sawdust, "Oops—sorry!" The ad was signed "Frederic March and Florence Eldrige." (I feel that theatrical advertising was more sprightly in those days—it was either that year or the next that Maurice Evans's uncut version of *Hamlet* was billed as "Longer than *Gone With the Wind*—and better!")

My game, of course, was to write a review of a new play before the papers came out the next day, and then compare my reactions with those of John Mason Brown, Brooks Atkinson, et alia. A couple of times John scared up fifty-five cents for a ticket and went with me; afterward we repaired to the Artists' and Writers' Restaurant on West 40th Street— universally known as Bleeck's, and frequented by *Herald Tribune* and *New Yorker* scribes—and each wrote a review over our beer; then we exchanged reviews and went home, to confer by phone in the morning and see who agreed with whom—though John had a tendency to write such scathing notices that they didn't agree with anybody. He did have a good opinion of Orson Welles, whose Mercury Theatre was flourishing that year with such productions as *Julius Caesar* and *Danton's Death*. In those days the expression "sneak preview" meant just that: the night we saw *Julius Caesar*, Welles came out after the final curtain and invited the audience to stay for the first public performance of Dekker's *The Shoemaker's Holiday*.

Meanwhile, John was producing poems at a good rate, yet having little success in getting them published. He would show them to me as they were finished, but I found that the old camaraderie that allowed me to offer critical suggestions was gone. "Goddamn it," he said in an anguished voice one day when I ventured to question a line or two, "I don't want you to *criticize* my work; I want you to *like* it!" He suffered when his poems were rejected, but kept grimly at the business of sending them out. I remember one cold Saturday in December when I arrived at the apartment around noon, and found Beryl, pale and bleak, huddled on a couch; John was pacing back and forth like a tiger in the middle of the big room, looking distraught and clutching a copy of Wordsworth's collected poems in one hand. "Listen!" he commanded me, and he read aloud the last four stanzas of "Resolution and Independence," about the old leech-gatherer who refused to be discouraged or deflected from his task, no matter what the obstacles nor how small the rewards. "That's the way I must be," John said. "That's the way I *will* be." I firmly commended this resolve but, feeling a bit stifled by the solemnity of the scene and the fact that John had been smoking countless Tareytons in a completely closed room, offered to take them to lunch at my favorite restaurant, Le Champlain, on 49th Street, where you got hors d'oeuvre, entrée, dessert, and a glass of wine for about a dollar. This brightened up the day considerably.

One of our diversions was to browse in bookstores, usually without buying anything. The exception was likely to be at Marboro's, where remaindered books were available for twenty-nine cents and up. There one day we found a book on the work of Peter Brueghel, with an introduction by Aldous Huxley and fuzzy but provocative reproductions of some of Brueghel's paintings, including the wonderful series on the four seasons. John and I each bought a copy (forty-nine cents), and a few days later he showed me "Winter Landscape," a rumination on art and time inspired by long and thoughtful looking at Brueghel's *Winter*. I have always been fond of the poem, one of the most lucid and eloquent that John had then written. (Malcolm Cowley published it in the *New Republic* about a year later, but only after John agreed, with some annoyance, that the words "After Brueghel" should be printed under the title. "The poem's not *about* the painting," he said; and when it was reprinted in *Five Young American Poets* [1940], he removed the explanatory phrase.)

I was naturally interested, that winter, in how the love affair between John and Beryl was holding up, especially since it was obvious that John's lack of money and a job, his mother's irritation at having to support him and her irascibility toward her potential daughter-in-law, John's volatile temper, and Beryl's firm habits of responsibility and self-control, all put the relationship under stress. There were times when the tension in the household would break into open and angry argument between John and his mother, and it was then that for the first time I witnessed the frightening phenomenon of John's swoons. A particularly bitter altercation arose one evening, and just as it seemed that there was no way of settling it, John suddenly sprawled on the floor, apparently senseless. He recovered after a few minutes, but was dazed and disoriented; the argument, of course, was not resumed.

John was reticent as to how things were going between him and Beryl, and I almost never saw her when he wasn't there. Once, when he was ill, she and I went for a long walk and stopped in for tea somewhere.

She said that although she loved John very much, she had doubts about their chances for a good marriage. She wasn't talking about "happiness," she said; that was something she did not really hope for; but John's instability and unreliability, and his sporadic arrogance and lack of tolerance, raised in her mind a picture of marriage that she knew she could never live with. It was her hope that when John got a job that suited his interests and abilities, their prospects together would look brighter.

I think the only other time I saw Beryl without John was early in the spring, when he was again ill and I invited her to a small party at my one-room apartment (the carnival on 79th Street had finally broken up in the fall). My old friend Winann was there with the devilishly charming young Austrian named Fritz, which prompted me to put a stack of Viennese waltzes on the phonograph. Beryl spoke fluent German and had been often to Vienna, and presently she and Fritz were swirling around the room in a most accomplished exhibition while the rest of us watched admiringly. As the last chord of the last record resounded, they pirouetted into a bow, and we all clapped. I was pleased to see Beryl so exhilarated, her winter pallor chased by spots of bright color in her lovely face.

Beryl went back to England in April 1939. John was morose, but continued to work hard. One day he called and said W. H. Auden and Louis MacNeice were giving a poetry reading up at Columbia; would I like to go? John had learned where Auden was staying, and that afternoon he telephoned, identified himself, and asked Auden if he would read "Our Hunting Fathers," a poem John thought highly of. We went up to Morningside Heights after dinner and waited impatiently; the performers were late in getting started. Eventually the two poets sauntered out onto the small stage, MacNeice big and well groomed, Auden smallish and disheveled. Auden read with such a heavy overlay of Oxford accent that I had to listen for ten minutes or so before I could clearly distinguish the words; but it was a moving occasion, for as an encore, he reached into his pocket and extracted a crumpled sheet of paper on which he had written out an unpublished poem. It was his elegy for William Butler Yeats, who had died late in January, and it was to become one of Auden's most famous poems. He also honored John's request, prefacing it with the remark, "Someone rang me up today and asked me to read 'Our Hunting Fathers.' " John was mildly indignant at having been referred to as "someone."

For me, the other surprise of that April 1939 was a phone call from Sally Pierce. She was in New York for spring vacation and wondered if I'd like to meet her for a drink. For about thirty seconds I struck the pose of the rejected lover too proud to show that he one jot of former love retains, and then agreed to be "under the clock" at the Biltmore—the Manhattan meeting place that always sprang to mind in those days—at 5 P.M.

She looked wonderful, and I knew in two minutes that the old feeling was still in my heart. Her affair with Fred James, she said as we sipped at our Tom Collins's, was on the way out—no explanation offered. But I shouldn't get my hopes up, she added quickly: she was quite sure she was going to marry David Dow, her high-school sweetheart, who had hovered tenaciously in the wings all these years and was now a successful young lawyer. I told her I had been planning to go back to Ann Arbor to pursue a Ph.D. anyhow (this was true), so I'd see her early in the summer. "Don't count on it," she said. "I don't count on anything any more," I said; and we then proceeded to have an enchanting evening together. ("Your letter scarcely surprised me," Bhain Champbell wrote after I had told him I was coming back to Michigan; "Brinnin said he saw you and Sally galloping along Fifth Avenue in a great mist of spring dream.")

The big problem about going back to Ann Arbor was money. My father, though pleased with the idea of higher learning, took the view that at the age of twenty-five I ought to be self-supporting: why had I not saved more from my earnings at the Institute of Foreign Travel? (I had a balance of $56.37 in my account at the Seamen's Bank for Savings.) Rumball-Petre also approved my educational goals, but said he thought I'd better quit work at the end of May if I was going to Michigan in June. He did come up with a farewell present that mightily impressed John: the third folio edition of the King James Bible, printed in 1634 and a replica of the famous 1611 edition. Not a man to do things half way, he had searched through his British catalogues until he found an ad for a copy that was inscribed on the flyleaf, "Thos Swift's Book, 1634." "I have conducted some research in the matter," Rumball-Petre wrote in a note tucked inside the cover, "and I find that in that year there were only two Thomas Swifts in England who were clergymen: the grandfather and the uncle of Jonathan. . . . Only the clergy attempted to own these large Black Letter folios, hence I deduct my conclusion that it must have been in that family."

The faint temptation I had to sell the Bible in order to finance my summer in Ann Arbor was quelled when I turned the handsome, heavy pages, still in sound condition after three centuries, and realized that they might well have been turned by the hand of twenty-five-year-old Jonathan Swift around the time he took his M.A. at Oxford in 1692.

Something, however, had to be done. The World's Fair had just opened in Flushing, and everyone said there were lots of jobs available. But nobody wanted to hire me for one month, and the only job I got was filling in for a few days at a stand where I guessed people's weights and, if wrong by more than three pounds, gave them a "free" teddy bear or doll. (Even with that brief on-the-job training I got to be quite good at weight guessing, especially when the subject was female; but I have never found it to be a skill that wins much enthusiasm when practiced, for instance, at parties.) John and I spent several afternoons and evenings just wandering through the great maze of exhibits and amusements at the fair, with special attention to those that didn't cost anything; we also made the remarkable discovery that we often could pick up girls at the roller coaster who were willing to pay for two tickets so as to have someone to hang on to (or vice versa) during the rather fearsome ride. One night we got our signals mixed, and John waited a long time for me at the roller coaster while I waited for him at one of the fairground gates. We were both angry, each thinking the other had failed to keep the appointment, but the contretemps did give rise to an interesting poem a week or so later—John called it, "The Instructor," but later included it (with emendations) in an early book of poems under the title "World's Fair."

Racking my wits for a way of getting money, I remembered that when I was much younger an uncle of my mother's, who had worked for many years in the U.S. Post Office, had given me a stamp which he said would some day be "very valuable." It had an engraving of an early-model automobile on it—printed upside down. Much to my mother's disappointment, I had never developed an interest in stamp collecting, but now my interest suddenly sprouted. I got out the stamp, in its neat little transparent envelope, and took it into one of the larger dealers listed in the Yellow Pages. The young man at the desk regarded me disdainfully until he looked at the stamp; then he disappeared behind a partition for a couple of minutes, and returned with the little envelope held carefully in one hand, and a brand new one-hundred dollar bill in the other. I had never seen one before in my life, and it looked to me like a map of Treasure Island. When I told Lois about the big sale, she said I was crazy: "I'll bet you could have gotten two hundred if you'd shopped around, and I'll bet in another ten years that stamp will be worth a thousand dollars." (To round out this parable, I must report that in 1977 I had lunch one day with Lois, and just as we were getting into a cold martini she remarked, "Say, did you see what your upside-down automobile stamp sold for at an auction yesterday?" "No," I said. "Twelve thousand dollars," she said.)

Toward the end of May, John went down to Maryland, where Mr. Berryman's sister had a farm:

> Fountain Valley
> Reisterstown, Maryland
> 25 May 1939

Dear Halliday,

I'd write you a paean to the birds and the bees and the trees, but there was a violent argument at breakfast, in which I encountered more blind fable and superstition than I've met in years, and I feel extremely sour. A walk over the hills since hasn't smoothed it out; I have just written Dillon, at *Poetry* [Magazine], the roughest letter he'll have this summer.

I came down here, among other things, to write verse and repair a year's correspondence, and despite the really marvellous weather, both are getting done. About three letters a day. . . . Not Campbell yet, though I've been rereading his messages and feel quite ashamed of my silence. He is growing up; even in the course of a year I can see a good deal of the accidental stupidity fall away. The verse too is better than I first thought it, or I have become more tolerant, which isn't likely. I am returning his letter to you, which I brought away by mistake. If you can, you ought to try to see him—whether I can get up is doubtful. [Bhain had written that he and Florence would be in New York briefly—

just at the time when I expected to leave.] I may as well copy
MICHIGAN PORTRAIT for you:

> There is a crazy man in Michigan
> Who laughs and chops his wood, studying Shelley
> And Shelley's bright preposterous ideas.
> The sun burns him, the late November snow
> Companions him with landscape, and the winds
> Blow from the lake a crazy blue for him.
> He has a wife, and she is twice as shy
> As he is mad or he is gay. They have
> A lovely time together, chopping wood,
> Examining poor Shelley in his time,
> Companioned with the sun and snow and winds,
> Great talk and drink, living and being landscape.*

Apparently I should have left New York earlier: a very welcome
letter from *The Kenyon Review*, promising a group [of John's poems]
next month and more later, wanting an essay, etc. 'We are very proud
to print your poems,' which I know is a formula and insist is genuine.

You can do me a favour if you will. I remember well but not
entirely Berkeley's poem ON THE PROSPECT OF PLANTING ARTS AND
LEARNING IN AMERICA, and find I badly need it. When you're near the
library, I'd greatly appreciate your copying it out: it's in the Oxford
Book of 18 c. Verse.

Good luck with all your arrangements. Write me.

John

---

*John's amusing poem gives a highly selective notion of the actual experience Bhain
and Florence had in Michigan in 1938–39: poor Bhain, who in the first flush of his
Marxist enthusiasm had sworn to me that he would never return to the bourgeois
academic life, had taken a miserably paid job teaching English at a junior college in
Highland Park and they had to live in an unheated, unplumbed cottage owned by his
parents at Union Lake, some thirty miles away.

Bhain and Florence Campbell,
1939. "They have / A lovely time
together . . . / Great talk and drink,
living and being landscape."
University of Minnesota Libraries

I sent John the Berkeley poem, and brought him up to date on my
plans for Michigan. A thank-you note from him carried the good news
that the *Nation* had agreed to take him on as their poetry editor; "I am
now selecting their verse, and damnably busy, poring over the works of
Charlotte Wilder and Oscar Williams, whoever they are." Three weeks
later he augmented this:

Excellent poems have been sent me by Wallace Stevens, John Peale
Bishop and W.H. Auden: apparently I can summon a good collection,
though this is a bad time of year to reach people. The collected works
of eighteen asses who long for print came down in a fat bundle from
the office on Saturday; from Florida to California, half of them with
the most gruesome confessional letters; I shudder and reject. Mark's
SHAKESPEARE is my solace; it's very good. . . .

B[eryl] sends her regards to you now and then. She plans to attend

St. Denis' London Theatre Studio this year, and is very optimistic about a West End production of [her play] THE INNOCENT, which is nearing final form. So am I.

If I told you soberly what I think of the poems I've written down here, you'd consider me vain; quite right, too; so I'll say nothing....

I had heard from Beryl myself: she was worried because John wrote her such sparse accounts of his present situation, and asked me to let her know "what's actually happening & how he is." She reported herself not very happy, though working hard on her play—"Life is *very* difficile. My brother says everyone should be retired until the age of 35."

THE TIME HAD finally come to put New York behind me, as I told John on June 20, 1939:

I have at last gotten all packed and ready to leave for Ann Arbor....

A fortnight ago someone (don't know who) sent me a clipping from the Ann Arbor paper announcing in certain terms Sally's engagement to Dow; "the wedding will take place in August." That was, of course, rather depressing; and since then I have done much pondering on the whole business and find that I have reached the end of my rope.... But of course she'll be there; and of course I'll run in to her fairly often. Don't suppose that it will be pleasant....

Did you write Campbell? I wrote him a few days before the date he had scheduled to leave for N.Y.; have not heard a word or seen a hair of his head. Or Florence's.... Alors,

Milt

Watching the landscape glide by the Wolverine the next day, I mulled over the kind of summer I was likely to have in Ann Arbor, and ways to make it pleasanter. I felt the certainty of doom for my pursuit of Sally, but decided that the saving thing would be to go to my fate with as much panache as possible. This explained my presence, the following morning, at a big used-car lot on Michigan Avenue in Detroit, giving a hard time to an overweight, lugubrious salesman who knew from the start that his profit on any sale he made to me was barely going to buy his lunch. After I had declined a 1932 Chevrolet at seventy-five dollars, and a 1931 Ford at sixty dollars, he fixed me with a penetrating but somewhat sympathetic look. "How much were you thinking of spending?" "Under fifty dollars," I replied. "Ah," he said. "You a student out at Ann Arbor?" "Yes," I said. "Ah," he said. "Here, take a look at this. Hudson Super-Six Coupe. Runs good. Rumble seat. Lot of miles on her yet. I could let you have it for . . ." he squinted up at the hot blue sky—"thirty-two dollars and fifty cents." "What year is it?" I asked. "1929. Good year. Just before the Crash." It was a very big car for a coupe, with headlights like kettle drums and a hood that seemed to stretch from *The Great Gatsby* to *The Sun Also Rises*. I got in and turned on the ignition: the engine came to life with a great roar. "Little hole in the muffler," the salesman shouted. "Nothing serious. Take her around the block." Half an hour later I was on my way to Ann Arbor, the Hudson Super-Six sailing along at sixty with the accelerator only half-way to the floor. It was, I realized even at the time, a great moment in a young American's life: his first automobile.

In Ann Arbor I found a tiny "apartment"—one small room with a kitchenette, no bath—in a monstrous old house of Victorian aspect at 555 South Division Street; the room I really wanted was on the third floor in a kind of tower, with Charles Addams Gothic windows and a narrow, twisting stairway up to a fourth-floor bedroom that could have been a belfry. But it had no kitchenette, which was essential for my summer budget. I settled in, paid a month's rent in advance to Mrs. Goldie Dawson, my worn-looking, widowed landlady, and drove around Ann Arbor to see how it felt, and who from the old crowd, if anyone, was still there. Someone told me John Malcolm Brinnin was running a bookstore in a room above Wahr's, the biggest textbook emporium in Ann Arbor, but the place seemed to be closed for the summer. Stopping off at the Michigan Union for a cup of coffee, I ran into Jim Doll. He said things were pretty quiet—

Art Miller and Norman Rosten were back in New York; he hadn't seen Bhain Campbell for a couple of months; the summer theater program hadn't started yet. Had I seen Sally? She was taking care of props for Valentine Windt at the theater, he said, but apparently wasn't planning to act: too busy getting ready...he paused discreetly....Had I heard that...? Yes, I said, I knew she was supposed to be getting married in August.

The next morning I got a copy of the *Michigan Daily* and drove out Washtenaw Avenue to a point half a block beyond Sally's home, where I parked. I half-read the paper, but kept an eye on her front porch; about ten o'clock she came out in a light blue summer dress and started walking toward the campus at a good clip. I put the Hudson in gear and eased up alongside her. "Want a ride?" I said, leaning across to open the door. Her surprise and her smile exceeded my hopes, and she even agreed to meet me for a Coke at one of our favorite rendezvous, the Betsy Ross, at four o'clock that afternoon.

Back in our old booth, she expressed admiration for the Hudson and for the affluence it implied (I did not tell her what I had paid), but hastened to assure me that the marriage to David Dow was very much on. No, of course she couldn't go out with me. Well, maybe for a swim at Loch Alpine some afternoon, before David arrived in August. But no *date* dates. She was enormously busy. She was glad I had decided to go for a Ph.D.; a good move, she said. I must come around and see the wedding presents soon: people were sending some wonderful stuff.

I knew I ought to give the whole thing up; and indeed, I told her repeatedly that I had done so—but I could not keep myself from fantasies that she might wake up some morning and know I was the man for her after all. Just about then, there came a poem-letter from John:

Dear Haliday,

If after all your conjuration, pleas,
Fraudulent calm and walking on your knees,
Still she will not be had, won, yours — move out,
Ease from that tangle your exhausted heart,
And to the steady, the unspeakable Dow
Let her go, let her go.

Say you would not have been happy with her,
Say she was inarticulate, could stir
But could not satisfy. Say anything
So you bring your heart home and still beating,
Say she was too good for you, too low —
Let her go, let her go.

This is what all men at one time have met,
An inexcusable error in the plot
Which nothing but day on day's work can set right.
Avoid being alone, keep in the light,
Release the crises history can show,
Let her go, let her go.

I was much touched by the poem and grateful to John for writing it, but just when its therapy might otherwise have worked, Sally phoned me on the Fourth of July, with the temperature about 100°, and said how about a swim this afternoon? I drove the Hudson, which I had now christened Matthew Arnold (because of its mysterious amalgamation of austerity and jaunty hauteur) around to her house, thinking sentimentally of the fact that it was precisely three years since our first date, back in 1936. About halfway to Loch Alpine a terrific thunderstorm hit, and since the Hudson's windshield wiper was inoperable, we had to pull off to the side of the road and wait.

There followed a scene of much passion, and when we came out of it we realized that the rain had long since stopped and it was getting late. Putting ourselves back together, we drove into Ann Arbor and had dinner downtown. She admitted that she thought we might have been happy together—but it was too late now, and she had to marry David; and besides, she said, "I do love David." I drove her back to her house with the refrain of John's poem echoing in my mind, and when we kissed just before she got out of the car, I knew that in all probability it was for the last time ever.

The era of good feelings that had prevailed between me and John since the previous autumn, when Beryl had come from England, suffered a setback in the middle of July. I was wandering around the Michigan League one Saturday evening when I suddenly spied Bhain Campbell cruising along the hall with Florence at his side. We exchanged enthusiastic greetings, and I was amazed to hear that John was outside in their car. I leaped out of the League, and found John nestling in the rear seat of an Oldsmobile with an oddly beautiful, rather exotic-looking creature—high cheekbones, slightly slanted eyes, sensual mouth—who turned out to be Florence's eighteen-year-old sister, Annette. They were all headed for a cottage on Lake Superior, Bhain explained, where they planned to luxuriate as a private literary salon for the summer while enjoying the salubrious air of Upper Michigan. We went down to the Pretzel Bell for a beer, and John took me confidentially aside to assure me that his liaison with Annette was merely temporary; I was not to assume that he was no longer in love with Beryl.

Watching Annette, I picked up the impression that she was not altogether happy with the arrangement: she took little part in the conversation and appeared to be in a melancholy humor. The following night, as we were all having dinner at the League cafeteria, she abruptly asked me to go for a walk with her. We went out into the cool of the evening and started to walk around the block. After a few steps Annette began to cry. I asked what the trouble was, and she gave me a short histoire: while she was a student in New York the year before, she had fallen in love with a medical student and had been sending him money as often as she could to help him through—money she had earned in modeling, under circumstances that she had found to be far tougher than she had expected. Recently he had told her that the prospect of their getting married was remote, which threw her into a deep depression, much disturbing her parents. At this point, Bhain and Florence had appeared on the family doorstep in Bronxville with John in tow. John had slipped into her bedroom one night and made love to her; and since both her parents and her doctor thought she ought to get away from the New York scene, she had accepted John's proposition to be his mistress for the summer.

Now, she said, the "highbrow" atmosphere of the entourage plus John's stiff British mannerisms were beginning to wear on her nervous system. She was still acutely unhappy over the medical student, and she felt she had made a grim mistake in coming along. John, she said, never paid any attention to her except when they were in bed. The upshot of all this was that she had decided she did not want to go on to Northern Michigan with John and the Campbells. She wanted to stay in Ann Arbor with me: I was the only one who could understand her; she could never relax with the others, and so on.

This was quite a surprise, and I hardly knew how to handle it. But it was certainly flattering to have this luscious young thing throwing herself on my mercy; and I confess that, remembering the incident over Jeanne Curtis the previous summer, I was not entirely displeased at what I knew would be John's great discomfiture. Since Annette refused to go back into the cafeteria, we climbed into my Hudson and drove to my little apartment. From there I telephoned the League and got Bhain on the wire. He said he was damned if he knew what to do; he'd let me talk to John. John began by being icily controlled, but when I told him Annette wanted to stay in Ann Arbor with me, he stormed into a rage.

"She's emotionally unbalanced!" he said. "She doesn't know what she's doing! Florence promised her parents we'd look after Annette for the summer; you're interfering with the entire plan! Bring her back here, Halliday!" I had been disposed toward negotiation, but this line of talk made me angry. "She wants to spend the night here," I said. "We can talk the situation over in the morning, when everyone's cooled down." This was like touching off a howitzer. "Halliday," John said, "I don't know whether she's told you anything about her life in New York, but I want to warn you! She may have syphilis! She very probably has syphilis!" He slammed the receiver onto the hook. Bhain called back a minute later. He had heard John's outburst and said that, however the incident might turn out, he wanted me to know that John's warning was "goddamn ridiculous."

Annette and I spent a good deal of the night talking about her problems, and I told her about my troubles with Sally: there was a lot of mutual empathy. In the morning she was still determined that she would not go back to the group, and asked if she could attend classes with me. I knew that Warner Rice and my professor of Anglo-Saxon would take a dim view of that, so I found her a good place in one of the library reading rooms, and went back there after lunch to put in two or three hours of reading before dinner.

I had felt in the morning that possibly Annette really could spend the rest of the summer in Ann Arbor with me. She would be a wonderful solace for my distress over Sally, and she was so sure she would be miserable with John that the thought of rescuing her made me feel like a combination of Jesus and Sir Lancelot. But now I was having severe doubts. Every time I looked up from my book, she was there across the table, gazing at me with her bright long-lashed eyes. I suddenly knew that if she stayed I would never pass my courses at the end of the summer.

So we talked and I tried to explain the problem, and Annette wept a little but seemed to understand. I drove her around to the rooming house where John and the Campbells were staying, and we all had a conference—or rather, Bhain and Florence and Annette and I did; John absented himself for a walk across the campus. Bhain, who was a solicitous brother-in-law, said he had not been fully aware of how unhappy Annette was about the arrangement for the summer, and that he and Florence would do all they could to see that she had a better time. They were vastly relieved at not having to deal with John *sans maîtresse*, or with Annette's parents over what had threatened to be an inexplicable change of plans. In the end, John and I shook hands, though stiffly, and they all drove off to Grand Marais in the Oldsmobile.

August came, and with it Sally's wedding to David Dow, which was attended by just about everyone I knew in Ann Arbor, but not by me. In an effort to make some repair in the breach between me and John over Annette, I wrote him a letter describing the finale, which was a reception in the Dows' back yard two doors away from the house I was living in:

I was upstairs trying to prepare for the morrow's final in Anglo-Saxon (I had not known about the reception) and the sounds of congratulatory laughter and pattering rice fell on my unready ears amid my own intonations of the most irregular verbs in the world. It was all a bit difficult, and I went downstairs to go for a walk just in time to meet the bridal car sweeping around the corner, the happy couple nuzzling each other in the back seat.

As a footnote almost too neat I might have added that in the concrete sidewalk of that very corner there were the linked initials D.D.—S.P., obviously engraved with a stick: Sally had shown this to me long before, explaining that she and David had been out roller-skating one day about 1926, and had stopped to register their juvenile fidelity in the wet cement. It was still there when I was in Ann Arbor a few years ago.

I WAS BACK in Michigan after a short visit to New York in September, when I heard from Bhain Campbell that he had a new job teaching freshman English at Wayne State University in Detroit, and that he had persuaded the department chairman to hire John in the same capacity.

The prospect looked pleasing to me: I liked the idea that all three of us would be launching ourselves on similar teaching careers at the same time and in such proximity. I expected to see a lot of John, for Bhain had said that he was enrolling in a writing course at the University of Michigan in order to qualify for entry into the Hopwood Contest. Bhain and Florence and John were sharing a roomy apartment near Wayne, and between my Hudson and Bhain's Oldsmobile it did not appear that transportation would be a problem even though John had never learned to drive. Weeks went by, however, without our getting together, nor did John answer a letter I wrote him in September after the start of hostilities in Europe, asking what he had heard from Beryl and how he thought the war was going to affect their plans. Eventually I phoned Bhain to find out what was going on. He explained that John's Hopwood course was conducted in Detroit, not Ann Arbor; moreover, John had four big sections of composition to teach, he was not getting on well with the other faculty members, most of whom he considered to be idiots, and he was sleeping badly and losing weight. "And I think he's still rather sore at you about Annette," he added. (Annette had enrolled at Michigan State in East Lansing that fall, and had come over to Ann Arbor a couple of times to visit me.)

Meanwhile I was having my own problems about teaching English composition. It is one of the ironies of American academic life that young men and women who are unusually fond of literature and good writing are subjected, as teachers of freshman English, to relentless inundations of dreadful prose. Nevertheless, I enjoyed my first semester of teaching. After a couple of weeks of terror in the classroom, when I was sure I would forget what I had planned to do or not have enough material to get through the hour, I began to savor my role. It was an astonishment to realize that in a gathering of twenty-odd bright young people, I was quite likely to know more about a good many subjects than anyone else in the room, and it was exciting to try to orchestrate the discussions toward reasonable conclusions.

I was in Detroit just once before Christmas, and briefly at that. I stopped in to see the Campbells and John, but the visit was not cheerful. John was in ill fettle and said the worst mistake he had ever made in his life was to take the job at Wayne. He looked haggard, and Bhain told me, aside, that he had swooned several times during the autumn, frightening them terribly since they had no idea what his ailment was—the doctor called it nervous exhaustion and recommended rest. The only bright spot on the horizon was one of Bhain's students, a most alluring nineteen-year-old named Mary Jane Christenson, who had become close friends with him and Florence. Lately, Bhain said, she had been administering to John's sexual needs once or twice a week—that is to say, she would come over for dinner, and sooner or later John would escort her into his bedroom. It was not a romance, according to Bhain, but he and Florence thought it might help John's *Weltanschauung*, and give Mary Jane an introduction to the world of literature and art that she much desired.

I went to New York for Christmas vacation and expected to see John there, but on one of the two occasions that I telephoned, John's mother said he was too ill to see anyone; on the other, she said he had gone to Princeton with the Allen Tates for the weekend. I returned to Ann Arbor with the feeling that our friendship was slowly foundering, for reasons not altogether clear.

Early in February 1940, Bhain phoned me and said John had just had a much worse fainting spell than usual, and a psychiatrist had diagnosed either epilepsy or incipient schizophrenia. John was unable to teach his classes; the department chairman was most upset about the situation; Bhain was trying to cover for him but was on the point of exhaustion himself; Florence was very near the end of her patience. We discussed the possibility of having John leave Detroit and live in Ann Arbor for the rest of the academic year, and we agreed that in any event, John's mother would have to be informed of how serious things appeared to be. I wrote her, telling as much as I knew, and she flew to Detroit for a day or two; I did not see her. The doctors decided that John's sickness was a form of petit mal; and this, since it was at least definite, seemed to raise his spirits enough so that he could go back to teaching. Yet Bhain and Florence reported that his domestic behavior grew more obnoxious. They decided they could no longer live with him, and moved out before the end of February, as Bhain indicated in a letter written on Washington's Birthday 1940:

263 East Ferry
Detroit

Dear Hal,

J. B. and the world are still versus, and I doubt the contest will ever be settled: at least, the world doesn't seem likely to cry uncle, and no other possibility offers itself. But he's still teaching. Mrs. B. did come out. We have moved, as you can see above. We're living, like yourself, in rooms—Christ, it seems I'm never to escape the primordial Victorian rooming house—with kitchenette. Pleasant place, however, one block north of the museum. . . . Please come and see it and us. Poor John, he's alone in that vast damned stripped apartment, paying forty a month for five rooms and living in one. I don't know, certainly at any rate, how he feels toward you. You may bring him around in time. . . . Oh, by the way, after five hundred bucks of medical attention for which he'll never have to pay a cent [the principal doctor was a comrade of Bhain's], John seems to need two teaspoons per day of calcium lactate, the milk of the mother, I take it, who has set him at war with the world. I'm tangled up in the symbolism. . . . See you soon—

B.

I was upset about the state of affairs in Detroit, and did not fully understand it. It seemed likely that there had been some trouble between John and Bhain that I had not been told about, and I could not help suspecting that John had made indecorous approaches to Florence. In any event there seemed to be nothing I could do about it, but I decided to have another try at restoring amicable relations with John myself by writing him a casual letter. I had been working on a long paper on "The Jest as an Element in Tudor Fiction," and I relayed a few extremely hoary jokes drawn from my research. "I hope you get out here soon and stay for a meal at least," I wound up—"better still, stay a night some weekend and we will drink beer and talk."

Before any answer to this came, I got a shocker from Bhain that shifted my concern from John to him with a snap:

> *March 11, 1940*
> *[postmarked March 21]*

Dear Hal,

I'm writing this from Grace Hospital, where I lie in bed, having suffered an orchidectomy, which is to say the removal of my great and tumorous left ball. You'll remember my mentioning last winter that a doctor had discovered a growth . . . a pendulous and spherical weight with which I have staggered for years so I'm told, but lately beyond the endurance of my abdominal and loinar musculature. . . . doctor called it a terratoma tumor, malignant, capable of enlarging to such a size that I could wheel it about in a wheelbarrow; capable at any moment of becoming active and murdering me upwards; doctor lopped it off, left poor scrotum on that side poor wrinkled and poor empty . . . final lab says tissue cancerous, localized. I've been here five days, out tomorrow, with one ball. . . .

We've bought a new car, and if I am as strong as I think I'll be we'll be over this weekend. . . . John has moved into a room, still considers me his enemy. Give my regards to Willum [Taylor] and Brinnin—tell them about my misfortune.

   —*B.*

Like most young people, I knew nothing about cancer except to be appalled by it and to feel sure I'd never get it. But I hung my optimism on Bhain's phrase, "tissue cancerous, localized." If it was localized, I fig-ured, it must be gone with the testicle. Bhain and Florence showed up in their new car the first weekend of spring, bringing Mary Jane Christenson with them. Bhain seemed to be his old, good-natured, debonair self, so I cheered up and we all went to the Pretzel Bell for a roast beef lunch. They had hardly glimpsed John, they said; he was meeting his classes but living a life apart and not seeing anyone. They thought his health was improved, but didn't know for sure. Riding around in the back of the car I had a tantalizing conversation with Mary Jane: she struck me as flirtatious but elusive, and I couldn't quite make out what she was up to, or why she had come out. She said she probably would be seeing John now and then, but did not "expect anything to come of it." I asked Bhain about it when we went to the men's room at the Pretzel Bell, and he said enigmatically, "Well, Florence and I thought you two would like each other, so we just brought her along."

A few days later I received from John the only letter he had written me since the start of the academic year:

2 April 1940

Dear Milt,

I've not been to Ann Arbor since I saw you last: indifferent health, editorial work and University work have kept me as perplexed and busy as a squirrel. My students are doing research papers, and it is a savage affair. I wanted to get up [to Ann Arbor] last week, during the vacation if such it can be called, but I had dozens of manuscripts and letters to deal with. Some were dated September; I spent a sorry time. My only diversion, except for writing, which is no diversion at all, has been buying books and reading them. I have found a lot of 'items' at absurd prices. So few persons here can read that when books are to be had they are to be had for almost nothing.

... Very little that is interesting has turned up for THE NATION: a long poem by Warren and a political satire by Blackmur: since the poets are not doing their job, the critics are. I have been writing ferocious letters to contributors, trying to jolt them into integrity or infuriate them into silence.

Tell me the mechanics of Hopwood Ms. preparation, how typed, how bound, nom-de-guerre, what formulas, etc. I am about to put

John and Bhain, Union Lake, 1940.
"John . . . was still hovering around
Detroit and coming out to the lake
now and then to see Bhain."
University of Minnesota Libraries

some stuff together for a typist. I don't like it at all, but having got this
far I may as well finish. If I should win something, the notion of any
publicity sickens me.

Come in when you can; I am at 4827 Second, with six windows at
one end of my room and incessant activity at the other. I may come up
week after next.

—John

It was not until I read this letter, written three weeks after Bhain's
operation but not mentioning it, that I realized fully what a gulf of non-
communication had opened between Bhain and John. I sent John the
Hopwood information but did not see him in Ann Arbor—though I heard
from Brinnin that John had appeared one April day at his shop to discuss
the advisability of one of them dropping out of the contest to make room
for the other.

May zephyred by in its usual green glory, and I was too busy shep-
herding my freshmen, playing tennis, and finishing seminar papers to
worry about anything much. Norman Rosten wrote from New York that
he and Hedda were "perilously close" to getting married, and that the
Theatre Guild had taken an option on his newest play, while Art Miller
was almost sure to have one on Broadway in the fall. He wanted to know

if Brinnin was still in Ann Arbor—which indeed he was, awaiting the results of the Hopwood, in which he had entered a major poetry manuscript.

Somewhat apprehensively, I went to the Hopwood lecture and announcement of awards in the plush new Rackham Auditorium at the end of May. I knew that John was going to be in a state of rage if he failed to win, and my apprehension grew as I looked around the audience and could not see him: if he had won he would have been notified that morning and surely would be there. The winners of major awards in poetry were John Malcolm Brinnin ($700), somebody named Burrows, and somebody named Arehart. Talking about it to Bhain the next day, I was partially relieved to hear that John had expressed utter contempt for the poetry judges, who that year were O. J. Campbell, Margaret Widdemer, and John Gould Fletcher. (This was, in fact, bad luck; for in earlier years such men as Mark Van Doren, Allen Tate, and Ezra Pound had been judges, and even though submissions were pseudonymous, it seems certain they would have been more sympathetic to John's poetic style.)

In mid-June 1940, Bhain and Florence moved back to the family cottage at Union Lake, taking Mary Jane with them as companion and helpmate. After summer school was well under way, a current girl friend and I drove out to the lake for an afternoon's visit. We had a nice swim and a cookout dinner, but I was disturbed to find that Bhain was sick again. He sat in a rocker on the porch and talked with animation and good cheer, but it was clear that he was in pain, and Mary Jane told me the doctors thought it was a recurrence of the cancer. John, she said, was still hovering around Detroit and coming out to the lake now and then to see her and Bhain, with whom he had made up. This was news to me, for I had heard nothing from him since the Hopwood.

SEVEN
World War II and After,
1940–72

Bhain Campbell was extracted from me
in dolour, yellow as a second sheet
& I have not since tried to be the same.
— "Relations"

I have never in my life been good at confronting
mortality. I concentrated on my summer-school courses, tried to convince
myself that the doctors were wrong and that Bhain would pull out of
whatever it was, and stayed put in Ann Arbor.

In mid-August my father and mother and my sister Dorothy stopped
to pick me up, and we headed for California. After a few days in San
Francisco, I hitchhiked to Los Angeles, stayed with a brace of ex-buddies
from Ann Arbor long enough to decide that L.A. was not for me, and
thumbed on to Sante Fe. I knew that a generous welcome awaited me
there: it was the home of Phoebe Stevens, the only friend from my dismal
summer in Iowa City in 1937 with whom I had stayed in touch.

I had planned just a few days in Sante Fe, but I happened to arrive
the day before the annual Mexican-American fiesta exploded. Phoebe put
me up in her adobe house, several miles out Canyon Road from the center
of town, and I soon became well acquainted with her husband, a private
of fortune named Fergus O'Mera; her six-year-old son (by an earlier marriage); their three sensitive Irish setters; and a goat named Henrietta. There
was a three-day drunk to celebrate my arrival, but as nearly as I could
make out, everyone in Santa Fe was in much the same mood so as to get
the fiesta off to a blazing start. What really detained me, however, was a
willowy, twenty-one-year-old, world-class blonde to whom Phoebe and
Fergus introduced me. NC—not Encie, as I had supposed when I first

heard her name; her father, Lt. James Breese, had been flight engineer of the NC-4 on its historic transatlantic hop in 1919—was the first authentic glamour girl of my acquaintance, and had she not been madly in love with a French ski instructor whom she hoped to rejoin soon, I might never have left. Her descriptions of skiing, illustrated with enticing snapshots, planted in my heart a desire to pursue the snowy sport which has never left me. She even aroused my interest in polo, but (though the sight of NC galloping down the green turf with her long golden hair flying and her stick swinging in great arcs was a stirring one) I decided to let that pass. By this time I was overdue for the fall semester in Ann Arbor, and with a good deal of regret I caught a ride to Chicago with a trio of young lawyers who had come down for the fiesta. The university seemed a bit dull after Santa Fe, but before long I was settled again in my tiny quarters at 555 South Division Street, and back to my worthy routine of teaching and study.

VERY EARLY IN the morning of Saturday, November 16, 1940, the quintessential Ann Arbor rooming house that I lived in caught fire from some antiquated electrical wiring, and burned for over three hours before the firemen got it out. Along with a score of other residents I had stumbled out into the cold in my nightclothes, which in my case consisted of a bathrobe and a pair of slippers. From the second-floor windows of the house next door we watched as the flames got into the stairwell and the cupola tower and transformed them into a roaring chimney: it was a spectacular fire and drew a large crowd of admiring spectators from the campus as well as downtown. At one point, fearing for my books, my file cabinet, a pile of unread freshman themes, my clothes, my Dinah Shore records, and a wonderful letter I had just received from NC Breese, I went out and tried to interest a couple of firemen in my corner of the house. Eventually I got them to put a ladder up there, and they poured a hundred gallons or so of water into my little apartment. I still have many curiously dappled books as mementoes of that morning; it took me weeks to get them dried out without the pages sticking together.

Living space was easy in Ann Arbor in those days, and by afternoon I and Jim Green, a graduate student and friend of mine who had also

Apartment House Flames Light Sky

BRILLIANT FLAMES LIGHT SKY: Nearly two hours after a 12-flat apartment house at 555 S. Division St. was discovered on fire at 5:20 this morning, flames shot high above the burning building, as shown in the above photograph taken at 7 a.m. Loss from the fire, cause of which was undetermined, was estimated at about $10,000. Twenty-three persons were left homeless, many with only their nightclothing.

"Very early in the morning . . . the quintessential Ann Arbor rooming house that I lived in caught fire. . . . " Ann Arbor *News*

lived at 555, had taken an apartment together just down the street in another old reconstructed house. Jim had lost everything, including a prized collection of Mozart records, in the holocaust on the third floor; I hauled my soaked and smoked belongings to the new abode in Matthew Arnold. Having salvaged what I could, I phoned Mary Jane Christenson in Detroit and told her to postpone her weekend visitation until the following Saturday.

I had taken up with Mary Jane in October, when she appeared one

Mary Jane Christenson, 1940. "There may have been an unconscious psychological component involving my relationship with John in my reaction to Mary Jane. . . ." Courtesy Mary Christenson Heming

Saturday with Gene Shafarman, Bhain's personal doctor, and his wife; they had come to Ann Arbor to ride horseback. We all had dinner together, and I got it straight from Gene, a very blunt fellow, that Bhain was "done for. He'll be lucky if he lasts till Christmas—or I should say, he'll be unlucky. It's going to be excruciating, and the only thing he'll have to live for will be morphine." I asked Mary Jane about John, from whom I'd heard nothing for six months. "He's in Cambridge," she said. "You knew Delmore Schwartz got him an appointment at Harvard this fall?" I asked her if she'd like to come out and spend the following weekend with me, and she said yes.

There may have been an unconscious psychological component involving my relationship with John in my reaction to Mary Jane, but certainly at the time I simply felt that she was extraordinarily attractive. She was so beautiful that it was an aesthetic experience merely to watch her take her clothes off or put them on, and her approach to sex was disarmingly innocent. It was her custom to bring with her one or another of the Winnie the Pooh books by A. A. Milne; these she liked to read aloud while we lay in bed, which tended to spin around the lovemaking an aura of sweet-natured children playing in a haystack. I asked her if she had done the same with John; yes, she said, but he didn't think much of Milne, and sometimes hurt her feelings by ridiculing her enthusiasm—like the time he had travestied Eeyore's response to Piglet's birthday gift: "A useful box to put things in." John, she said, was very "importunate"—a word she had learned from him—about sex, and when they were out at Union Lake in the summer she had felt chagrin over making love with him in one room "while Bhain was slowly dying in the next," but somehow she had not been able to do anything about it.

Mary Jane, that fall, became not only my liaison with Bhain, to whom she conveyed my desperately wishful messages of encouragement, but herself a principal in trying to ease his last days on earth. She had taken a job as Dr. Shafarman's secretary, and he was lenient in allowing her time to visit the Campbells' Detroit apartment daily to help Florence manage the painful domestic chores. I went in to Detroit just once, in mid-November. Bhain was horribly emaciated and twisted: the cancer had so overwhelmed his body that almost no part of him was unaffected, and it was only with great difficulty that he could take any nourishment. Yet the old gallantry glimmered through; he managed a feeble smile and exchanged with me a few broken sentences that I knew were attempts at quips. Mary Jane said John had written that he'd be coming out for a last visit during the Thanksgiving weekend. I considered meeting him there, but it seemed likely that the strain that had now developed between us might worsen a dolorous occasion. I wrote to Van Doren to see if he could throw any light on John's current state of mind, but he replied that he had not seen John for a year and a half, and really didn't understand what was going on. "Take notes at Thanksgiving and decide where we all stand," he wrote; but in the end I decided not to go in.

Bhain Campbell died on December 3, 1940. A few days later there was a memorial service, and a small contingent of his old friends went in from Ann Arbor. The mourners in the funeral parlor were divided into two groups that did not fully correspond to the seating arrangements: on the one hand Florence, Mary Jane, the Shafarmans, and our Ann Arbor group; on the other Bhain's mother and her friends from Royal Oak and Detroit. The minister delivered a fulsome eulogy which culminated, "Robert was twenty-nine. In recent years he had been led into paths of false political and philosophical beliefs, but we have reason to believe that in his last days he returned to the faith of our fathers." This was pure—or impure—fabrication.

A week or two before Christmas, Florence asked me if I'd like to help her drive her car to New York. A graduate student at Ann Arbor, a friend of mine named Harry Garvin, had offered to do it, and Florence had accepted. She then began to understand that Harry was brimming over with love for her, and she thought it would be well to have someone else along on the trip. It all worked out fine: Harry was happy to do most of the driving as a demonstration of his devotion to Florence, and we made lively conversation about everything in the world except the ordeal she had passed through in the last few months. It was my first direct insight into the fact that the death of someone you love who has been in prolonged and mortal pain is a blessed relief.

IN NEW YORK, John telephoned me just before Christmas to hear my account of Bhain's funeral. I related what I could, and then suggested that we go together to Morningside Heights and see if any of the old Columbia crowd was around. We met, as we often had before, by an enormous clock in the Times Square IRT subway station and went up to 116th Street. He looked far healthier than he had the previous year, but was in a dark mood because of Bhain's death and also, I found, because Harvard had turned out to be "not much better than Wayne." The only person in Cambridge who gave him any consolation, he said, was Delmore Schwartz, for whom he had developed a large admiration. Up at Columbia, we tried to call on several people but found nobody home, and instead went for a beer at the Gold Rail. Somehow there didn't seem to be much to say to each other. John took from a big envelope a copy of his first book publication, *Five Young American Poets*, which New Directions had just brought out, and handed it to me. I looked in the front; he had inscribed it, "To Milt—remembering a better time—John, 21 December 1940." I murmured appreciation, but he waved it aside; he was not pleased with the book.

I asked what he heard from Beryl. "Very little," he said. "She writes only sporadically. She's extremely busy working for the BBC and doing other war work. She could be killed any day in an air raid." After one beer we went out and got on the subway again and started downtown. It was crowded, and we stood in the middle of the car hanging onto the poles. One or the other of us made some remark about a girl further down the car who had a nice figure, whereupon John suddenly said, "Mary Jane has the most beautiful breasts I've ever seen." I didn't know whether he had heard about her weekends with me in Ann Arbor, but decided that if this was a test, I'd better take it. "Yes," I said, "they're extraordinary." He turned toward me, the pupils of his eyes executing the narrow, flickering oscillation that you noticed when he looked straight at you. "You've seen them?" "Yes," I said. The train was just pulling in to Times Square, and I had thought we might get off for a cup of coffee and to make some plans for New Year's Eve. But as the doors slid open John said, "Happy New Year," and stepped out onto the platform. The doors closed, and I went on to Brooklyn Heights.

I WOULD HAVE BEEN surprised but not astonished if I had known then that I would not see John again for well over two years. The winter and spring of 1941 brought to my life a steadily growing sense of the end of a chapter. I worked fairly hard at my graduate courses and my teaching, but more and more I felt that it was in some measure just a ploy against time. The draft was looming, and though I was no student of international affairs, I did not see how the country was going to avoid the war.

This slightly fatalistic turn of mind, paradoxically, gave life a strange and pleasurable intensity. Jim Green and I, who never in the world would have been roommates except for the fire, were working up a grudging admiration for each other. We had a good time cooking elaborate meals, drinking more than we could afford, playing tennis, having long arguments about history and literature, and pursuing various girls. (Mary Jane, that spring, had worked herself into a serious involvement with someone in Detroit, so our friendship was suspended for the duration.) Life seemed so valuable during those months that Jim and I fell into the habit of staying up very late so as not to miss too much of it. This fitted in nicely with the routine of our friend Bill Menger, a perpetually skeptical graduate student who earned a marginal living as a night watchman for the university. We were close to the campus, and about one in the morning Bill was likely to drop in between punches of his time clock and have a swig of his favorite drink, which was grape juice mixed with vodka. I was fond of Menger, not least for his addiction to the art of parody; it was he who came up with the immortal transformation of A. E. Housman's famous lines:

By broads two bucks for leaping
The lads like me get laid,
While rose-lipped girls are keeping
The boys who made the grade.

ABOUT THE TIME of the Nazi invasion of the USSR in June 1941, I met a fantastic girl named Harriet who was attending summer school in Ann Arbor. Within a week I was overboard in love as I had not been since Sally. When she went back to Berkeley at the end of the summer, I hitchhiked out there with the draft board snapping at my heels, and we got married just a month before I was inducted.

One of the few compensations of being incarcerated in a California field artillery training camp for the paranoiac months following Pearl Harbor was that all sorts of people back in civilian life sent me unexpected letters. Among them was John, and to my surprise his tone was much like that of the old days:

> *49 Grove Street*
> *Boston*
> *Tuesday 3 Febr 1942*

Dear Milt,

It is amusing is it not that after all this time I should be in a hurry when I write to you. However, je suis. I have only just got your address from your parents and I am going tomorrow to New York for several days: a place from which I never can write a letter to anyone. And I have a heavy cold and it is fairly late and I am this moment back from one of the best concerts I have ever heard—the Budapest playing a late Haydn quartet, Mozart's K. 387, and the first Razoumovsky, in case you care enough to be jealous. I must take a hot bath and go to bed.

Probably it is just as well, the hurry. What the devil are we to say to each other after such a lapse and at this moment of the world's

history? I don't know even whether you want to hear from me. I hope
you do. But what to say is a puzzle: I feel nine-tenths out of touch. I
could ask you some familiar questions with unfamiliar intensity. For
example, are you really married? The concept reached me but I have
not been able to do anything with it. If it is true it is immensely
important, as important as the concept and the fact that I am not
married; but it can't be understood as a piece of news. . . . I could ask
about You And The Army, and I do. And what your state of mental
health is. . . .

. . . What would you like to know about me? (That 'about,' that
external 'about,' really touches the attitude.) My life goes on in the
interesting path you know; but it has got very far down in the past
year, in spite of the addition of Rusty and the addition of music. . . . I
live alone in a comfortable, filthy apartment on Beacon Hill. I am still
teaching at Harvard, a college I like less every hour. My health oscillates
between the indifferent and the unspeakable; the Army have rejected
me. I try to write and I don't often succeed; I publish almost nothing, I
see almost nobody. I am very gloomy. Well! Have I missed anything? If
I have, ask me about it in the letter you are going to write me—
immediately, my boy.

Yours as usual, John

Although I was pleased to get John's letter, my general mood at this
point was mightily depressed, and I did not answer it for many weeks.
The group of draftees I was in had completed basic training, and we all
waited tensely every day for news of our assignments. First it was said we
would be shipped to the Aleutians; then it was Burma. Then somebody
in my barracks came down with measles, and we were quarantined for
thirty days. Meanwhile, up in Berkeley, my new wife was vivaciously
wending her way through graduate school, attended every day—nay, pursued, I was certain—by a dozen or so young men who for one reason or
another were not in the military. Harriet was the kind of girl who made

Harriet Halliday, 1942. "... the kind of girl who made halfbacks long to take up Renaissance literature...."

halfbacks long to take up Renaissance literature and professors of linguistics daydream of leaving their wives, and her New York intellectual background had led her to marry me only on the understanding that neither of us was to be bound by middle-class prohibitions of extramarital sexual freedom. The inevitable result was a series of agonizing scenarios to which I subjected myself while standing guard duty in the rain or bivouacking in the cold California hills, all of them featuring Harriet in stunning déshabille while she brilliantly explained to a breathless companion the principles of free thought and free love. These fantasies proved, later on, to have been without foundation, but at the time they helped induce in me a profound irritation with the civilian world I had been forced to leave.

The measles quarantine, however, brought me an unexpected break: by the time it was over someone had looked at my qualifications record, noticed that I was a good typist with some experience in journalism, and assigned me to army public relations. Harriet joined me, and feeling as if we had miraculously been reprieved we took the train as ordered to Fort Sill, Oklahoma, where I was to be a reporter and feature writer for the *Fort Sill Army News*. It was even better than we had hoped: we were allowed to live in an apartment in nearby Lawton, Harriet got a job on the post, and suddenly we seemed to have dropped into a world that was only half military. We did soon learn, however, that the stiff army hierarchy of rank prevailed even off-duty. Harriet, planting a little garden out in back of our house that spring, struck up a pleasant acquaintance with a young woman neighbor who was, like her, a graduate of the University of Wisconsin; she invited us to a cocktail party the following weekend. We were not yet fully aware of the social chasm separating enlisted men from officers, and although I knew the young woman's husband was a captain, I was amazed when we went to the party to witness the effect created by my corporal's uniform. Conversation subsided to embarrassed silence, followed by excruciatingly polite efforts to get us out of there as quickly as possible. We had broken the code.

All of this in some part explains my failure to answer John's letter promptly, and the tone of my reply when I finally did write in June:

Your letter came when things looked hopeless; and if you remember, you began with a lush description of how you felt after just returning from one of the finest concerts ever heard by man. Then you groused a bit about what a dog's life you were living on Beacon Hill or some such high cultural plateau, mentioned books, mentioned a mistress or two. . . . well, somehow the whole thing seemed vastly and ghastly irrelevant.

. . . We had a furlough two weeks ago, and were in New York for about ten days. I accumulated a quiet fury by the time we came back: the city seemed too much the same, with all the goddamned civilians enjoying the war immensely and making more money than they ever will again. . . . Not that I begrudge them their lives; it's the realization of the fabulous web of graft, politics, and capricious discrimination beneath the surface of the whole 'war effort' that gets me. . . . Remember how we felt and spoke, you and Beryl and I, one night in 1938 or 39, when we came out from seeing "All Quiet on the Western Front"? I still feel pretty much the same way.

There were a few quiet and pleasant interludes, such as an hour we spent at Mark's one afternoon. Guess who had just dropped in to see him before we got there—Aylward. Mark says he puts forth a tremendous effort to appear unpriestlike: swears like a pirate, etc. . . . I saw none of the old crowd . . . didn't even call up Winann, which shows how things went.

Do you still hear from Beryl, and how is she? What have you been teaching this last year? . . . The whole idyllic university world seems like a dream to me now. . . . Let me know your mind and mien, and if we get another furlough (should be around Christmas) let's try to get together.

Milt

The summer went by with no answer to this, but in October an engraved wedding invitation arrived. This stirred me to write again:

Lawton, Oklahoma
Sunday, October 11, 1942

Dear John,

I wonder whether you were more startled to hear of my having been married than I to hear of your having set the date. My memory for names is appalling, but I assume that Eileen Patricia [Mulligan] is Rusty; is that right? If she's the girl I'm thinking of, I met her about a year and a half ago in the company of J[ean] Bennett, a girl from whom, in turn, I have never heard since she offered to have the Daisy Air Rifle Company fly me [from Michigan] to New York and back. I accepted, and am still waiting for the ride.

I don't know why I haven't had an answer to my last letter, sent to you at Boston, although I have an idea I may have been rather nasty therein. Everybody in the Army is nasty, you know. If that was it I apologize, and hope you'll now write and fill in the abyss with selected bits of information so that we'll know who we are even if not why.

So many things about the war disgust me literally beyond words that I don't talk much about it. . . . (Actually an Army camp is the best place for this: the soldiers in training never think of the war, talk of it, or speculate as to its outcome. They speculate as to the outcome of their next Saturday night in town.) . . . I am still in what is known as the Public Relations Office, writing "news" releases about what goes on at Fort Sill. Harriet and I know *personne* whom we like well enough to see them often, so we live in practical isolation, reading, talking, making love and good meals. It's not a bad life, since the Field Artillery School Library is surprisingly good as well as almost untouched by human hands. . . . It is, however, in all probability merely a reprieve: I shall be in an officer-candidate school perforce before spring, I think.

I have no idea what to say about your marriage except that if you are happy about it I am very glad. I don't really know Rusty any better than you know Harriet, and of course I have often wondered about Beryl, whom I remember with clarity and affection. It's a funny damned world, except that it's not very funny.

. . . In any case, here are congratulations, which is about as traditional as I can get when it comes to a wedding (Harriet and I were married at 8:22 in the morning at Reno, Nevada, by a large judge with red eyebrows: time, eight minutes). Please convey my good wishes for happiness to Rusty, and tell her we are very sorry but the Army wants us in Oklahoma on October 24 (why, neither we nor anyone else can tell). I hope everything goes off splendidly; I should like to be there.

Milt

The very day I dropped this into the mail box, a letter came from John:

49 Grove St., Boston
8 October, 1942

Dear Milt,

Your phrase 'mentioned a mistress or two' put me off, & other
things intervened; so that I never expressed my pleasure in your letter
& my sympathy with your very disagreeable lot. But even civilian life
can be unpleasant—men have killed themselves to be rid of it, for
instance—& I hope you will forgive me.

Even this is a note (I am as busy as you are & not well) to say that
Rusty & I are to be married, presumably, in New York on the 24th of
this month, and I wish you were to be there. . . . B's utter breaking off
our engagement, & the whole terrible story, I will tell you some day,
not now. Even (even—3rd) the damned have their reticences.

Whether I deserve it or not, tell me your plans. . . . Perhaps we can
meet at Xmas. . . . My sympathy to Harriet, who has to deal with you;
send yours to Rusty, who may have to deal with me. A flood of memory
comes up. . . . Ou sont les neiges d'antan? I agree with you absolutely
about this war. . . . My students go off every day—it isn't pleasant to
watch. . . .

John

[P.S.] . . . Do you get, ever, to Medicine Park—or does it still exist? I
loved to swim there once—My father was a captain of artillery and was
at Sill often in the summer. I remember it well.

We did not get to New York for Christmas, or indeed anywhere else,
as I explained to John on December 27, 1942:

Harriet has been in the hospital since Dec. 7, a date which I
should prefer to skip entirely next year. She caught her pajamas on fire
that morning from the goddamned gas heater we have in our bedroom;

I already had gone to the post. By the time she got the flames out she
was horribly burned on her legs and thighs. Fortunately, although they
cover an extensive area, the burns appear to be mostly second degree
not third: there should be little scarring [this turned out to be
overoptimistic]. But it has been an unspeakably painful experience for
her. The doctors at Ft. Sill . . . say she will probably be there another
week at least [she was there until February].

. . . What are you teaching this year? I presume you are now an
assistant professor or something. I may make it myself at the age of fifty
or so. . . . I guess I'll be lucky to live to be thirty, let alone fifty. . . . They
are hot after us able-bodied boys now, and I'll either have to go to
OCS or go over as an enlisted man. . . . At least I then will be doing
something more palpable towards winning the war; the only trouble
being that it's only at intervals that I can go about trying to win a war
with any heart for the matter at all. I am very much inclined to view
the entire affair as weary, flat, stale and unprofitable.

. . . Happy New Year to you both—

   Milt

   John replied almost immediately:

                                                        5 January 1943

Dear Milt,
   The Spirits Ironic & Sinister must have spent their force on you by
now. That is the only bearable inference I can draw from Harriet's
accident, for which I am as sorry as you can imagine. I hope she is
mending quickly now or is quite well, and marked as little as possible.
Our helpless sympathy to both of you.
   The best I can do is to write you an amusing letter, but je n'en
peux plus. My thoughts just now would amuse nobody but Satan who

has a taste I am told bizarre bizarre; they make him howl. Later, if a certain View is correct, they will make me howl. So much for metaphysics. . . .

Your surmise that I am now an assistant professor amuses Satan too. Halliday! I am precisely what I was three years ago, an Instructor, and I am paid less money, and the money buys less. If I were not by now unfitted by the universities for serious existence, I would get a job as a Postman. Fortunately I have as little desire for academic distinction as I have to become a Captain of Artillery; but unfortunately I early acquired a taste for food & clothing, et cetera, of which I find it difficult to rid myself. Shit upon Harvard is what I always say.

Have you ever tried to buy a bar of cooking chocolate in Boston & its environs on the fourth of January 1943? It shouldn't happen, as the Jew says, to a dog.

I hope you won't go overseas. Explain to them that you never wanted to travel. But why do you hesitate about Officers' Training. . . . Non-coms get killed quick, I hear, and I want you to live a long time. My feeble congratulations, en route, on another birthday—November was it? Old, old, Master Shallow, both of us old & neither of us gay. Let us hear about Harriet.

John

[P.S.] Don't think I am joking when I ask you to send us, if you can get it there, some Baker's Chocolate. Several bars. And say how much it is. Chocolate at night (hot chocolate) has been our only resource against the bloody housewives who have stocked up on all the meat & butter & everything in the country and who stand in front of us in line at the grocery shops paying for their loot with twenty-dollar bills. I am now engaged on the sixth volume of my work entitled *A La Recherche Du Temps A Manger*; I call it *Chocolat Disparu*.

This month, or so, my boy, you and I have been friends for ten
years. Find me ten worse years in human history and I will give you an
ounce of butter (my last). Hands under the table. Drink to the next
ten. "This is only the beginning" mutters Satan.

IN MAY 1943, with Harriet in New York working for *Time*—her burn
wounds having finally been healed at the Cornell Medical Center—I went
to an officer candidate school at Fort Washington, Maryland, for a ninety-
day training course. One hot weekend in Washington, I was cooling off
in an air-conditioned piano bar when I heard Mrs. Berryman's distinctive
voice trilling at me from across the room. We had a conversation, and
sometime in July I was called into headquarters at camp: a civilian was
out at the gate and wanted to see me. I hiked out there and found John
sitting on the curb by the guardhouse. We were very pleased to see each
other, and shook hands and grinned a lot, but I had been granted a total
of only half an hour off, and it was difficult to know what to talk about.
John looked pale and underweight. He explained that he had not been
reappointed at Harvard for 1943–44; he and Rusty were broke and in
debt, and they were having "an Inferno of a summer" in New York trying
to stay alive. No other academic job seemed to be available, and he had
even tried selling encyclopedias from door to door (a spectacle I found
hard to envisage) without getting "one goddamned order." Although I
thought myself miserable at officer candidate school and had rather hoped
that I would flunk out and thus be allowed to take an assignment I had
been offered as an overseas correspondent for *Yank*, the army magazine,
I walked back to a pretty good dinner at the mess hall realizing that in
some respects John had reason to envy me.

In August 1943, emerging from the OCS cocoon a second lieuten-
ant, I was gratefully surprised to be ordered to Bozeman, Montana, as
adjutant of a college training unit. Harriet was to join me in November;
meanwhile she went on working for *Time*, and saw John at least once in
New York. She reported that he finally had landed a teaching job at
Princeton through R. P. Blackmur, the literary critic, but only after a
distressing interlude at a Westchester prep school where he had been

obliged to teach Latin. John filled me in on this in a letter from Princeton on December 2, 1943:

I resigned that infernal idiotic job (of which Harriet will have told you) just before my mind disintegrated; or just afterwards: it is not quite clear which.... began teaching here on November 1st. For a time I felt, remembering Hell, as if I were at leisure, but actually I am busy enough: classes six days a week.... Basic English it is, Army and Marine, and the boys are overworked, bored, ignorant and illiterate. I have 110 of them and like them very well, although I am unable to remember their names.

We like Princeton, too, which is a place altogether, morally & humanely, superior to Harvard. Through the accident of friendship with Blackmur, who has been here for two years and has carefully gone through the University looking for interesting people, being the most obsessive conversationalist of our time, we have got to know automatically an extraordinary group of men, mathematicians, historians, philosophers, refugee novelists, musicians—I suppose it sounds entertaining; and it is; but I am not in repair for it. I never felt the need of solitude so sharply as now when it is absolutely inaccessible.

... Eileen is working for the League of Nations, at the Institute for Advanced Study outside Princeton, and sees Einstein at precisely 10:30 every morning.... I have been reading *Finnegans Wake*, and as Jute says "I can beuraly forsstand a weird from sturk to finnic in such a patwhat": 17 years of 9/10 wasted labour....

And so farewell, Mr. and Mrs. Halliday. Truly we have enjoyed this interlude. I congratulate you on the passing without incident of December 7th, day of Fire, and I advise you to stay in bed all day, rigid, in prayer, thanks giving that the grieving world is not wars always from day to day, but faintly sometimes to the unquiet solitary spirit words of friends come.

John

I sent John a description of life in Bozeman, a town then so remote that except for the presence of my unit the war seemed almost not to exist. The aura of civilian tranquillity, in fact, was sometimes too pervasive. On New Year's Day 1944, skiing carelessly on a nearby mountain, I took a bad fall and broke my leg. The bone was set by the only available doctor, who until lately had been a veterinarian, and it was set very badly. When a subsequent X ray revealed the grievous fault, I was sent to a big army hospital near Salt Lake City where the whole thing was done over again, this time expertly. I revealed all this to John in a tardy second letter, adding that I had barely returned to Bozeman when the Army Specialized Training Program, of which my unit was a part, had been abruptly canceled by the government. (One consequence of this was that thousands of the ASTP soldiers, who had been carefully selected for brains and college aptitude, were shipped off in big bunches to combat units instead of being more widely dispersed. A disproportionately large number of these excellent young men were killed or wounded in the forthcoming Battle of the Bulge.) On the personal level, the result was that I was assigned to a traveling team of interviewers and examiners whose job was to tour infantry replacement-training centers, winnow out a few men highly qualified in physics, chemistry, or mathematics, and send them to Oak Ridge, Tennessee, where a supersecret research project was under way. It turned out to be the famous Manhattan Project, but at the time we could only guess what it was all about.

With me constantly on the move, Harriet went back to New York and landed a great job at *Newsweek* as assistant to Tom Wenning, the drama critic. This put her within John's orbit:

Princeton, 31 October 44

... Harriet came down for part of a day recently, as she probably has told you; and liked the appearance of Princeton so well—the place is superficially very agreeable, there is no doubt of it, I was ravished when I came here—that she explained to me that my life is a very pleasant one! Mine! In the ferocious argument which ensued on this madness, however, she kept her temper so much better than I did—brilliantly, indeed—that my respect finally overcame my anger. Except for a war with Blackmur one evening about a year ago, and one with an Australian novelist a few months earlier, I have been as mild as a dove since I left Harvard, publicly I mean mild. "Tempest thee nought al croked to redresse."*

I was thirty last week and took from the same great poem my emblem for the next decade: "Savour no more than thee bihove shal."** I hope that it will be less continuously horrible than the last decade but I don't think it will, so I mean to cut down the area of operation. What were your feelings on passing that point? I had been speechlessly gloomy for a long time, but a few days before the anniversary I came suddenly out waving a pencil and have been writing so busily since that I hadn't any proper sentiments at all. Work work & the flowing of emotion: these are the only things that interest me.

. . . Who are you voting for, the Roos or the Dew, in this (ruined) Garden idyl? I don't much care, but as [Dwight] Macdonald says I can't vote for the Prohibition candidate because I am in favour of alcoholic beverages, and I want Thomas' hold on the Socialist party to be shaken by an unusually small vote, and I must do something. Still, there is self-respect to consider. May the Dew melt. Reactionary & ancient Rose, go forward!

Now all this tyme lat us be mirry
And sett nocht by this warld a chirry

as saith Dunbar. Let me know whether this admirable philosophy is practicable where you are, and how you enact it.

---

*"Don't try to set straight everything that's wrong."
**"Taste no more than you need." John's quotes are from William Dunbar (c. 1460–1520).

Proofs of the strange story I wrote in the summer ["The Lovers"] have just come from the Kenyon Review, and not having looked at it since, I have reread it with appropriately strange emotion. I predict that it will cause general chaos in the hearts of its readers.
Always,

John

I was amused to see—and not for the first time—John's fierce determination to assert the misery and anguish of his life even when the outward circumstances were balmy. I had come to recognize it as a corollary of his conviction, which I did not share, that great art emerges only from pain and suffering by the artist.

I was less amused by a letter from Harriet about this time, telling of how John had phoned her one night after having dinner with someone in New York, and asked insistently if he could drop in for a nightcap at her apartment. He came up, drank several, and then announced that she had become "an area of conflict" for him. Although she did not elaborate in her letter, I knew what he meant, of course; later I learned that he had been obnoxiously stubborn, eventually rushing into her bedroom, climbing into the bed shoes and all, and declaring that he was going to stay there until she joined him.

Considerably annoyed by this behavior, I was not mollified by another letter from John later that fall, expressing birthday wishes but proceeding to a violent denunciation of a book by Llewelyn Powys, *Impassioned Clay*, which I admired and had recommended to John years before but which he had only now gotten around to: "I never read such a tissue of superstitious animistic hedonistic nonsense. . . . The opinions of Mr. Russell . . . communicated in the language (horresco referens) of a Baptist pulpit. . . . His Greek-worship particularly is insufferable in an olio which would have excited homicidal contempt in Athens. . . . Consider, consider, Milt: 'to have had an unhappy life is to have failed in life. It is the one consummate error,' he says, this animal . . . and if I were to speak of him from a *Christian* point of view, I should never be done." While I had lost some of my teenage enthusiasm for Powys I was still in basic agreement with him, and it was clear to me that John and I were off on quite different philosophical trajectories, probably irreversibly.

MY MARRIAGE TO Harriet survived the war, but in such battered condition that we gave up in 1946. By that time I was back in Ann Arbor, teaching again and working on a doctoral dissertation on Ernest Hemingway. It was good to be back, but a haze of nostalgic melancholy hung over everything, it seemed to me.

One day somebody told me that Sally Pierce was in Ann Arbor, visiting her parents, and I called her. We met at the same old place, the Betsy Ross, in the same old booth, for a lemon Coke. But she looked thin and tired. She and David Dow had spent most of the war at Los Alamos, New Mexico, where David was special assistant to Dr. Robert Oppenheimer. She told me a little about her children, but did not seem to be happy, and I could not figure out what was really wrong. "I don't know," she said, "—everything seems to turn to dust and ashes." A little over two years later, just before my own first child was born, I heard that Sally had died of leukemia. She was thirty-four.

MY SECOND WIFE was a splendid Canadian girl named Beverley who also had just canceled a war marriage. We spent a lot of time in 1947 explaining to each other why we would never marry again. We were married in the spring of 1948, and at Christmas time, with Bev several months pregnant, we made a trip to New York.

I had not heard from John for a couple of years except for the arrival of a copy of The Dispossessed, a book of his poems published earlier in 1948. One day between Christmas and New Year's the phone rang, and it was John. Would we like to meet him for a drink at Penn Station before he took the train to Princeton?

I was delighted at the prospect, and Bev of course was curious. We waited at the appointed bar for half an hour or so, and John finally showed up. He was a bit disheveled and clearly had been drinking somewhere else before coming to meet us, but he rapidly downed a scotch and ordered another. Our conversation kept running aground on non sequiturs, and I was irritated by the fact that John paid so little attention to Bev that she might just as well not have been there. I brought up my work on Hem-

ingway, which I thought would interest him because I knew he was working on Stephen Crane, but he was barely responsive. "By the way," he
said abruptly, "I've been talking to Bhain."

I took this to be some kind of figure of speech. "Yes," I said, "I've
been thinking about him a lot myself. Have you seen the book of his
poems that Norman Rosten put together for Farrar & Rinehart?"*

"No," John said, "you don't understand. I've actually been talking to
Bhain."

"What the hell do you mean, John?" I said.

"He calls me on the telephone. Very late at night. It's happened several
times lately. It's Bhain, no mistake. You know how recognizable his voice
is."

To this I could think of no adequate reply. We all had another drink
and spoke of nothing much, and John checked his watch and said he must
go for his train. Bev waited at the bar while I walked him into the station
proper and found his gate. We shook hands and wished each other luck,
and he went down the steps to the platform, walking somewhat unsteadily,
carrying his head tipped to one side as I had seen him do a hundred times
before, and was lost in the crowd.

AS THE YEARS went by I was able to keep some track of John's career,
which was slowly edging into the realm of public knowledge. *The Dispossessed* aroused little stir, but his study of Stephen Crane, published in
1950, got generally good reviews, including kudos from Edmund Wilson.
There were rumors of alcoholism and of a breakup with his wife Eileen;
there was a garbled story about a drunken fracas in Iowa City, where I
had known my own miseries seventeen years earlier; then I heard that
Allen Tate had taken John under his wing at the University of Minnesota.
John's long poem, *Homage to Mistress Bradstreet*, which already had excited
favorable comment when it was published in the *Partisan Review*, came
out as a much praised book in 1956; after that it was clear that my old
friend had become a literary celebrity on a national scale.

Now and then one or the other of us would make a gesture toward
reviving our friendship, and as a matter of fact I always thought it *would*

The Task (New York, 1945).

revive sooner or later. In a North Carolina hospital in 1957 for a hernia operation (during which a young Egyptian surgeon, who had promised me he would perform a casual vascectomy at the same time, nearly came to a scalpel duel with his assistant, a born-again Christian who would not allow this kindest cut of all), I whiled away my convalescence by writing John an amiable account of the episode and of what else I had been up to. It was forwarded to him from Minnesota, and a month or two later I received a genial response from Madrid, where John was sojourning with his second wife, Ann, and their baby boy, Paul—beings of whose existence, until then, I had not been aware.

Other sporadic stabs at correspondence occurred over the next few years, usually ending on each side with notations of our telephone numbers and promises to call; but some kind of mutual reluctance prevailed, and we did not phone each other. An exception was the day John won the Pulitzer Prize for *77 Dream Songs* in May 1965. When I got to my suburban home that night—I was working in New York as a magazine editor—I had a bourbon on the rocks and then telephoned John in Minneapolis, where he was living with his third and last wife, Kate Donahue, and their little daughter, Martha. He came on the line after a minute or two, his voice sounding perfectly familiar as of old. Instead of welcoming my congratulations, however, he loudly insisted that the Pulitzer was nothing to be proud of: "*You're* the one who should be proud, Milt—you have your great job at *Heritage*; you have your great wife, you have your great children . . . *I'm* congratulating *you!*" This sounded like drunken nonsense or drunken sarcasm, and I soon said good-bye, ill at ease and disgruntled.

WHEN THE NEWS of John's suicide hit the papers on January 8, 1972, I felt a sharp pang of remorse at not having made greater efforts to keep in touch with him. Reports of the acute illness and anguish of his last months made me feel worse. We had often shared the ability to cheer each other up; was it conceivable that if I had just taken a plane to Minneapolis sometime in 1971 I would have been able to help him?

It is doubtful that I would have, but I wish I had tried.

In one of the last letters he wrote to Mark Van Doren, a few months before his death, John compared himself to A. E. Housman: "The man I identify with is Housman, pedantic & remorseless (though with a lyric style far superior to mine), a really bifurcated personality—and I mean to deal with him some time." I suspect that when John decided to end his life by jumping from the Mississippi bridge in Minneapolis, Housman's line, "By brooks too broad for leaping," with all of its poignant metaphorical burden, must have entered his mind. His bold irascible spirit had encountered many such brooks in his tempestuous life, despite the triumph with which he had leaped many others. And one such brook, slowly but inexorably broadening, had flowed between John and me, defeating both of us and pushing back into a golden distance the days of our youthful friendship.

Afterword

The unique thing about this memoir, of course, is that no one else but E. M. Halliday could have told its story. First of all, we have the extraordinary good fortune of Halliday's having saved every letter he ever received from Berryman at a time when Berryman's fame was not even equal to that of the young Pound at a similar age or of his hero, Odysseus, swept by the gods about the Mediterranean trying to find his way home: a man without a fortune and with a name to come. Second, we have someone—Berryman's exact contemporary—who was there either by geography or as privileged listener: in either case there by proximity to Berryman's heart. For nearly a decade—the decade when Berryman by dint of sheer hard work began to turn himself into an artist—Halliday was there to listen and to respond. True, there were other correspondents, but none to whom Berryman revealed himself as fully as he did to Milt Halliday.

Consider for a moment the other characters in Berryman's bildungsroman. There was Berryman's mother, and the letters he wrote her from Cambridge, England, are full and fulsome, so much so that when Berryman later reread them he gagged on the overt oedipal content he saw revealed there. Moreover, he lived at home for most of his Columbia years and again after he returned from Cambridge, at which point the relationship went into a sharp downward spiral, especially when "Mum," who by then had farmed out Berryman's stepfather, Uncle Jack, that is, John Berryman the elder, insisted (less than half-jokingly), on being introduced to her son's friends and acquaintances not as his mother but as his older sister. Moreover in that correspondence there were also long silences when Berryman simply could not bring himself to write to the woman he had once called "Darling" and "Bebe Dirl." He had to learn to survive as best he could.

There was also Mark Van Doren, his English professor at Columbia, the man who became the first of his chosen surrogate fathers, the one responsible for turning him toward his lifelong study of Shakespeare and toward the writing of poems. But in this instance, too, Van Doren was on the scene at Columbia, and the letters Berryman wrote to his teacher from England and Wayne State and Harvard are those of the brilliant ephebe to a mentor whom he wishes to impress and please. Or they are letters asking for help in getting started on the road to imitating the father as teacher and as scholar. Van Doren's letters, in return, while friendly and increasingly intimate, maintain the classic reserve of a father for a favorite son. Berryman's letters to Van Doren are always circumspect and hardly touch on his inner life, except as the life of the mind. Even Van Doren had to admit in the early 1940s that he knew almost nothing of Berryman's personal life, and he said so to Berryman in such a way as to suggest that it was probably better to keep things that way.

Then, too, all—or nearly all—of Berryman's letters to his various loves as well as to his first fiancée, Jean Bennett, were apparently long ago burned. And even if they hadn't been, it is possible now to see that Berryman simply did not know how to be very straightforward with any of his women. In truth it would be another twenty years and more before he began to see them in the complexity of their individual selves. The first woman—his mother the Amazon—continued to stand between him and every other woman he knew, and this was to include, sadly, all three of his wives.

There were no other male friends to whom he wrote as he wrote to Halliday, not his only sibling, Robert Jefferson, five years his junior, nor any of his classmates from his four years at South Kent School, nor any of his other Columbia classmates. Not even Robert Giroux, who would later, after Halliday's path had led elsewhere, come to mean so much to Berryman as his fame began to grow. As for Bhain Campbell, as intense as that relationship was to be—more intense even than his relationship with Halliday—its very brevity and tragic closure were what gave it its almost preternatural heat and light. And again, the letters between Berryman and Campbell are few since they either lived with or in proximity to each other. There was also the estranged silence between them after Campbell and his wife left the apartment they shared in Detroit, forced to make the move by Berryman's prolonged depression. By the time the relationship resumed it was clear to everyone that Campbell was dying, falling down and backward from the white dunes of that nearly perfect summer into the final Absence waiting. Only Halliday remains, then, as eyewitness to tell us what was on the young Berryman's mind and in his heart.

We are also fortunate to have in Halliday a witness who can spin a story and who had the documents at hand to help refresh his memory at nearly every turn: Berryman's letters to him, as well as his letters to Berryman, which Berryman kept, now among the Berryman papers at the University of Minnesota, a mile from where Berryman lived, two miles from where he died. And there are the wonderful early photographs of Halliday and Campbell and Beryl Eeman and Berryman and the other attendant players, Columbia's Riverside tower and (yes) Grant's Tomb in the background of one, Hitler's prewar Heidelberg for backdrop in another—Nazi Germany with its dark, hypnotic, terrifying Wagnerian promise which would cost, in less than ten years, nearly twenty million lives.

What Halliday wants to tell, in large part, is the story of a friendship. Let someone else, he says by his absences, talk of Berryman's intellectual sea change at Cambridge which left Berryman forever after altered as well as altared. Let someone else sing of those strange and sudden masks Berryman tried on after he left Columbia, when the Tradition rose up in the figure of a Blakean Yeats visiting Berryman in a waking vision which even Berryman could hardly bring himself to describe to Halliday and which Halliday—fearing for his friend's sanity—would have preferred not to hear of anyway. The Halliday who emerges in these pages is after all a pragmatist interested in women with an intensity only heightened by the mores of the thirties, by the Janus-faced repression of prohibition and the fear of early pregnancy and its attendant (economic) dishonor. Too, there is the intensification of male bonding among these young middle-class American hunters consoling each other over the repeated failures of their "charms" to help them snare their prey. In truth these women are too fast, too intelligent, for these young men. The women have their own agendas and it seems clear by the close of the memoir that they—and not the men— have pretty much understood what was at stake and what action was called for in the skirmish of the sexes. The Restoration dramatists would have understood the unraveling of the plot from the opening scene. Berryman's character was, indeed, his fate.

The story of two young men at Columbia and the University of

Michigan, at Clare College, Cambridge, and Wayne State and Harvard is told swiftly and told well. It is an intimate and honest portrait, more honest than Berryman as a young man could have brought himself to admit and a wonderful corrective to the young old man, as he called himself, who looks down and inward in a 1939 photograph meant to capture the very essence of the *poète maudit*. It is but another mask and not a very pleasant one, though those who loved him would forgive him. But he was funny and fun to be with much of the time, as Eileen Simpson, his first wife, has reminded us in her published memoir, *Poets in Their Youth*, which takes up the story soon after the moment when Berryman walked off the subway that Christmas of 1940, and—feeling betrayed by Halliday's disclosures—said good-bye to the early intimacy of their friendship.

A word too about the subtext of this memoir. If at first *John Berryman and the Thirties* seems to be little more than a picaresque retelling of mostly failed sexual exploits and exploitation, it is all the while gathering to itself a growing darkness: the cross-purposes and cross-interests of two men going too often after the same women, and the growing sense of friendship turning to betrayal. When Berryman learned that Christmas of 1940 that Halliday had slept with "his" woman from his Detroit days, the woman Bhain Campbell—just three weeks dead then—had introduced to Berryman, it was too much. That Berryman himself—engaged at the time—had betrayed Halliday's trust earlier Berryman chose either to overlook or to forget. In any event, though Berryman and Halliday continued to write each other during the war years and, occasionally, afterward, by the time Berryman returned from England in the summer of 1938 the great change had already occurred.

Halliday himself knew this. Like Mark Van Doren, he found it hard to talk to Berryman during that summer of 1938, when Berryman—hating New York and all it represented—wore British tweed and sported a beard and an accent which strained after Cambridge and the Great Tradition Incarnate, though it sounded like no living Englishman's talk. That amalgam of the King's English laced with the vernacular subsided, altered, but never left him. It was an idiom—cut through with many linguistic layers—that no man but Berryman, master ventriloquist, ever spoke. It was a language his students for the next thirty years and more could not help mimicking, though many of them admired and even loved him.

In fact, a good part of Berryman's story concerns the struggle to come to terms not only with his own voice but also with the story of his life. Here was a man who in his twenties and thirties hated even to be photographed, who refused outright to send the various anthologies, pictures or information about himself, who would not even autograph his books, who wrote of himself at the age of thirty-eight that he was "a man of griefs & fits / trying to be my friend." And yet it was this same man who later allowed himself to be photographed—wild beard flashing as if wired for electricity—by *Life*'s and *Time*'s photographers ad nauseam and who, in successive volumes, revealed more and more about himself until even the reviewers and critics turned their faces from some of the disclosures of *Love & Fame* and of *Recovery*.

It is fitting, then, that Halliday should quote several passages from Berryman's late work in the headnotes to his various chapters, for if Halliday appears as a character in *Love & Fame*, he reverses the mirror here, re-creating this version of his friend. In fact, much of Halliday's memoir acts as an extended and welcome gloss on Berryman's own portrait of the artist as a young dog in the first half—dedicated to Mnemosyne—of Berryman's *Love & Fame*. We understand better now what Berryman chose to remember, exaggerate, forget, and misremember. And reading the two against each other, we understand better the limits of each eyewitness. Halliday emerges as more the blessed hedonist, as a man who, in rejecting his minister father's way of life for a life of pleasure, follows, perhaps, the Paterian ethic.

Berryman, on the other hand, whose father for most of his life was a ghost not unlike the one who stalked Hamlet in the predawn mists, turned in *Love & Fame*, by long-delayed necessity I would guess, to something approximating the Augustinian paradigm: the Prodigal Son turning at last to a rescuing Father. But to such a place Halliday will not follow him. Instead, as with Saul Bellow who also feels uncomfortable with that side of Berryman, Halliday has attempted to reconstruct a Berryman friendlier to his own memory. Weirdly, even that preemptive strategy seems only to intensify the tragedy of this brilliant, tormented poet who fell at last from a great height in the winter of 1972 and who now belongs to the long shadows of that Past which claimed him almost from his start.

Paul Mariani
Montague, Massachusetts
7 February 1987